The Editor

DOUGLAS C. LANGSTON is Professor of Philosophy and Religion
at New College of Florida. He is the author of *God's Willing
Knowledge: The Influence of Scotus' Analysis of Omniscience* and
Conscience and Other Virtues: From Bonaventure to MacIntyre.
His articles have appeared in *The Journal of Religious Studies,
Franciscan Studies, Medieval Philosophy and Theology,* and *The
Southern Journal of Philosophy,* among others.

NORTON CRITICAL EDITIONS IN THE HISTORY OF IDEAS

A NORTON CRITICAL EDITION

Boethius

THE CONSOLATION
OF PHILOSOPHY

AUTHORITATIVE TEXT
CONTEXTS
CRITICISM

Edited by

DOUGLAS C. LANGSTON

NEW COLLEGE OF FLORIDA

W. W. NORTON & COMPANY
New York • London

W. W. Norton & Company has been independent since its founding in 1923, when William Warder Norton and Mary D. Herter Norton first published lectures delivered at the People's Institute, the adult education division of New York City's Cooper Union. The firm soon expanded its program beyond the Institute, publishing books by celebrated academics from America and abroad. By mid-century, the two major pillars of Norton's publishing program—trade books and college texts—were firmly established. In the 1950s, the Norton family transferred control of the company to its employees, and today—with a staff of four hundred and a comparable number of trade, college, and professional titles published each year—W. W. Norton & Company stands as the largest and oldest publishing house owned wholly by its employees.

The text of this book is composed in Fairfield Medium
with the display set in Bernhard Modern.
Manufacturing by Maple Press
Book design by Antonina Krass.
Composition by TexTech, Inc.
Production manager: Eric Pier-Hocking.

ISBN: 978-0-393-93071-9

W. W. Norton & Company, 500 Fifth Avenue
New York, N.Y. 10110
www.wwnorton.com

W. W. Norton & Company Ltd., Castle House
75/76 Wells Street, London W1T3QT

2 3 4 5 6 7 8 9 0

Contents

Preface

I have spent most of my scholarly career working on the late Middle Ages, especially the writings of Thomas Aquinas, Duns Scotus, and William of Ockham. While I have taught Boethius's *The Consolation of Philosophy* (mainly Book 5) in my survey course on the philosophy and religious thought of the Middle Ages, I had never really focused much scholarly energy on it. The opportunity to produce this edition of the work for Norton has given me a chance to study the work intensely and read wide-ranging scholarship on it. I have been struck by both the unity of Boethius's work and the striking ambiguities in it. I have tried to capture my double reaction in my introduction to the text as well as in the secondary sources I have chosen for the volume.

My thanks go out to Jeff Stout, who originally suggested me as an editor for this volume. Carol Bemis of Norton has acted as the general editor for the project, and her assistant, Rivka Genesen, has been the specific liaison for it. I particularly wish to thank John Marenbon for his generous contribution to this volume as well as his outstanding scholarship on Boethius in general. I also want to thank James Stock at Wipf and Stock Publishers for his generosity in allowing the reprinting of chapter one from Nelson Pike's *God and Timelessness*. Finally, I wish to acknowledge the material support New College of Florida has given me in completing this project.

Introduction

Boethius (Anicius Manlius Severinus Boethius) was born around 476 C.E. into the noble Roman family Anicii. At the death of his father during his childhood, he was adopted by Symmachus, whose own family was even more esteemed than the Anicii. With this background, it is no surprise that Boethius was afforded an excellent education in Greek and Roman literature and philosophy. At a time when knowledge of Greek was becoming rarer in the Western Roman Empire, Boethius set himself the task of translating the works of both Plato and Aristotle into Latin. He did, in fact, translate Aristotle's logical works but none of Plato's *Dialogues*. While he may never have finished the ambitious task of translating the works of both men, his decision to enter into public service certainly impeded his translation task. His service as Consul in 510 allowed him considerable leisure to continue his studies in Rome since the post had become more or less ceremonial. In 522, during the consulship of his two sons, he became the "Master of Offices" for Theoderic the Ostrogoth and moved to the administrative capital of the Western Roman Empire in Ravenna.

Since 395, there had been two Roman Emperors administering the Roman Empire: one in the West and one in the East. While the Eastern Emperor enjoyed considerable power, the Western Emperor had to rely increasingly on paid barbarian armies to support his reign. In 476, Romulus Augustulus, a Roman, was deposed by the barbarian general Odoacer. While Odoacer became the Western Emperor, the situation was extremely complex. Odoacer controlled and administered the Western Empire and was regarded as king by the dominant barbarian armies. But the Roman citizens of the Western Empire saw themselves as citizens of the Roman Empire and, in principle, subject to the Roman Eastern Emperor. Obviously, various tensions arose between the administering court of Odoacer and the Roman citizenry. The Roman Senate continued to exercise what it saw as its prerogatives, even though it had little actual power. These tensions persisted after Odoacer was overthrown by Theoderic the Ostrogoth. Moreover, since Roman Christians were Catholic, there was religious tension with the Arian Ostrogoths. It was the job of the Master of Offices to coordinate between the Ostrogothic emperor and the other officials at the court and to mediate between the Roman citizenry and Senate and the Ostrogothic administration. The position was fraught with difficulties and Boethius was imprisoned and accused of various offenses. Ironically, his imprisonment saved him from the demands of his office and gave him time to compose his most famous work, *The Consolation of Philosophy*. His execution around 526, as well as the subsequent execution of Symmachus, was perceived as a low point in Theoderic's reign, which came to an end in 532 when the Eastern emperor, Justin, fulfilled Theoderic's fears by trying to reconquer the Western Empire in what has been called the Gothic Wars.

Intellectually, Boethius draws much of his thought from classical sources. *The Consolation of Philosophy* contains many references to the works of Plato, Aristotle, Cicero, and other classical writers. As we shall see, the work is a major source for medieval references to various Greek and Roman legends and myths. Although Boethius is a product of classical thought, he is, like Augustine, regarded as a medieval thinker since his influence on the period is so profound.

Boethius wrote works on arithmetic, astronomy, geometry, and music—which he termed the "quadrivium" since they are four mathematical paths to objects of intelligence—as well as translations and commentaries on various logical works by Aristotle, Cicero, and Porphyry. While only the works on arithmetic and music (incomplete) survive from his quadrivium studies, his logical works were highly valued in the Middle Ages and provided much of what was known of Aristotelian logic in Europe until the twelfth century. Boethius also wrote very influential works on logic and rhetorical reasoning. He was particularly influenced by Cicero's work, *Topics*, and his own work seemed to be aimed at giving practical advice about reasoning that could benefit anyone interested in argument—whether philosopher or lawyer.

In part as a response to contemporary disputes about theological issues, Boethius composed five treatises on a variety of theological issues: the nature of the trinity, the hypostatic union, competing notions of what a nature is, the nature of evil, and the content of Christian doctrine. As he did in his more philosophical works, Boethius combined the insights of Platonic and Neoplatonic thought with the logical method and distinctions of Aristotle. Using terminology from Aristotle's *Categories* and syllogistic logic, Boethius in one of the treatises defends the orthodox Chalcedonian definition of Christ as one person with two natures against the heresies of Nestorius and Eutyches. While some have questioned the unity of these treatises and their philosophical (in contrast to theological) nature, they are indicative of the line of reasoning Boethius follows in *The Consolation of Philosophy*: pursuing basic Christian doctrines by examining closely related philosophical doctrines that capture the Christian point of view while moving it beyond a purely Christian perspective.

The five books of *The Consolation of Philosophy* can be divided into three closely related parts: Books 1–3; Book 4; Book 5. The main topics of the first part (Books 1–3) are the nature of goods and what the ultimate good is. The second part (Book 4) moves from the identification of the ultimate good as God, established in the first part, to ask about the role of evil as well as divine planning in the world. The third part (Book 5) builds on the views about Providence and Fate in the second part to address the issue of the relationship between God's knowledge and human freedom. The discussion of the third part introduces notions not seen before but is rooted deeply in the answers to Boethius's complaints in the first part and the view of God's Providence presented in the second part. Thus the work is a carefully crafted whole that stresses different issues in its different parts. If one isolates Boethius's discussion of God's knowledge and his postulation of God's timelessness from the rest of the text (as many contemporary thinkers do), one does a disservice to Boethius and runs the risk of misunderstanding his views.

Part One (Books 1–3)

The first part of the text begins with a poem of lament spoken by Boethius himself. He is miserable for reasons he will soon elaborate. His sole comfort seems to be the Muse of Poetry and it is fitting that he initially expresses himself in poetry, for he thinks it provides comfort. (It is important to note, however, that this is one of the few times Boethius himself speaks poetically in the text. For the most part, it is Lady Philosophy who speaks in poetry and Boethius who speaks in prose.)

Lady Philosophy suddenly appears to Boethius. Her appearance is both fantastical and metaphorical. She is old and young, bright and dark, of ordinary height and yet her head touches the heavens. Her garments are torn and neglected and the Greek letter Θ appears at the top of her robe and the Greek letter Π appears at the bottom. This is an unusual appearance, to say the least, but Boethius is trying to communicate several things in Lady Philosophy's appearance. In the first place, he is acknowledging that there are various philosophical schools with competing doctrines. So, philosophy will have various forms. Yet, the torn garments indicate an abuse of philosophy, and Boethius wants to maintain that many of these schools of philosophy are really misuses of philosophy. As we shall see, in the *The Consolation of Philosophy* itself, Boethius regards a Platonic-Aristotelian line of thinking as true philosophy and, while drawing from other schools of philosophy, he sees such schools as Stoicism and Epicureanism as misguided philosophy.

Almost immediately, Lady Philosophy dismisses the Muses of Poetry. This is a symbolic move on her part because the dismissal signifies the falsity of the comfort poetry offers to Boethius and this first part of the text is concerned with separating false, earthly goods from true, ultimate goods. As it turns out, only when Boethius is able to see the difference between temporary goods and permanent goods can he be truly comforted. Lady Philosophy's elaborate proof of this to Boethius combines philosophical reasoning from Plato and Aristotle with basic Christian doctrine.

Boethius needs comfort because he has lost what he cherishes: his office, his wealth, his honor, his freedom. And he has lost these not for any wrongdoing on his part. On the contrary, we learn that he had been punished for doing his job well. He has discharged his duties fairly and compassionately; but in doing so he has run afoul of evil men who have falsely accused him of magic and conspiring to undermine the court of Theoderic. Of course, he is not the first honest man to be falsely accused. In his conversations with Lady Philosophy in this first part, he provides various examples of upright men who have been persecuted unfairly by various Roman emperors. He is but the latest example of unjust persecution. Yet, this does not give him comfort, for seeing that injustice has happened to other just men does not explain why there is injustice at all, why just men suffer the loss of their possessions, honors, and lives. And Lady Philosophy understands this. To answer Boethius's complaints of unfairness, she asks the question: what is truly worthwhile?

After listening to Boethius's recounting of his unjust treatment in Book 1 and emphasizing in Book 2 that Fortune (the events that happen to one in the world) constantly changes, Lady Philosophy in Book 3, Prose 2 looks at what goods human beings pursue: riches, honor, power, fame, and pleasure. Reflecting arguments from Plato's dialogue, *Gorgias*, and the first book of Aristotle's *Nicomachean Ethics*, Lady Philosophy argues that none of these goods is truly good. Riches do not eliminate the needs of hunger and thirst. On the contrary, they create the avarice to have even more riches and never provide satisfaction. Honor seems to cover over weakness and wickedness rather than cure them. Moreover, it deteriorates over time and can never provide blessedness. Power frightens those who have it and traps them into trying to preserve it or expand it. It cannot rid a person of anxieties and, in fact, increases them. Fame is often given by the masses to those who are completely unworthy. It does not improve the person but leaves the person unchanged. Bodily pleasures only end in misery since appetites can never be fulfilled. At the root of these so-called goods is the fact that they are pursued not for themselves but for what they might bring: happiness. They are instrumental goods that are sought to the extent that they bring the highest good. This highest good, which is happiness, must be perfect. As perfect it must be self-sufficient and one. Moreover, all the imperfect goods must be good to the extent that they participate in the perfect good. Given all of these characteristics, it is clear that the highest good can only be God since only God is a perfect, self-sufficient unity that is the cause of all goodness. Happiness must then be connected with God: it is participating in God's divinity. To be with God is the good that human beings strive for as the highest good attainable for them. All other goods must be judged in relation to how they lead to this greatest good. Losing imperfect goods is not really a loss so long as one is able to attain the highest good. To mourn over the loss of imperfect goods is to lose sight of one's real goal.

So at the end of the first part of *The Consolation of Philosophy* Lady Philosophy has answered Boethius's laments by philosophical reasoning and shown him that what he is lamenting is not worth lamenting. On the contrary, he needs to view his life in relation to the pursuit of the highest good and take comfort in his progress towards it even if he has lost imperfect, temporal goods. Boethius seems satisfied with the reasoning she provides. But he does wonder if there is the divine order Lady Philosophy points to. Would there be the evil we see if God is directing everything toward the good? Would there be the seeming misfortunes if God is directing all? The existence of a final happiness answers his laments, but aren't there reasons to question whether there is the order leading to a final happiness?

Part Two (Book 4)

In the second part of the work, consisting of Book 4, Boethius addresses the doubts he has raised: the problem of evil and the seeming disorder of the world. As he presents it at the beginning of Book 4, the problem of evil is the puzzle why, if God is all-knowing and all-powerful and desires only good, there is evil and evil goes unpunished. His answer, although somewhat difficult to trace in the text, is fairly simple. Evil never goes unpunished. Either the evildoer harms himself by his pursuit of evil and is punished or, if the evildoer avoids punishment in this life, he is punished by God in the next. In explaining her answer, Lady Philosophy shows how the evil persons are actually weak because they desire the good but their actions do not lead them to what is truly good. Since we consider a person who is able to get what he wants as stronger than a person who does not get what he wants, the evildoer is weaker than the good person. If the evildoer is not punished in this life, the evildoer is not corrected in his path away from the ultimate good. When the next life comes, the unpunished evildoer finds himself cut off from the ultimate good and suffers. So the issue of evil not being punished is not a problem since evil is always punished and good is always rewarded.

But why should there be evil at all? Boethius's answer is a fairly traditional one (it can be found in the Book of Job, for example). Since human beings do not comprehend the ways of God, we do not know the purposes that evil serves. Sometimes evil strengthens the good person. The supposed success of evildoers reinforces for the good the lesson that temporal goods are not the ultimate good. Human beings can only accept the fact that since there is a good God the plan God has for everything is good and so for every case of evil there must be a reason God has that leads to the eventual rewarding of the good and the punishing of the evil.

In elaborating on this last point, Lady Philosophy draws a distinction between Providence and Fate. Providence is the plan for everything that God has in his mind. Fate is the execution of God's plan in time. It is quite clear that God's Providence brings about Fate since Fate is nothing but God's plan in time. But since God is good, God's plan is good. It then follows that Fate must also be good. That is to say, since the events in the world are nothing but the execution of God's plan, which is good, the order of events in time must be good and lead to the reward of the good and the punishment of the evil. Thus, at the end of Book 4, Lady Philosophy has reaffirmed for Boethius the answer to his laments that she provided in the first part of the text (Books 1–3). Yet, the reaffirmation has opened up the question of how human beings operate in an order that an all-knowing God has set up. The final part of *The Consolation of Philosophy* aims to discuss this issue.

Part Three (Book 5)

Book 5 of *The Consolation of Philosophy* presents one of the most influential discussions of the relationship between God's knowledge and human freedom in medieval thought. Boethius seems to dissolve the problem of determination through the relationship by stressing that God is eternal and from eternity sees all that occurs as if it were present. Since knowledge of an activity when it occurs is clearly non-deterministic, God's knowledge in eternity has no deterministic implications for human activity.

It is important, however, to contextualize Boethius's discussion in Book 5. At the end of Book 4, in Prose 6, Boethius distinguishes between Providence and Fate:

> The generation of all things, and the whole course of mutable natures and of whatever is in any way subject to change, take their causes, order, and forms from the unchanging mind of God. This divine mind established the manifold rules by which all things are governed while it remained in the secure castle of its own simplicity. When this government is regarded as belonging to the purity of the divine mind, it is called Providence; but when it is considered with reference to the things which it moves and governs, it has from very early times been called Fate. It is easy to see that Providence and Fate are different if we consider the power of each. Providence is the divine reason itself which belongs to the most high ruler of all things and which governs all things. Fate, however, belongs to all mutable things and is the disposition by which Providence joins all things in their own order.

Boethius clearly thinks that God's Providence brings about the order of causes in the world. As we learn at the beginning of Book 5, there is no chance in the world, if chance is understood as "an event produced by random motion and without any sequence of causes." On the contrary, as Aristotle points out in *Physics*, Book 2, chapter 4, "Whenever anything is done for one reason, but something other than what was intended happens on account of other reasons, it is called chance." There are clear causes for whatever takes place and these causes are brought about through God's Providence.

Having established that Fate operates in the world, Boethius immediately asks in Book 5, Prose 2: "But, within this series of connected causes, does our will have any freedom, or are the motions of human souls also bound by the fatal chain?" Boethius states unequivocally that there is free will. Interestingly, his main support for this affirmation is that there could not be a reasoning nature without free will, for a reasoning being must be able to distinguish between objects to be shunned and objects to be desired. Moreover, he also claims that human beings are more free to the degree that they maintain themselves in the contemplation of the divine mind and less free to the degree that they turn from this contemplation. Boethius does not here link freedom or free will with the ability to do otherwise.

When Boethius proposes to Lady Philosophy the problem of the relationship between God's knowledge and human freedom at the beginning of Book 5, Prose 3, he explicitly rejects a possible solution he has encountered:

> I cannot agree with the argument by which some people believe that they can solve this problem. They say that things do not happen because Providence foresees that they will happen, but, on the contrary, that Providence foresees what is to come because it will happen, and in this way they find the necessity to be in things, not in Providence.

Boethius says that the difficulty with this argument is that it grants that what happens in the world happens of necessity, even if the necessity does not come from God's knowledge. As he states a few paragraphs later, the problem with this necessity is that it renders in vain all rewards and punishments for good and bad actions since it eliminates the "free and voluntary" actions that would warrant praise and blame. Thus it is clear that Boethius will only accept a solution to the problem of the relationship between God's knowledge and human freedom that does not render human actions necessary. But what is meant by "necessity" in Boethius's discussion?

At the beginning of Book 5, Prose 4, Lady Philosophy wonders why Boethius found the solution he discusses in Prose III inadequate. She suggests that the reason Boethius thinks that future things are necessary is because he thinks they are rendered necessary by divine foreknowledge:

> First, let me ask why you regard as inconclusive the reasoning of those who think that foreknowledge is no hindrance to free will because it is not the cause of the necessity of future things. For do you have any argument for the necessity of future events other than the principle that things which are known beforehand must happen? If, as you have just now conceded, foreknowledge does not impose necessity on future events, why must the voluntary outcome of things be bound to predetermined results?

Lady Philosophy then suggests a thought experiment. Assume that there is no foreknowledge. Any thought Boethius has that events resulting from free will are necessary would be eliminated. Assume further that foreknowledge exists but imposes no necessity on things. Then freedom of will continues to exist and is not infringed by necessity.

What emerges from this exchange between Boethius and Lady Philosophy is that Lady Philosophy believes Boethius should not think that future human actions are necessary in a sense that infringes upon human freedom. To solidify her point, Lady Philosophy suggests to Boethius that he think of God's foreknowledge as a sign of future events. This is important, for a sign merely indicates what is the case and does not bring it about. So if there is necessity associated with divine foreknowledge about future human acts, it must be a reflection of the necessity found in the events themselves. But are the human acts necessary? Lady Philosophy suggests that we think about the status of those things we know that are immediately in front of us. She says that we are certain of them (since we see them immediately) but our certitude does not render them necessary since our certitude does not compel them. So Lady Philosophy has linked the necessity that infringes on human freedom with compulsion and she stresses that knowledge that is contemporaneous with what is known does not compel what is known.

Obviously, this line of reasoning by Lady Philosophy is important for the dissolution of the problem of God's foreknowledge that Boethius offers. Since God's knowledge in the eternal now is as if present to what is known, God's knowledge does not compel what is known and render it necessary in a way inconsistent with human freedom. Indeed, Lady Philosophy stresses at the end of Book 5, Prose 4 and in Proses 5 and 6 that the mode of being of an agent determines its mode of knowing. Temporal beings know objects sequentially in time. An eternal being, who completely possesses an endless life enjoyed as one simultaneous whole, knows all of time—past, present, and future—as if it were taking place in the present. Such present knowledge does not necessitate what is known but leaves its nature unaffected:

> Therefore, this divine foreknowledge does not change the nature and properties of things; it simply sees things present before it as they will later turn out to be in what we regard as the future. His judgment is not confused; with a single intuition of his mind He knows all things that are to come, whether necessarily or not. Just as, when you happen to see simultaneously a man walking on the street and the sun shining in the sky, even though you see both at once, you can distinguish between them and realize that one action is voluntary, the other necessary; so the divine mind, looking down on all things, does not disturb the nature of the things which are present before it but are future with respect to time.

This last quotation is particularly interesting. Boethius draws a contrast between necessary natural agents (for example, the sun) and voluntary agents (human beings and other rational agents) to explain how God's knowledge does not conflict with human freedom. As we saw in Book 5, Prose 2, Boethius assumes that all rational agents are free agents. These agents are not subject to a necessity that infringes on their freedom. In the present passage, Boethius links the relevant freedom from necessitation to being a voluntary agent. Once again he does not explicitly link freedom with an ability to do otherwise.

At the end of Book 5, Prose 6, Boethius returns to the solution to the problem of God's knowledge that he had rejected in Book 5, Prose 3:

> God has this present comprehension and immediate vision of all things not from the outcome of future events, but from the simplicity of his own nature. In this way, the problem you raised a moment ago is settled. You observed that it would be unworthy of God if our future acts were said to be the cause of divine knowledge.

Lady Philosophy's reply is that "Now you see that this power of divine knowledge, comprehending all things as present before it, itself constitutes the measure of all things and is in no way dependent on things that happen later." This response suggests both that God's knowledge is unchanging (since it is eternal) as well as that God's knowledge determines each thing's mode of existence. This echoes Boethius's comments in Book 4, Prose 6, that Providence creates Fate in the world. God's providence (his providing knowledge) creates the system of causes (including the activities of rational agents in the world) that is inconsistent with chance defined as the lack of causes. Such a view is difficult to reconcile with a view of freedom that equates freedom with an agent's ability to act otherwise than he does. It is far easier to reconcile with a view that links freedom of rational agents with their being voluntary agents. In short, Boethius's dissolution of the problem of God's knowledge seems closely connected with seeing freedom in terms of voluntary action.

The Message of the Text

Many have puzzled over the philosophical nature of *The Consolation of Philosophy*. It does not seem particularly Christian since it never mentions Christ. But the work is profoundly Christian, although it uses philosophy and Classical literature to deliver its Christian message. Although Boethius cites various Greek and Roman legends and uses examples of non-Christians to lament the injustices that Roman emperors have caused to just men, Boethius strongly affirms in Book 3, Poem 6 that the Christian God is the source of all things and must be seen as the ultimate author behind all the non-Christian stories:

> The whole race of men on this earth springs from one stock. There is one Father of all things; One alone provides for all. He gave Phoebus his rays, the moon its horns. To the earth He gave men, to the sky the stars. He clothed with bodies the souls He brought from heaven.

Boethius has thus united the Classical stories and legends with a Christian perspective. Moreover, his using philosophical arguments from Plato and Aristotle to show that instrumental goods are not ultimate goods ends in the claims that God is the ultimate good and that the ultimate happiness for human beings consists of being with God in the next life. So Boethius is using philosophy to deliver a Christian message.

In fact, Boethius even uses Lady Philosophy to undercut philosophy in its attempt to explain God's preservation of human freedom. The problem of the relationship of God's knowledge to human freedom is introduced as a philosophical problem. Its answer requires an analysis of the nature of time and how the nature of one's knowledge depends upon the status of one's existence. And Boethius is thus able to show that human freedom and divine knowledge are compatible. But this philosophical problem turns out not to be the chief threat to human freedom. Rather, the Christian belief that God is the cause of all through Providence seems to be by far a more serious problem. Yet, Boethius ends up affirming God's Providence and, very similar to Augustine, maintains that God's Providence preserves human freedom. It preserves human freedom because Providence creates human beings as voluntary agents who are the sources of their own actions. They make decisions in a world of necessary agents whose activities are controlled by a good creator.

The consolation of *The Consolation of Philosophy* is, in fact, a religious one. While the text is buttressed by philosophical arguments and uses philosophical arguments to answer philosophical problems, the answer to Boethius's laments—what he seeks consolation for—is a religious conviction in God's goodness and the good order following from this goodness.

Secondary Sources

The selected secondary sources to Boethius's text are of two types. The first type consists of selections from texts that Boethius drew upon for his work. These include selections from two of Plato's *Dialogues*, a selection from the first book of Aristotle's *Nicomachean Ethics*, and a selection from Book 3 of Augustine's *On Free Choice of the Will*.

In his dialogue *The Gorgias*, Plato presents his notion that evildoers cause more harm to themselves than to others through their evil actions as well as his notion that it is better for evildoers that they be punished for their evil deeds than escape punishment. These notions are reflected in Boethius's discussions of the nature of the true Good in Books 2 and 3 of *The Consolation of Philosophy*.

The dialogue *The Timaeus* presents Plato's view of the origin of the world order. Like most ancients, he claims that the Earth is round, "having its extremes in every direction equidistant from the center." Boethius refers in Book 3 (Prose and Poem 9) to the section selected from the dialogue in which Plato discusses the World Soul animating the World and explains the everlasting, temporal existence the world has. Boethius uses the world's perpetual temporal existence to contrast with God's timeless and eternal existence.

In the selection from Book 1 of *The Nicomachean Ethics*, Aristotle claims that all human beings desire the good. In determining what the good is, Aristotle argues that the goods of pleasure, wealth, and acclaim are sought not for themselves but for the sake of happiness, which he claims is living and faring well (*eudaimonia*). Boethius uses similar arguments in Books 2 and 3 to claim that worldly goods are not the highest goods we are really seeking.

Augustine's *On Free Choice of the Will* deeply influenced Boethius's thought in *The Consolation of Philosophy*. Book 1 of *On Free Choice of the Will* offers a ranking of types of goods as well as the notion that evil is nothing. The passage excerpted is from Book 3, chapters 1–8. Here Augustine distinguishes natural from voluntary agents and argues that God's foreknowledge is consistent with human freedom since such knowledge guarantees the voluntary acts human beings perform. The influence on Book 5 on *The Consolation of Philosophy* is very clear.

Although Boethius drew from many other sources in his text, these four selected texts were major influences. The selections from Plato are from Benjamin Jowett's translations of the Platonic dialogues. The selection from the *Nicomachean Ethics* is from J. E. C. Welldon's translation. The selection from Augustine's *On Free Choice of the Will* is from Thomas Williams's translation. There are multiple translations of the full texts of these works available. An online source is the Internet Classics Archive <http://classics.mit.edu/>.

The second type of selections consists of essays written by recent and contemporary scholars of Boethius. The first two selections offer standard views about *The Consolation of Philosophy*. Henry Chadwick's "Introduction" from *Boethius: His Life, Thought, and Influence* offers a general introduction to Boethius's life and writings. Chadwick stresses the influences on Boethius as well as his influence on subsequent thinkers. He emphasizes the importance for Boethius's stature of works other than *The Consolation of Philosophy*, giving stress to the translations of Aristotle, the treatise on music, and the theological tractates. Chadwick presents the standard view of Boethius as an honest functionary during his time as Master of Offices under Theodoric.

Nelson Pike's essay "The Predicate Timeless," from his *God and Timelessness*, offers a very clear interpretation of what Boethius means by saying that God is eternal (timeless). Drawing comparisons with spatial notions, Pike explains how a being can lack both temporal location and duration. Nonetheless, such an eternal being can have all of time present to it. Pike's articulation of Boethius's view and its influence on other thinkers helps to clarify the traditional interpretation that Boethius is claiming that God's knowledge is not foreknowledge and in itself, i.e., in isolation from God's causal activity, does not determine human actions.

The final three selections depart from traditional readings of *The Consolation of Philosophy* in significant ways. In his essay "Theodoric vs. Boethius: Vindication and Apology," William Bark argues that Boethius's interest in the theological issues he discusses in his theological tractates has political motivations. Boethius, in fact, is involved with the Byzantine Emperor's attempts to overthrow Theoderic (Theodoric) the Ostrogoth and reunite the Empire. According to Bark, Boethius is guilty of treason and this fact explains his execution by Theoderic.

In "The Fall of Boethius and the Fiction of the *Consolatio Philosophiae*," Edmund Reiss questions reading the text at face value. Most people see Boethius's comments in the first three books of the text as describing real historical events and persons. Reiss urges us to regard many of Boethius's claims as symbolic. They are not intended to talk about Boethius's own personal predicament so much as about the general situation of human beings, attracted by worldly goods and suffering various misfortunes. Among those influenced by Reiss's article is Nathan Basik whose essay "The Guilt of Boethius" claims that Boethius was guilty of treason. Both Reiss and Basik are indebted to William Bark's essay.

John Marenbon's essay "Anicius Manlius Severinus Boethius" is abridged from his longer article on Boethius in the Stanford Encyclopedia of Philosophy. Marenbon is the leading contemporary scholar of Boethius and his thought. In this selection, he discusses the importance of Boethius's theological tractates and provides a detailed analysis of *The Consolation of Philosophy*. In particular, after summarizing the essential notions of Books 1 to 4, he focuses on Boethius's treatment of the problem of the determination of human actions through God's knowledge. Marenbon suggests that Boethius's argument does not rest on the fact that God is an atemporal (timeless) being, contrary to the usual understanding of Boethius's solution. Moreover, Marenbon indicates that Boethius, on the last page of the text, complicates his position by pointing out that God causally necessitates all events in the world, including human actions. But this situation suggests that human beings are not free in the sense that they can do other than they do. Reacting to this seeming about-face in Boethius's thought about the existence of human freedom, Marenbon suggests a different way of reading the text: it is intended to emphasize the limits of philosophy when dealing with theological matters.

While there are countless works on Boethius and his writings, the selections are intended to show the importance and complexity of the text. *The Consolation of Philosophy* was one of the most significant works of the early Middle Ages and merits careful and creative thought.

Translator's Preface

This translation is based on the critical edition of *The Consolation of Philosophy* by William Weinberger in the Corpus Scriptorum Ecclesiasticorum Latinorum (Vienna, 1934). I have checked my translation against the now standard critical edition by Ludwig Bieler, *Boethii Philosophiae Consolatio* (Turnhout, 1957). I have also used the excellent and convenient edition and translation prepared for The Loeb Classical Library by E. K. Rand and H. F. Stewart (Cambridge, Mass., 1918), both for comparing the Latin texts and as a check on my own readings of ambiguous passages. My purpose in this translation has been to provide students and the general reader with an accurate version of this famous medieval book in modern, idiomatic English.

The translator of *The Consolation* faces a number of serious problems. Boethius is one of the makers of the vocabulary of medieval philosophy, and employs many technical terms for which the English of the twentieth century provides no corresponding terms or, at best, terms that miss or confuse the precise meanings and distinctions of the medieval author. In many instances, Boethius's context makes the meaning of his philosophical terminology reasonably clear. Where it does not, I have tried to represent his ideas as nearly as I could in the language at my disposal.

The metrical parts of *The Consolation* raise further problems. Translators who have rendered these in verse have inevitably been forced by the demands of their art rather far from the meaning of the original. Since fidelity to the author's ideas, rather than imitation of his forms, has been my primary concern, I have chosen to translate his poems in prose and as literally as I could. In addition, this decision was influenced by my concern to preserve for the student of late medieval literature the figures and metaphors of this very influential book. I hope that what is gained in fidelity to the historical language of the metrical passages will compensate for the loss of poetic reach and elegance that a good verse translation can provide.

Boethius was a devoted and learned reader of the ancient Latin authors and an expert medieval imitator of the prose style of Cicero, the Roman whom he most admired. As a consequence, his own prose is consciously mannered in ways that resist literal translation into modern English. I have not hesitated to alter the structure of his sentences where this could be done without changing his meaning.

Like all modern students of *The Consolation of Philosophy*, I am indebted to the work of E. K. Rand, Howard R. Patch, Helen M. Barrett, Edmund T. Silk, and Pierre Courcelle, and would like here to acknowledge generally points which might have been noted specifically in my Introduction and translation. In addition, I wish to thank my friends, Professors Alba H. Warren, Jr., and D. W. Robertson, Jr., for their careful reading of the translation, and for suggestions which have made it more accurate and graceful than it would otherwise have been.

RICHARD H. GREEN

Baltimore, Maryland
April, 1962

The Text of
THE CONSOLATION OF
PHILOSOPHY

Book 1

Poem 1

I who once wrote songs with keen delight am now by sorrow driven to take up melancholy measures. Wounded Muses tell me what I must write, and elegiac verses bathe my face with real tears. Not even terror could drive from me these faithful companions of my long journey. Poetry, which was once the glory of my happy and flourishing youth, is still my comfort in this misery of my old age.[1]

Old age has come too soon with its evils, and sorrow has commanded me to enter the age which is hers. My hair is prematurely gray, and slack skin shakes on my exhausted body. Death, happy to men when she does not intrude in the sweet years, but comes when often called in sorrow, turns a deaf ear to the wretched and cruelly refuses to close weeping eyes.[2]

The sad hour that has nearly drowned me came just at the time that faithless Fortune favored me with her worthless gifts. Now that she has clouded her deceitful face, my accursed life seems to go on endlessly. My friends, why did you so often think me happy? Any man who has fallen never stood securely.

Prose 1

Lady Philosophy appears to him and drives away the Muses of poetry.[3]

While I silently pondered these things, and decided to write down my wretched complaint, there appeared standing above me a woman

---

1. Boethius, in fact, wrote several poems, and the poetic parts of the *Consolation* testify to lifelong interest in poetry.
2. Since he was born around 476 C.E. and the *Consolation* was composed in 524 (two years before his death in 526), Boethius was about 48 years old when he composed the work. It is not at all clear that, when he wrote the *Consolation*, Boethius thought he would be put to death.
3. Within the framework of Boethius's narration, Professor Green has added quotation marks to the dialogue between Lady Philosophy and Boethius, thus identifying the speakers. He has also provided explanatory headings to the prose sections.

of majestic countenance whose flashing eyes seemed wise beyond the ordinary wisdom of men. Her color was bright, suggesting boundless vigor, and yet she seemed so old that she could not be thought of as belonging to our age. Her height seemed to vary: sometimes she seemed of ordinary human stature, then again her head seemed to touch the top of the heavens. And when she raised herself to her full height she penetrated heaven itself, beyond the vision of human eyes. Her clothing was made of the most delicate threads, and by the most exquisite workmanship; it had—as she afterwards told me—been woven by her own hands into an everlasting fabric. Her clothes had been darkened in color somewhat by neglect and the passage of time, as happens to pictures exposed to smoke.[4] At the lower edge of her robe was woven a Greek Π, at the top the letter Θ, and between them were seen clearly marked stages, like stairs, ascending from the lowest level to the highest.[5] This robe had been torn, however, by the hands of violent men, who had ripped away what they could.[6] In her right hand, the woman held certain books; in her left hand, a scepter.

When she saw the Muses of poetry standing beside my bed and consoling me with their words, she was momentarily upset and glared at them with burning eyes. "Who let these whores from the theater come to the bedside of this sick man?" she said. "They cannot offer medicine for his sorrows; they will nourish him only with their sweet poison. They kill the fruitful harvest of reason with the sterile thorns of the passions; they do not liberate the minds of men from disease, but merely accustom them to it.[7] I would find it easier to bear if your flattery had, as it usually does, seduced some ordinary dull-witted man; in that case, it would have been no concern of mine. But this man has been educated in the philosophical schools of the Eleatics and the Academy.[8] Get out, you Sirens; your sweetness leads to death. Leave him to be cured and made strong by my Muses."

4. This is a fantastical description of Lady Philosophy. Her varying height might well be a metaphor for different types of philosophy. The darkness and neglect of her garments surely indicates neglect of philosophy by many thinkers.
5. The Greek letters Π (pi) and Θ (theta) are usually taken to stand for the two-fold division of philosophy into Theoretical (Θ) Philosophy and Practical (Π) Philosophy. Theoretical Philosophy is seen as a higher discipline than Practical Philosophy in Boethius's image of Lady Philosophy.
6. Lady Philosophy's torn garments suggest the misuse of philosophy by various philosophical schools.
7. Boethius presents a conflict between Philosophy and the Muses, suggesting that only philosophy offers a true solution to the misfortunes he experiences. The conflict also indirectly reaffirms Boethius's appreciation of poetry since Lady Philosophy clearly thinks of poetry as a pretender to solving Boethius's misfortunes.
8. The traditional name for Plato's school of philosophy in Athens; the Eleatics: a group of Greek philosophers who emphasized rational argument. Zeno and Parmenides are two of the most famous Eleatics.

And so the defeated Muses, shamefaced and with downcast eyes, went sadly away. My sight was so dimmed by tears that I could not tell who this woman of imperious authority might be, and I lay there astonished, my eyes staring at the earth, silently waiting to see what she would do. She came nearer and sat at the foot of my bed. When she noticed my grief-stricken, down-cast face, she reproved my anxiety with this song.

Poem 2

"Alas! how this mind is dulled, drowned in the overwhelming depths. It wanders in outer darkness, deprived of its natural light. Sick anxiety, inflated by worldly winds, swells his thoughts to bursting.

"Once this man was free beneath the ocean heaven, and he used to run along heavenly paths. He saw the splendor of the red sun, the heaven of the cold moon. And any star that pursued its vagrant paths, returning through various spheres, this master understood by his computations.

"Beyond all this, he sought the causes of things: why the sighing winds vex the seawaves; what spirit turns the stable world; and why the sun rises out of the red east to fall beneath the western ocean. He sought to know what tempers the gentle hours of spring and makes them adorn the earth with rosy flowers; what causes fertile autumn to flow with bursting grapes in a good year.

"This man used to explore and reveal Nature's secret causes. Now he lies here, bound down by heavy chains, the light of his mind gone out; his head is bowed down and he is forced to stare at the dull earth.

Prose 2

Seeing his desperate condition, Philosophy speaks more gently and promises to cure him.

"But," she said, "it is time for medicine rather than complaint." Fixing me with her eyes, she said: "Are you not he who once was nourished by my milk and brought up on my food; who emerged from weakness to the strength of a virile soul? I gave you weapons that would have protected you with invincible power, if you had not thrown them away. Don't you recognize me? Why don't you speak? Is it shame or astonishment that makes you silent? I'd rather it were shame, but I see that you are overcome by shock." When she saw that I was not only silent but struck dumb, she gently laid her hand on my breast and said: "There is no danger. You are suffering merely from lethargy, the common illness of deceived minds. You have forgotten yourself a little, but you will quickly be yourself again when you recognize me. To bring you to your senses, I shall quickly wipe the dark cloud of mortal things from your eyes." Then, she dried my tear-filled eyes with a fold of her robe.[9]

Poem 3

Then, when the night was over, darkness left me and my eyes regained their former strength; just as when the stars are covered by swift Corus, and the sky is darkened by storm clouds, the sun hides and the stars do not shine; night comes down to envelop the earth. But if Boreas, blowing from his Thracian cave, beats and lays open the hiding day, then Phoebus[1] shines forth, glittering with sudden light, and strikes our astonished eyes with his rays.

Prose 3

Boethius recognizes Lady Philosophy. She promises to help him as she has always helped those who love and serve her.

In a similar way, I too was able to see the heavens again when the clouds of my sorrow were swept away; I recovered my judgment and recognized the face of my physician. When I looked at her closely, I saw that she was Philosophy, my nurse, in whose house I had lived from my youth. "Mistress of all virtues,"[2] I said, "why have you come, leaving the arc of heaven, to this lonely desert of our exile? Are you a prisoner, too, charged as I am with false accusations?"

She answered, "How could I desert my child, and not share with you the burden of sorrow you carry, a burden caused by hatred of my name? Philosophy has never thought it right to leave the innocent man alone on his journey. Should I fear to face my accusers, as though their enmity were something new? Do you suppose that this is the first time wisdom has been attacked and endangered by wicked men? We fought against such rashness and folly long ago, even before the time of our disciple Plato. And in Plato's own time,

---

9. Wiping his eyes with her robe is symbolic of Philosophy curing Boethius's unhappiness and continues the metaphor of note 6 above by regarding Lady Philosophy's garments as representing philosophical doctrines.
1. The sun; *Corus*: the northwest wind; *Boreas*: the north wind; *Thracian*: Thrace is thought of as an extreme northern land.
2. The virtue ethics of Plato and Aristotle was very influential on classical and medieval thought. Virtue ethics emphasizes the agent's development of states of character that lead the agent to act in the best ways to lead to happiness (*eudaimonia*).

his master Socrates, with my help, merited the victory of an unjust death.[3] Afterwards, the inept schools of Epicureans, Stoics, and others, each seeking its own interests, tried to steal the inheritance of Socrates and to possess me (in spite of my protests and struggles), as though I were the spoils of their quarreling. They tore this robe which I had woven with my own hands and, having ripped off some little pieces of it, went away supposing that they possessed me wholly.[4] Then, when traces of my garments were seen on some of them, they were rashly thought to be my friends, and they were therefore condemned by the error of the profane mob.

"Perhaps you have not heard of the banishment of Anaxagoras, the poisoning of Socrates, the torments of Zeno, for these men were strange to you.[5] But you probably know about Canius, Seneca, and Soranus,[6] for their fame is recent and widely known. They were disgraced only because they had been trained in my studies and therefore seemed obnoxious to wicked men. You should not be surprised, then, if we are blown about by stormy winds in the voyage of this life, since our main duty is to oppose the wicked. But, even though our enemies are numerous, we should spurn them because they are without leadership and are driven frantically this way and that by error. And if they sometimes attack us with extraordinary force, our leader withdraws her followers into a fortress, leaving our enemies to waste their energies on worthless spoils. While they fight over things of no value, we laugh at them from above, safe from their fury and defended by a strength against which their aggressive folly cannot prevail.

Poem 4

"The serene man who has ordered his life stands above menacing fate and unflinchingly faces good and bad fortune. This virtuous man can hold up his head unconquered. The threatening and raging

---

3. Socrates was condemned to death by the city state of Athens in 399 B.C.E. His student, Plato, used Socrates as a character in the *Dialogues*. Plato's depiction of Socrates's trial and death in the *Apology* and the *Phaedo* presents Socrates as unjustly accused of impiety and corruption of the youth of Athens.

4. Epicureanism, founded by Epicurus, emphasized the pleasure of the senses. Stoicism, founded by Zeno of Citius, taught that happiness is the result of becoming part of the order of Nature. Both systems were founded in the fourth century B.C.E. in Athens. Lady Philosophy suggests that these are false philosophical schools, and this passage refers back to the passage at note 6 above, where false schools of philosophy tear at Lady Philosophy's garments.

5. Zeno of Elea (famous for his paradoxes) was said by Diogenes Laertius in his *Lives, Teachings, and Sayings of Famous Philosophers* to have been tortured and killed after a failed attempt to remove a tyrant from Elea. Anaxagoras, a naturalistic philosopher, was exiled from Athens in 450 B.C.E. for suggesting that the stars were not divine. Socrates' method of execution was poisoning by hemlock.

6. Julius Canius was executed in 40 C.E. by the Roman Emperor Caligula. Seneca, a celebrated Roman poet and philosopher, was forced to commit suicide in 65 C.E. by the Roman Emperor Nero as was Barea Soranus, a Roman senator, in 65/66 C.E.

ocean storms which churn the waves cannot shake him; nor can the bursting furnace of Vesuvius, aimlessly throwing out its smoky fire; nor the fiery bolts of lightning which can topple the highest towers. Why then are we wretched, frightened by fierce tyrants who rage without the power to harm us? He who hopes for nothing and fears nothing can disarm the fury of these impotent men; but he who is burdened by fears and desires is not master of himself. He throws away his shield and retreats; he fastens the chain by which he will be drawn.

Prose 4

Boethius gives an account of his public career and especially of the causes of his present misery.

"Do you understand what I have told you," Philosophy asked; "have my words impressed you at all, or are you 'like the ass which cannot hear the lyre'? Why are you crying? Speak out, don't hide what troubles you. If you want a doctor's help, you must uncover your wound."

I pulled myself together and answered: "Do I have to explain; isn't the misery of my misfortune evident enough? I should think this place alone would make you pity me. Compare this prison with my library at home which you chose as your own and in which you often discussed with me the knowledge of human and divine things. Did I look like this? Was I dressed this way when I studied nature's mysteries with you, when you mapped the courses of the stars for me with your geometer's rod, when you formed my moral standards and my whole view of life according to the norm of the heavenly order? Are these miseries the rewards your servants should expect? You yourself proposed the course I have followed when you made Plato say that civil governments would be good if wise men were appointed rulers, or if those appointed to rule would study wisdom. Further, you decreed in the words of the same philosopher that government of the commonwealth ought to be in the hands of wise men; that if it should be left to unscrupulous and wicked men, they would bring about the ruin of the good.

"On this authority, I decided to apply to public administration the principles I had learned privately from you. You, and God who gave you to the minds of wise men, know that I became a magistrate only because of the unanimous wish of all good men. For these reasons I have become involved in grave and hopeless trouble with dishonest men; and, as always happens to the administrator of independent conscience, I have had to be willing to make powerful enemies in the interest of safeguarding justice.[7]

"I have often opposed the greed of Conigastus in his swindling of the poor. I have condemned the crimes of Triguilla, Provost of the King's house, both in their beginnings and after they had been committed.[8] At grave risk to my position I have protected the weak from the lies and avarice of cruel men in power. No man ever corrupted my administration of justice. I was as depressed as those who suffered the losses when I saw the wealth of our citizens dissipated either by private fraud or oppressive taxation. At the time of the severe famine, when prices were set so exorbitantly high that the province of Campania seemed about to starve, I carried on the people's fight against the Praetorian Prefect himself and, with the King's approval, I won—the fixed prices were not enforced.[9]

"I saved Paulinus, the former Consul, from the howling dogs of the court who hoped to devour his wealth. In order to save Albinus, another former Consul, from unjust punishment, I risked the hatred of his accuser, Cyprian.[1] One would think I had stirred up enough opposition. But I ought to have been defended by others, especially since, through devotion to justice, I had given up the favor of the courtiers who might have saved me. But who were the accusers who overthrew me? One of them was Basil who had earlier been expelled from the King's service and was now forced by his debts to testify against me.[2] My other accusers were Opilio and Gaudentius, also men banished by royal decree for their many corrupt practices.[3] They tried to avoid exile by taking sanctuary, but when the King heard of it he decreed that, if they did not leave Ravenna by a certain day, they should be branded on the forehead and forcibly expelled. How could the King's judgment have been more severe? And yet on that very day their testimony against me was accepted. Why should this have happened? Did I deserve it? Did their criminal records make them just

---

7. Boethius is recounting significant details of his life. He indicates that, following Plato's advice in the *Republic* that the State should be governed by rulers who have studied philosophy, he left his preferred studies of philosophy to enter civic service. While faithfully discharging his duties in as fair a manner as possible, he has run afoul of many less honest men.

8. Boethius is recounting his encounters with two "dishonest men," Conigastus and Trigulla, Ostrogoths and favorite officers of Theoderic the Ostrogoth, ruler of the Western Roman Empire in Boethius's time.

9. Faustus, the Praetorian Prefect (head of the civil and judicial administration of the empire), during a time of famine and high food prices, proposed compulsory purchase of food from farmers in Campania at excessively low prices.

1. Albinus, Roman consul, was accused by Cyprian (who himself later became a high official (*comes sacrarum largitionum*), of writing unfavorably of Theoderic to Justin, the Emperor of the Eastern Roman Empire.

2. Basil was forced to accuse Boethius to escape debt.

3. Opilio and Gaudentius were exiled from Ravenna (Western Roman Empire Administrative Capital) on pain of branding. They sought asylum in a church and accused Boethius on the day they were to leave the city.

accusers? Fortune[4] ought to have been shamed, if not by the innocence of the accused, then at least by the villainy of the accusers.

"Finally, what am I accused of? They say I desired the safety of the
Senate.[5] But how? I am convicted of having hindered their accuser
from giving evidence that the Senate is guilty of treason. What is
your judgment, my teacher? Shall I deny the charge in order to avoid
shaming you? But I did desire to protect the Senate, and I always
will. And how can I confess, since I have already stopped hindering
their accuser? Shall I consider it a crime to have supported the
integrity of the Senate? It is true that the Senate itself, by its decrees
against me, has made my position a crime. But folly, driven by self-
deception, cannot change the merits of the case; nor, following the
rule of Socrates, can I think it right either to hide the truth or concede a lie. I leave it to you, and to the judgment of the wise, whether
my course of action is right. I have put this in writing so that posterity may know the truth and have a record of these events.

"Why should I even mention the spurious letters in which I am
charged with having hoped for Roman liberty?[6] That fraud would
have been exposed had I been permitted to use the confession of my
accusers, the strongest evidence in any case. But there is now no
hope for freedom of any kind—I only wish there were. I should have
answered in the words of Canius when Gaius Caesar, son of Ger-
manicus, accused Canius of having known of a conspiracy against
him: 'If I had known of it,' Canius said, 'you would never have
known.'[7] But I am not so discouraged by what has happened to me
that I complain now of the attacks of wicked men against virtue; the
reason for my surprise is that they have accomplished what they set
out to do. The desire to do evil may be due to human weakness; but
for the wicked to overcome the innocent in the sight of God—that is
monstrous. I cannot blame that friend of yours who said, 'If there is
a God, why is there evil? And if there is no God, how can there be
good?'[8] It is not surprising that evil men, who want to destroy all just
men, and the Senate too, should try to overthrow one who stood up
for justice and the Senate. But surely I did not deserve the same
treatment from the Senators themselves.

---

4. A personification of Fate; Fortune dictates the order of events in the world and is ultimately the result of God's Providence.
5. The accusation of "desir[ing] the safety of the Senate" needs to be regarded in terms of
   the opposition between an indigenous Roman population and the ruling Ostrogothic
   tribes. Support for the prerogatives of the Roman Senate can easily be seen as treason by
   the ruling Ostrogothic dynasty.
6. Letters supposedly exchanged between Boethius and the court of the Eastern Roman
   Emperor, Justin, in which Boethius advocates Roman liberty.
7. Canius was accused by the Roman Emperor Caligula. (See note 6, p. 7) Boethius is the
   only source we have for this quotation.
8. Epicurus is the author of these words. Calling him "friend" seems sarcastic given the considerations of note 4, (p. 7).

"You remember well that you always directed me in everything I said and everything I tried to do or say. You recall, for example, the time at Verona when the King wanted to overturn the government and tried to involve the whole Senate in the treason of which Albinus was accused; then, at great risk to my personal safety I defended the innocence of the whole Senate.[9] You know that this is true, and that I have never acted out of a desire for praise; for integrity of conscience is somehow spoiled when a man advertises what he has done and receives the reward of public recognition. But you see where my innocence has brought me; instead of being rewarded for true virtue, I am falsely punished as a criminal. Even the full confession of a crime does not usually make all the judges in the case equally severe; some, at least, temper their severity by recognizing the errors of human judgment and the uncertain conditions of fortune to which all mortals are subject. If I had been accused of plotting the burning of churches, the murder of priests, even the murder of all good men, even then I would have been sentenced only after I had confessed and been convicted, and when I was present before the court. But now, five hundred miles away, mute and defenseless, I am condemned to proscription and death because of my concern for the safety of the Senate. The Senate deserves that no one should ever again be convicted for such a 'crime'!

"Even my accusers understood the honor implicit in the charges they brought against me, and, in order to confuse the issue by the appearance of some crime, they falsely alleged that I had corrupted my conscience with sacrilege[1] out of a desire for advancement. But your spirit, alive within me, had driven from my soul all sordid desire for earthly success, and those whom you protect do not commit sacrilege. You have daily reminded me of Pythagoras' saying: 'Follow God.' It is not likely that I would have sought the protection of evil spirits at a time when you were forming in me that excellence which makes man like God. Moreover, the innocence of my family, the honesty of my closest friends, the goodness of my father-in-law, who is as worthy of honor as yourself—all these ought to have shielded me from any suspicion of this crime.[2] But the worst is that my enemies readily believe that wisdom itself is capable of the crime of ambition, and so they associate me with such misconduct because I am imbued with your knowledge and endowed with your virtues. So,

9. See notes 5 (p. 10) and 1 (p. 9) above.
1. The misuse of sacred objects. A few lines later, the accusation is linked to alliances with evil spirits.
2. Symmachus became Boethius's father-in-law after Boethius married his daughter, Rusticiana. He was also Boethius's guardian after the death of Boethius's father. Symmachus was himself a man of great intellect and learning; he corresponded with Priscian, a renowned Latin grammarian. Symmachus was executed by Theoderic shortly after Boethius.

my reverence for you is no help; their hatred of me leads them to dishonor you.

"Finally, and this is the last straw, the judgment of most people is based not on the merits of a case but on the fortune of its outcome; they think that only things which turn out happily are good. As a result, the first thing an unfortunate man loses is his good reputation. I cannot bear to think of the rumors and various opinions that are now going around; I can only say that the final misery of adverse fortune is that when some poor man is accused of a crime, it is thought that he deserves whatever punishment he has to suffer. Well, here am I, stripped of my possessions and honors, my reputation ruined, punished because I tried to do good.

"It seems to me that I can see wicked men everywhere celebrating my fall with great pleasure, and all the criminally depraved concocting new false charges. I see good men terrorized into helplessness by my danger, and evil men encouraged to risk any crime with impunity and able to get away with it by bribery. The innocent are deprived not only of their safety, but even of any defense. Now hear my appeal.

Poem 5

Boethius concludes with a prayer.

"Creator of the star-filled universe, seated upon your eternal throne You move the heavens in their swift orbits. You hold the stars in their assigned paths, so that sometimes the shining moon is full in the light of her brother sun and hides the lesser stars; sometimes, nearer the sun she wanes and loses her glory. You ordain that Hesperus, after rising at nightfall to drive the cold stars before him, should change his role and, as Lucifer,[3] grow pale before the rising sun.

"When the cold of winter makes the trees bare, You shorten the day to a briefer span; but when warm summer comes, You make the night hours go swiftly. Your power governs the changing year: in spring, Zephyrus renews the delicate leaves that Boreas, the wind of winter, had destroyed; and Sirius burns the high corn in autumn that Arcturus[4] had seen in seed.

"Nothing escapes Your ancient law; nothing can avoid the work of its proper station. You govern all things, each according to its destined purpose. Human acts alone, O Ruler of All, You refuse to restrain within just bounds. Why should uncertain Fortune control our lives?

3. The "Morning Star," the last celestial body visible in the morning. *Hesperus*: the "Evening Star," the first celestial body visible in the evening. They are both, in fact, the planet Venus.
4. The brightest star in the constellation Boötes (The Bear Watcher); *Zephyrus*: the west wind; *Boreas*: the north wind; *Sirius*: the dog star.

"Harsh punishment, deserved by the criminal, afflicts the innocent. Immoral scoundrels now occupy positions of power and
unjustly trample the rights of good men. Virtue, which ought to
shine forth, is covered up and hides in darkness, while good men
must suffer for the crimes of the wicked. Perjury and deceit are not
held blameworthy as long as they are covered by the color of lies.
When these scoundrels choose to use their power they can intimi-
date even powerful kings, because the masses fear them.

"O God, whoever you are who joins all things in perfect harmony,
look down upon this miserable earth! We men are no small part of
Your great work, yet we wallow here in the stormy sea of fortune.
Ruler of all things, calm the roiling waves and, as You rule the
immense heavens, rule also the earth in stable concord."

Prose 5

*Philosophy suggests that the source of the prisoner's trouble is within
himself and begins to reassure him.*

While I poured out my long sad story, Philosophy looked on ami-
ably, quite undismayed by my complaints. Then she said: "When I
first saw you downcast and crying, I knew you were in misery and
exile. But without your story I would not have known how desperate
your exile is. You have not been driven out of your homeland; you
have willfully wandered away. Or, if you prefer to think that you have
been driven into exile, you yourself have done the driving, since no
one else could do it. For if you can remember your true country you
know that it is not, as Athens once was, ruled by many persons;
rather 'it has one ruler and one king' who rejoices in the presence of
citizens, not in their expulsion. To be governed by his power and
subject to his laws is the greatest liberty. Surely you know the oldest
law of your true city, that the citizen who has chosen to establish his
home there has a sacred right not to be driven away. The man who
lives within the walls of that city need not fear banishment; but if he
loses his desire to live there, he loses also the assurance of safety.
And so, I am not so much disturbed by this prison as by your attitude. I do not need your library with its glass walls and ivory decoration, but I do need my place in your mind. For there I have placed
not books but that which gives value to books, the ideas which are
found in my writings.

"What you have said about your merits in the commonwealth
is true; your many services deserve even more than you claim.
And what you have said about the truth or falsity of the accusations against you is well known to everyone. You were right to speak

sparingly of the crimes and deceit of your enemies; such things are better talked about by the man in the street who hears about them. You have sharply protested the injustice done you by the Senate; and you have expressed sorrow for the accusations against me and the weakening of my place in the public esteem. Finally, you protested against Fortune in sorrow and anger, and complained that rewards are not distributed equally on the grounds of merit. At the end of your bitter poem, you expressed the hope that the same peace which rules the heavens might also rule the earth. But because you are so upset by sorrow and anger, and so blown about by the tumult of your feelings, you are not now in the right frame of mind to take strong medicine. For the time being, then, I shall use more gentle treatment, so that your hardened and excited condition may be softened by gentle handling and thus prepared for more potent remedies.

Poem 6

"The fool who plants his seed in the hard ground when summer burns with the sun's heat must feed on acorns in the fall, because his hope of harvest is in vain. Do not look for violets in purple meadows when fields are blasted by winter winds. And do not cut your vine branches in the spring if you want to enjoy the grapes, for Bacchus brings his fruit in autumn.

"God assigns to every season its proper office; and He does not permit the condition He has set to be altered. Every violent effort to upset His established order will fail in the end.[5]

Prose 6

Philosophy begins to remind Boethius of certain basic truths which will place his misfortunes in proper perspective.

"First," Philosophy said, "will you let me test your present attitude with a few questions, so that I can decide on a way to cure you?"

"Ask whatever you like," I replied, "and I will try to answer."

"Do you think," she began, "that this world is subject to random chance, or do you believe that it is governed by some rational principle?"

"I cannot suppose that its regular operation can be the result of mere chance; indeed, I know that God the Creator governs his work,

5. Boethius, through Lady Philosophy, is claiming that there is a proper order, established by God, to Nature and the changes in Nature. This notion will recur most prominently in Books 4 and 5 of the *Consolation*.

and the day will never come when I can be shaken from the truth of this judgment."[6]

"That is true," Philosophy answered, "and you said as much in your poem a while ago when you deplored the fact that only men were outside God's care. You did not doubt that all other things were ruled by reason. Strange, isn't it, that one who has so healthy an attitude should be so sick with despair. We must search further, because obviously something is missing. Tell me, since you have no doubt that the world is ruled by God, do you know *how* it is governed?"

"I don't quite get the point of your question, so I am unable to answer."

"You see, I was right in thinking that you had some weakness, like a breach in the wall of a fort, through which the sickness of anxiety found its way into your soul.

"But tell me, do you remember what the end, or goal, of all things is—the goal toward which all nature is directed?"

"I heard it once," I answered, "but grief has dulled my memory."

"Well, do you know where all things come from?"

I answered that I knew all things came from God.

"How then," she went on, "is it possible that you can know the origin of all things and still be ignorant of their purpose? But this is the usual result of anxiety; it can change a man, but it cannot break him and cannot destroy him.

"I want you to answer this, too: do you remember that you are a man?"

"How could I forget that," I answered.

"Well then, what is a man? Can you give me a definition?"

"Do you mean that I am a rational animal, and mortal? I know that, and I admit that I am such a creature."

"Do you know nothing else about what you are?"

"No, nothing."

"Now, I know another cause of your sickness, and the most important: you have forgotten what you are. And so I am fully aware of the reason for your sickness and the remedy for it too. You are confused because you have forgotten what you are, and, therefore, you are upset because you are in exile and stripped of all your possessions. Because you are ignorant of the purpose of things, you think that stupid and evil men are powerful and happy. And, because you have forgotten how the world is governed, you suppose that these changes of your fortune came about without purpose. Such notions are enough to cause not only sickness but death. But be grateful to the Giver of health that nature has not entirely forsaken you. For you have the best medicine for your health in your grasp of the truth

6. Again, God's governing activity is emphasized.

about the way the world is governed. You believe that the world is not subject to the accidents of chance, but to divine reason. Therefore, you have nothing to fear.[7] From this tiny spark, the living fire can be rekindled. But the time has not yet come for stronger remedies. It is the nature of men's minds that when they throw away the truth they embrace false ideas, and from these comes the cloud of anxiety which obscures their vision of truth. I shall try to dispel this cloud by gentle treatment, so that when the darkness of deceptive feeling is removed you may recognize the splendor of true light.

Poem 7

"Stars hidden by black clouds send down no light. If the wild south wind churns up the sea, the waves which once were clear as glass, as clear as the bright days, seem muddy and filthy to the beholder. The flowing stream, tumbling down from the high mountain, is often blocked by the stone broken off from the rocky cliff.

"So it is with you. If you want to see the truth in clear light, and follow the right road, you must cast off all joy and fear. Fly from hope and sorrow. When these things rule, the mind is clouded and bound to the earth."

---

7. Lady Philosophy is laying the groundwork for her answer to Boethius's despair: ultimately, the purpose of things—God's plan to reward the good and punish the evil—will answer Boethius's laments.

Book 2

Prose 1

Philosophy reminds Boethius of the nature and habits of the goddess Fortune.

Philosophy was silent for a while; then, regaining my attention by her modest reserve, she said: "If I understand the causes of your diseased condition, you are suffering from the absence of your former good fortune. What you regard as a change has greatly upset you. I am well acquainted with the many deceptions of that monster, Fortune. She pretends to be friendly to those she intends to cheat, and disappoints those she unexpectedly leaves with intolerable sorrow. If you will recall her nature and habits, you will be convinced that you had nothing of much value when she was with you and you have not lost anything now that she is gone. But I do not suppose that I have to labor this point with you.

"When Fortune smiled on you, you manfully scorned her and attacked her with principles drawn from my deepest wisdom. But every sudden change of fortune brings with it a certain disquiet in the soul; and this is what has caused you to lose your peace of mind. Now is the time for you to take some gentle and pleasant remedy which may prepare you for stronger medicine. I shall use the sweet persuasion of rhetoric, which is suitable enough if it does not contradict the truths of philosophy, and I shall add the grace of Music, a servant of mine whose songs are sometimes happy and sometimes sad.[1]

"What is it, my friend, that has thrown you into grief and sorrow? Do you think that you have encountered something new and different? You are wrong if you think that Fortune has changed toward you. This is her nature, the way she always behaves. She is changeable, and so in her relations with you she has merely done what she always does. This is the way she was when she flattered you and led

---

1. Boethius composed a treatise on Music. However, these comments by Lady Philosophy seem tongue-in-cheek, for she does not really believe that either Rhetoric or Music will offer proper consolation for Boethius.

17

you on with the pleasures of false happiness. You have merely discovered the two-faced nature of this blind goddess. Although she still hides herself from others, she is now wholly known to you. If you like her, abide by her conditions and do not complain. But if you hate her treachery, ignore her and her deceitful antics. Really, the misfortunes which are now such a cause of grief ought to be reasons for tranquility. For now she has deserted you, and no man can ever be secure until he has been forsaken by Fortune.

"Do you think that your lost happiness is a precious thing? Can present good fortune be dear to you, even though you know that you may lose it, and that the loss will bring sorrow? If you cannot keep her, and if it makes you miserable to lose her, what is fickle Fortune but a promise of future distress? It is not enough to see what is present before our eyes; prudence demands that we look to the future. The double certainty of loss and consequent misery should prevent both the fear of her threats and the desire of her favors. Finally, once you have submitted yourself to her chains, you ought to take calmly whatever she can do to you. If you were to wish for a law to control the comings and goings of one whom you have freely taken for your mistress, you would be unjust and your impatience would merely aggravate a condition which you cannot change. If you hoist your sails in the wind, you will go where the wind blows you, not where you choose to go; if you put seeds in the ground, you must be prepared for lean as well as abundant years.

"You have put yourself in Fortune's power; now you must be content with the ways of your mistress. If you try to stop the force of her turning wheel, you are the most foolish man alive. If it should stop turning, it would cease to be Fortune's wheel.

Poem 1

"When Fortune turns her wheel with her proud right hand, she is as unpredictable as the flooding Euripus;[2] at one moment she fiercely tears down mighty kings, at the next the hypocrite exalts the humbled captive. She neither hears nor cares about the tears of those in misery; with a hard heart she laughs at the pain she causes. This is the way she amuses herself; this is the way she shows her power. She shows her servants the marvel of a man despairing and happy within a single hour.

2. A narrow strait that separates the island of Euboea from the coast of Boeotia.

Prose 2

Philosophy shows that it is the nature of Fortune to change.

"Let me confront you with the arguments of Fortune herself; then you will see that she is right. She might say to you: 'Why do you bother me with your daily complaints? What have I taken from you that belonged to you? You may argue your case against me before any judge; and if you can prove that riches and honors really belong to any mortal man, I will freely concede your ownership of the things you ask for.

"'When nature produced you from your mother's womb, I found you naked and lacking in everything. I nourished you with my abundant gifts, and, being inclined to favor you (an attitude which you now seem to hold against me), I endowed you with all the affluence and distinction in my power. Now it pleases me to withdraw my favor. You should be grateful for the use of things which belonged to someone else; you have no legitimate cause for complaint, as though you lost something which was your own. Why then are you so sad? I have done you no injury. Riches, honors, and all good fortune belong to me. They obey me as servants obey their mistress; they come with me, and when I go, they go too. I would even say that, if the things which you complain about losing had really been yours, you would never have lost them.

"'Why should I alone be deprived of my rights? The heavens are permitted to grant bright days, then blot them out with dark nights; the year may decorate the face of the earth with flowers and fruits, then make it barren again with clouds and frost; the sea is allowed to invite the sailor with fair weather, then terrify him with storms. Shall I, then, permit man's insatiable cupidity to tie me down to a sameness alien to my habits? Here is the source of my power, the game I always play: I spin my wheel and find pleasure in raising the low to a high place and lowering those who were on top. Go up, if you like, but only on condition that you will not feel abused when my sport requires your fall. Didn't you know about my habits? Surely you had heard of Croesus, King of Lydia, who was a formidable adversary to Cyrus at one time and later suffered such reverses that he would have been burnt had he not been saved by a shower from heaven.[3] And you must have heard how Paulus wept over the calamities suffered by Perses, King of Macedonia, whom he captured.[4] What else

---

3. Herodotus recounts how Croesus was captured by Cyprus, King of Persia, in 548 B.C.E., was condemned to be burned on a pyre of wood, and was saved from death by a rainstorm sent by Apollo.
4. Amelius Paulus, Consul of Rome, defeated Perses in 168 B.C.E.

does the cry of tragedy bewail but the overthrow of happy realms by the unexpected blow of Fortune?

"'You must have learned as a boy that on Jupiter's doorstep there are two barrels, one holding good things, the other bad.[5] What if you have drawn more abundantly from the barrel of good things? What if I have not deserted you completely? What if my very mutability gives you reason to hope that your fortunes will improve? In any case, do not lose heart. You live in the world which all men share, so you ought not desire to live by some special law.

Poem 2

"'If free-handed Plenty should dispense riches from her cornucopia as plentiful as the sands cast up by the storm-tossed sea, or as the stars that shine in heaven on clear nights, men still would not stop crying their miserable complaints.

"'Even though God were overgenerous with treasures of gold and deigned to satisfy every plea, if He favored the ambitious with the greatest honors, still all this would not satisfy.

"'Ravenous greed would devour everything and then discover other wants. No bridle can restrain man's disordered desires within reasonable bounds. Even when he is filled with great favors, he burns with thirst for more. No man can be rich who cries fearfully and considers himself to be poor.'

Prose 3

Philosophy reminds the prisoner of his former prosperity and of the precious gifts he still has.

"If Fortune should argue her case in this way, you would be unable to answer her. But, if you do have something to say in support of your complaint, I will be glad to listen."

"You have made a persuasive argument," I replied, "and presented it with sweet music and rhetoric. But it satisfies only while it is being spoken. Those in misery have a more profound awareness of their afflictions, and therefore a deep-seated pain continues long after the music stops."

---

5. At *Iliad*, Book 24, Achilles mentions the two barrels of Jupiter to Priam (King of Troy), who has come to the Greek encampment to beg for the body of Hector, Priam's son killed by Achilles.

"You are quite right," Philosophy answered, "for these words are not supposed to cure your disease but only to kill the pain of your obstinate sorrow. At the proper time I shall apply more deeply penetrating medicine. Still, you ought not to consider yourself completely miserable if you recall your many great joys.

"I will not mention that when you lost your father you were adopted by very prominent people and were chosen to become closely associated with the most powerful figures in the city.[6] You soon were more dear to them by love than you had been close before by relationship, and that is the most precious bond. Everyone considered you most fortunate to have so noble a father-in-law, such a chaste wife, and such fine sons. I pass over such trivial things as the fact that in your youth you received honors which most men never achieve even in old age.

"But I want to stress the greatest of your joys. If any mortal achievement can make a man happy, is it possible that any amount of misfortune can dim the memory of that brilliant occasion when you saw your two sons made Consuls and carried from their house in the company of the Senators and acclaimed by the people? They sat in the Senate in the chairs of consulship while you made a speech in honor of the King which earned high praise for its wit and elegance. You stood between your two honored sons and surpassed the expectations of the great crowd with your triumphant generosity. You pledged yourself to Fortune while she pampered you and favored you with her gifts. You got more from her than any private citizen ever received—and now do you think you can bargain with her?

"This is the first time she ever frowned on you with her evil eye. If you balance the number and kinds of your joys and misfortunes, you must admit that up to now you have been a happy man. If you think yourself unfortunate because you have now lost the things which seemed to make you happy before, still you should not make yourself miserable, because this sorrow will also pass. Do you imagine that you have just come on the stage of life as an unexpected pilgrim? Surely you do not expect to find stability in human affairs, since the life of man himself is often quickly ended. Although it is true that things which are subject to fortune can hardly be counted on, nevertheless, the last day of a man's life is a kind of death to such fortune as he still has. What difference does it make, then, whether you desert her by dying, or she you by leaving?

6. Boethius was adopted by Symmachus. He married Symmachus's daughter, Rusticiana, and his two sons became the Roman Consuls in 522 C.E. The consulship was established in the Roman Republic to replace the power of the king. Eventually, there were two consuls: one for the Western Empire, the other for the Eastern Empire. Under the Roman Emperors the office became more ceremonial than powerful.

Poem 3

"When Apollo in his rosy cart begins to spread light across the sky, the stars grow pale and fade before the rushing flame.[7] When the warm west wind blows, the woodland is radiant with spring roses; but the rage of the cold east wind can blast their beauty and leave only thorns. The calm sea often gleams in serene stillness; but often, too, angry storms out of the north throw up huge waves.

"If the form of this world cannot stay the same, but suffers so many violent changes, what folly it is to trust man's tumbling fortunes, to rely on things that come and go. One thing is certain, fixed by eternal law: nothing that is born can last."

Prose 4

Boethius protests that the worst sorrow is the remembrance of lost joys. Philosophy answers that the only true joy is self-possession in the face of adversity.

Then I answered: "Everything you say is true, dear nurse of all virtues. I do not deny that I came quickly to great prosperity. But the memory of it is what causes me most pain; for in the midst of adversity, the worst misfortune of all is to have once been happy."

"You are being punished for having misjudged your situation," Philosophy answered. "Therefore you have no right to blame the things which bother you. But if you are so impressed by this rather silly notion of happiness based on good fortune, let us consider how very well off you are. Then, if you find that among all the gifts of Fortune your most precious possessions are still safely yours, thanks to God's providence, can you justly complain of misfortune?

"Your father-in-law, Symmachus, one of the finest men who ever lived, and one for whom you would gladly give your life, is still unharmed. That most wise and virtuous man lives in safety to lament the injuries you are suffering. Your wife, so gracious, so chaste, so like her father in excellence of character, still lives, though now she is weary of life and goes on only for your sake. Even I must concede that in her case your happiness is greatly marred since her sorrow for your misfortunes is killing her.

"Think of your sons, the Consuls, who already at their age show the character of their father and grandfather. You are a happy man, if you consider what you still have. The greatest concern of mortals is

---

7. Phoebus Apollo carries the sun in his chariot. He is often identified with the sun. See note 1, pg. 6.

to preserve life, and you still possess things which everyone agrees are dearer than life itself. So, dry your tears. Fortune has not yet done her worst to you; you have not become a derelict in the storm since those anchors of present comfort and future hope hold fast."

"And I pray that they will continue to hold," I said, "for as long as they do I shall not go down, no matter how bad things get. Still, you see yourself how much I have lost."

"We have made some progress anyway," she answered, "if you have found something to be happy about. But I find your self-pity hard to bear when you moan childishly over the loss of some of your happiness. No one is so completely happy that he does not have to endure some loss. Anxiety is the necessary condition of human happiness since happiness is never completely achieved and never permanently kept. The man who enjoys great wealth may be scorned for his low birth; the man who is honored for his noble family may be oppressed by such poverty that he would rather be unknown. Someone else may enjoy both wealth and social position, but be miserable because he is not married. Still another may be happily married but have no children to inherit his fortune. Others have children, only to be saddened by their vices. Therefore, no one is entirely satisfied with his lot; each finds something lacking, or something which gives pain.

"Besides, those most blessed are often the most sensitive; unless everything works out perfectly, they are impatient at disappointment and shattered by quite trivial things. It takes very little to spoil the perfect happiness of the fortunate. Just think how many people would consider themselves lucky to have only a small part of your remaining good fortune. This very place which you call a land of exile is home to those who live here: nothing is miserable unless you think it so; and on the other hand, nothing brings happiness unless you are content with it. No one is so completely happy that he would not choose to change his condition if he let himself think about it impatiently. The joy of human happiness is shot through with bitterness; no matter how pleasant it seems when one has it, such happiness cannot be kept when it decides to leave.

"You see, then, how shoddy is the enjoyment provided by mortal things. They forsake those who are content with them, and they do not satisfy those who are discontented. Why then do men look outside themselves for happiness which is within? You are confused by error and ignorance and so I will point out to you the source of perfect happiness. Is anything more precious to you than yourself? You will agree that there is nothing. Then if you possess yourself, you have something you will never want to give up and something which Fortune cannot take from you. If you will consider carefully the following argument, you will have to admit that happiness cannot depend on things which are uncertain. If happiness is the highest good of rational natures, and if nothing which can be lost can be a supreme good (because it is obviously less good than that which cannot be lost),[8] then clearly unstable Fortune cannot pretend to bring happiness. The man who enjoys fleeting happiness either knows that it is perishable, or he doesn't. If he does not know it, his condition is unhappy because it rests on blind ignorance; if he knows his happiness is perishable, he must live in fear of losing what he knows can be easily lost—and such constant fears will not let him be happy. And if he should lose it, would he think that a trivial matter? Whatever can be given up without regret is indeed a thing of little worth. Now, you are a man fully convinced by many proofs that human souls are in no way mortal. It is clear, then, that if transitory happiness ends with the death of the body, and if this means an end of all happiness, the whole human race would be plunged into misery by death. But if we know that many men have sought the enjoyment of happiness not only in death, but also in the sorrows and pains of life, how can this present life make us happy when its end cannot make us unhappy?

Poem 4

"The prudent, steady man who wants a lasting place, immune from blasting winds and dangerous waves, should avoid high mountain peaks and the shore's shifting sands. For the mountain tops are lashed by terrifying gale-winds; and the loose sand of the beach will not bear his weight. Leave then the dangerous places of delight, and make your home safely on the low rocks. Though the wind trouble the sea with threats of destruction, you will live a serene life, happy for having built a strong house in the quiet valley, and laughing at the wrath of the elements.

Prose 5

Philosophy evaluates the things men strive for and concludes that material possessions bring neither true credit nor safety.

"Now that I see that the soothing medicine of my discourse is taking effect, I think I may risk somewhat stronger remedies. Even if

---

8. That a good that cannot be lost is greater than a good that can be lost can be found in the writings of Augustine and Plato. Lady Philosophy will use this fact to argue that eternal reward will outweigh any temporal good Boethius might have lost during his life.

the gifts of Fortune were not momentary and uncertain, there is
nothing about them that can ever really be made your own, and they
are vile in themselves if you look at them carefully. Are riches naturally precious, or are they precious because of some virtue of yours?
What is precious about them, the gold metal or the pile of money?
Wealth seems better when it is spent than when it is in the bank, for
avarice makes men hated, but liberality makes them popular. But
that which is given away is no longer possessed, so that money is
more precious when it is generously got rid of. And if all the money
in the world were acquired by one man, everyone else would be penniless. The sound of a voice can be given equally to many hearers,
but money cannot be distributed among many persons without
impoverishing those who give it up. Riches, then, are miserable and
troublesome: they cannot be fully possessed by many people, and
they cannot be acquired by some without loss to others.

"The brilliance of jewels is eye-catching, but the thing of special
value is in the light of the gems rather than in the eye of the beholder.
I am amazed that men prize them so highly. For what is there about a
thing which lacks the life of the soul and the articulation of the body
which can rightly be thought beautiful by human beings who have
living, rational natures? It is true that all things derive a certain
beauty from the Creator and from their own variety; but they are too
far beneath your excellence for you to marvel at them.

"You are, of course, delighted by the beauty of the open fields. And
why not, since this is a beautiful part of a very beautiful creation. In
the same way we are pleased by a serene sea, we admire the sky, the
stars, the sun and the moon; but do any of these things belong to
you? How then can you glory in their splendor? You are not adorned
with spring flowers, nor are you laden with summer fruit. When you
act as though such external goods are your own, you are deluded by
foolish satisfaction. Fortune can never make things yours which
nature made foreign to you. No doubt the fruits of the earth are
given to animals and men for their food; but, if you simply wish to
satisfy the demands of nature, there is no reason why you should
struggle for the superfluities of Fortune. For nature's needs are few
and small; if you try to glut yourself with too many things, you will
find your excesses either unpleasant or positively harmful.

"Or perhaps you pride yourself on fine clothes. Well, if they are
handsome to look at, I would admire either the quality of the material or the skill of the tailor. Possibly you think that a large number of
servants can make you happy. But if they are unreliable or dishonest,
they are a pernicious influence in the house and extremely troublesome to their master; on the other hand, if they are good, how can
their honesty be considered any virtue of yours?

"Therefore, it ought to be clear that none of these things which you are inclined to take credit for really belong to you. And if there is no desirable beauty in these things, why should you regret losing them, or be particularly elated to possess them? If they are beautiful by nature, what is that to you? They would be pleasing to you even if they belonged to someone else. They are not precious because you have them; you desire to have them because they seem precious.

"What then do you want from Fortune with all your strident demands? I suppose you are trying to avoid poverty by acquiring possessions. But you will find just the opposite: you will need more in order to keep the various valuable things you have. Those who have much, need much; and, on the contrary, those who limit their possessions to their natural needs, rather than to their excessive ambitions, need very little. Do you try to satisfy your desires with external goods which are foreign to you because you have no good within you which belongs to you? What an upside-down state of affairs when a man who is divine by his gift of reason thinks his excellence depends on the possession of lifeless bric-a-brac! Other creatures are content with what they have; but you, made in the likeness of God by virtue of your reason, choose ornaments for your excellent nature from base things, without understanding how great an injury you do to your Creator. God wished the human race to be superior to all earthly things, but you have lowered your dignity below the level of the most trivial things. For, if it is true that the good thing in which something else finds its good is more precious than the something else which counts it his good, then when you judge vile things to be your goods, you lower yourself beneath them by your own estimate and so deservedly become so. For man is constituted so that when he knows himself he excels all other things; but when he forgets who he is, he becomes worse than the beasts. It is natural for other living things not to know who they are, but in man such ignorance is vice. Your error is painfully evident if you suppose that a man can improve himself by adding ornaments that are not his own. It cannot be done; for if a thing attracts attention by added decoration, that which is added is praised, but that which is covered and disguised remains as base as before.

"Moreover, I deny that anything can be considered good which harms the one who has it. I am sure that you will agree. And riches are frequently harmful to those who possess them. Desperate men are greedy for things that belong to others and think that possession alone is enough to make a man worthy of riches and jewels. Now you are fearful of losing your life; but, if you had walked the road of life as a poor pilgrim, you could laugh in the face of thieves. What a blessing worldly riches are: when you have them, you have lost your safety!

Poem 5

"Men were most happy in former ages, content with the yield of fertile fields, and not yet ruined by indolent luxury. Their hunger was easily satisfied by acorns. They did not know the potent mixture of wine and honey; they had not learned to color fine silk of Syria with Tyrian dye. They slept soundly on the soft grass, drank from the running streams, and rested in the shade of the high pines.

"Travelers had not yet sailed the high seas to visit foreign ports with their merchandise. Trumpets of war were silent, and blood had not with fierce hate dyed red the gory fields. For how could hostile fury drive men to take up arms when war offered no rewards for gaping wounds except the blood that was spilled?

"Would that our age could return to those ancient virtues; but now man's avarice burns more fiercely than Aetna's fires. Who was he that first dug up the buried gold, the gems that wished to remain hidden, and with them all our costly dangers?[9]

Prose 6

Philosophy goes on to show that Fortune's gifts of honors and power are transitory and not good in themselves.

"I shall now speak about honors and power which you praise to the sky because you are ignorant of the nature of true honor and power. If these gifts of Fortune are given to a wicked man, they can cause more harm than floods or Aetna's eruptions.[1] Surely, you recall that your ancestors first freed the city from monarchy on account of the pride of kings, and then wanted to abolish consular government, even though it stood for the beginning of their liberty, because of the pride of the consuls. And even in those rare cases when honor and power are conferred upon good men, we are pleased not by the honor and power but by the probity of those who possess them. Thus, honor is not paid to virtuous men because of their rank; on the contrary, it is paid to rank because of the virtue of those holding it.

"What, indeed, is this power which you think so very desirable? You should consider, poor earthly animals, what it is that you seem to have in your power. If you should see a mouse seizing power and lording it over the other mice, how you would laugh! But if you consider only his body, what is weaker than a man who can be killed by the

---

9. This poem conflates a number of common views drawn from, among others, Vergil's *Georgics* and Ovid's *Metamorphoses.*
1. Plato argued in several dialogues that evil persons can be further harmed by receiving goods rather than punishments for their evil deeds.

bites of insects or by worms finding their way into him? For who can force any law upon man, except upon his body, or upon his fortune which is less than his body. You can never impose upon a free spirit, nor can you deprive a rationally self-possessed mind of its equanimity. Once, when a certain tyrant tried to torture a free man into betraying the partners of his conspiracy against the tyrant the man bit off his tongue and spat it in the raging tyrant's face.[2] In this way the torments which the tyrant inflicted as the means of his cruelty, this wise man made the means of virtuous action. Indeed, what can any man do to another which another may not do to him? We recall that Busirus, who was accustomed to kill his guests, was himself slain by his guest, Hercules.[3] Regulus had bound many of his African captives in chains; but before long he was himself chained by his captors.[4] How slight is the power of a man who cannot prevent someone from doing to him what he does to others.

"Moreover, if honor and power were by nature good in themselves, they would never be found in wicked men. For opposites are rarely found together, and nature abhors the union of contraries. Since there is no doubt that wicked men are often honored, it is obvious that the kind of honor which can be achieved by the wicked is not good. And this is even more obviously the case with all the other gifts of Fortune which are freely given to vicious men. It may also be said in this connection that no one doubts the courage of a man in whom he sees the marks of bravery; nor the swiftness of a man who obviously can run fast. Similarly, music makes musicians, medical skill makes doctors, rhetoric makes rhetoricians; for each thing does what is proper to its nature. It is not mixed with the characteristics of contrary things; indeed, it repels its opposites. Therefore, riches cannot be separated from insatiable avarice, nor can power make a man master of himself if vicious desires bind him with unbreakable chains. Honor bestowed upon wicked men does not make them honorable; on the contrary, it betrays and emphasizes their dishonor. And why does this happen? It happens because you choose to call things by false names, even though the things in question may be quite different, and the things are then found to contradict their names by their effects. Therefore, material possessions are not rightly called riches, worldly power is not true power, and public honor is not true honor.

"In the end, we reach the same conclusion about all the gifts of Fortune. They are not worth striving for; there is nothing in their

---

2. Diogenes Laertius provides this story of the philosopher Anaxarchus and Nicocreon, King of Cyprus.
3. Busirus, King of Egypt, sacrificed a stranger on the altar of Zeus once a year. Hercules, about to be sacrificed, killed Busirus instead.
4. Cicero relates that Regulus, a Roman consul during the First Punic War, was captured by the Carthaginians. He, under oath, was sent by them to Rome to negotiate an exchange of prisoners. After ensuring that the exchange was rejected, he returned to Carthage, where he was tortured to death.

natures which is good; they are not always possessed by good men, nor do they make those good who possess them.[5]

Poem 6

"Everyone knows the horrors done by Nero: he burned the city and murdered the Senators; he cruelly killed his own brother, and stained his hands with his mother's blood. He casually looked at her cold body and did not weep, as though he were merely the judge and critic of her dead beauty.[6] Yet this man ruled all the people under the sun from its rising in the east to its setting beneath the waves—all those under the cold northern stars and those scorched by the dry heat of the south winds which roast and burn the hot sands. But all this great power could not subdue the madness of this depraved man. When the evil sword of power is joined to the poison of passion, the commonwealth must groan under an intolerable burden."

Prose 7

Even the fame won by virtuous men in the performance of honorable public service is of slight value.

Then I said, "You know that ambition for material things has not mastered me; but I have desired the opportunity for public service so that my virtue should not grow old and weak through lack of use."

Philosophy answered, "Indeed, this is the only ambition which can attract minds which are excellent by nature but have not yet achieved perfect virtue. Such minds can be led on by desire for glory and the fame of having deserved well of their commonwealth. But think how trivial and empty such glory is. You know from astrological computation that the whole circumference of the earth is no more than a pinpoint when contrasted to the space of the heavens; in fact, if the two are compared, the earth may be considered to have no size at all. Moreover, as you learned from Ptolemy,[7] only a quarter of this tiny part of the universe is known to be inhabited by living things. And if you mentally subtract from this quarter of the earth all of the area occupied by seas, marshland, and arid deserts, there is almost no space left for human habitation. Do you, therefore, aspire to spread your fame and enhance your reputation when you are confined to

---

5. Lady Philosophy has now shown that the goods of the world are not truly good. To be deprived of them is not necessarily a misfortune.
6. The reign of the Roman Emperor Nero was marked by a number of atrocities. He was reputed to have executed many Roman senators and set fire to Rome itself.
7. A famous mathematician, astronomer, and geographer who taught in Alexandria, Egypt, in the middle of the second century.

this insignificant area on a tiny earth? How can glory be great that is severely limited by such narrow boundaries.

"Then, too, this small inhabited area is occupied by many nations which differ in language, customs, and philosophy of life. Do you suppose that the fame of individual men, or even of cities, can reach nations so remote and different, nations with which there is very little contact? In the time of Cicero, as he says himself somewhere, the fame of the Roman republic had not reached beyond the Caucasus Mountains even though at that period Rome was a mature nation, feared even by the Parthians and others.[8] Do you see now how small and petty the glory is which you strive to extend and increase? Certainly the fame of an individual Roman cannot reach where the fame of Rome herself has not penetrated.

"Moreover, since the customs and institutions of the different nations differ so much, what is praised by some may be condemned by others. The result is that though a man is pleased by the extension of his fame, he is unable to make himself known among many nations. Therefore, a man must be content with a reputation recognized among his own people, since the noble immortality of fame is confined within the boundaries of a single nation.

"Many men who were famous during their lifetime are now forgotten because no one wrote about them. But even written records are of limited value since the long passage of time veils them and their authors in obscurity. When you think about future fame, you imagine that you assure yourselves a kind of immortality. But, if you consider the infinite extent of eternity, what satisfaction can you have about the power of your name to endure? If you compare the duration of a moment with that of ten thousand years, there is a certain proportion between them, however small, since each is limited. But ten thousand years, however many times you multiply it, cannot even be compared to eternity. Finite things can be compared, but no comparison is possible between the infinite and the finite. And so, however long a time fame may last, it must seem not merely brief but nothing at all if it is compared to eternity.

"You mortals, however, know how to act justly only when you have the support of popular opinion and empty rumor; you are not satisfied with the assurance of conscience and virtue but seek your reward in the hollow praise of other men. Did you ever hear the joke about the folly of such arrogance? One man was ridiculing another who falsely called himself a philosopher; he called himself this not because he practiced true virtue, but because of vanity. The first man claimed that he would find whether or not the other was a philosopher by the way

---

8. The reference is to Cicero's *Republic*, 6, 22. This sixth book was known as the Dream of Scipio. Macrobius wrote an influential commentary on the work.

the other humbly and patiently put up with insults. The would-be philosopher bore the insults patiently for a while and then said, 'Now do you think that I am a philosopher?' His tormentor laughed and replied, 'I would have thought so, if you had kept silent.' But seriously, what sort of fame is there for the kind of excellent men I am talking about—those who seek glory through virtue? What do they get from fame after they die? For, if men perish completely in death, a thing which our reason prevents us from accepting, then there is certainly no glory when the man who is supposed to have it no longer exists. But, if the soul, in full awareness of its virtue, is freed from this earthly prison and goes to heaven, does it not disregard all earthly concerns and, in the enjoyment of heaven, find its satisfaction in being separated from earthly things?

Poem 7

"The man who recklessly strives for glory and counts it his highest goal should consider the far-reaching shores of heaven and the narrow confines of earth. He will be ashamed of a growing reputation which still cannot fill so small a space. Why do proud men try in vain to throw this world's burden from their shoulders? Though their fame spread to remote lands and be sung by many voices, though their proud families acquire high honors, still death is contemptuous of such glory and treats the humble and proud in the same manner. Death equalizes the high and the low.

"Where now are the bones of faithful Fabricius? What has become of Brutus and stern Cato?[9] Their slight surviving fame entrusts their empty names to some few books. But, although we know these fair words, we cannot know the dead. Then lie there, quite unknown, for fame will not keep fresh your memory. If you hope to live on in the glow of your mortal name, the day will come at last to take that too, and you will die a second death.

Prose 8

Philosophy argues that misfortune is more beneficial than good fortune, for good fortune deceives, but misfortune teaches.

"But do not think that I am engaged in total war with Fortune; for there is a time when that goddess no longer deceives, and then she

---

9. Marcus Porcius Cato (the Greater) was Consul in 195 B.C.E. He was a model and proponent of strict private and public morality. Gaius Fabricius Luscinus, Consul in 282 and 278 B.C.E., was noted for his austerity and incorruptibility. Lucius Junius Brutus, Consul in 509 B.C.E., was the founder of the Roman Republic.

deserves well of men. That is the time when she unmasks herself, when she shows her face and reveals her true character. But perhaps you do not yet understand what I mean. What I am about to say is so strange that I scarcely know how to make my meaning clear. I am convinced that adverse fortune is more beneficial to men than prosperous fortune. When Fortune seems kind, and seems to promise happiness, she lies. On the other hand, when she shows herself unstable and changeable, she is truthful. Good fortune deceives, adverse fortune teaches. Good fortune enslaves the minds of good men with the beauty of the specious goods which they enjoy; but bad fortune frees them by making them see the fragile nature of happiness. You will notice that good fortune is proud, insecure, ignorant of her true nature; but bad fortune is sober, self-possessed, and prudent through the experience of adversity. Finally, good fortune seduces weak men away from the true good through flattery; but misfortune often turns them around and forcibly leads them back to the true good.

"Do you think it a small matter that your terrible misfortunes have revealed the feelings of those friends who are faithful to you? Fortune has separated your true friends from two-faced ones; when she left you, she took her followers with her and left you your own. Think how much you would have given for this knowledge when you were still on top and thought yourself fortunate. Now you complain of lost riches; but you have found your friends, and that is the most precious kind of wealth.

Poem 8

"That the universe carries out its changing process in concord and with stable faith, that the conflicting seeds of things are held by everlasting law, that Phoebus in his golden chariot brings in the shining day, that the night, led by Hesperus, is ruled by Phoebe,[1] that the greedy sea holds back his waves within lawful bounds, for they are not permitted to push back the unsettled earth—all this harmonious order of things is achieved by love which rules the earth and the seas, and commands the heavens.

"But if love should slack the reins, all that is now joined in mutual love would wage continual war, and strive to tear apart the world which is now sustained in friendly concord by beautiful motion.

"Love binds together people joined by a sacred bond; love binds sacred marriages by chaste affections; love makes the laws which join true friends: O how happy the human race would be, if that love which rules the heavens ruled also your souls!"

---

1. Phoebe is the moon, who rules the night.

Book 3

Prose 1

Philosophy promises to lead Boethius to true happiness.

When her song was finished, its sweetness left me wondering and alert, eager to hear more. After a while I said, "You are the perfect comforter for weak spirits. I feel greatly refreshed by the strength of your ideas and the sweetness of your music; in fact, I think I may now be equal to the attacks of Fortune. And those remedies you spoke of earlier as being rather harsh—I not only do not fear them, I am quite eager to hear them."

Philosophy answered, "I knew it when I saw you so engrossed, so attentive to what I was saying. I waited for you to achieve this state of mind, or, to put it more truly, I led you to it. You will find what I have yet to say bitter to the taste, but, once you have digested it, it will seem sweet. Even though you say that you want to hear more, your eagerness would be even greater if you knew where I am about to lead you."

"Where?" said I.

"To true happiness, to the goal your mind has dreamed of. But your vision has been so clouded by false images you have not been able to reach it."

"Tell me then," I said. "Show me quickly what true happiness is."

"I will gladly, for your sake. But first I must try to make something else clear, something you know much more about. When you have understood that, you may turn your attention in the opposite direction and then you will be able to recognize the nature of true blessedness.

Poem 1

"The man who wants to sow a fertile field must first clear the ground of brush, then cut out the ferns and brambles with his sharp hook, so that the new grain may grow abundantly.

"Honey is sweeter to the taste if the mouth has first tried bitter flavors. Stars shine more brightly after Notus has stopped his rainy blasts. Only after Hesperus[1] has driven away the darkness does the day drive forward his splendid horses.

"Just so, by first recognizing false goods, you begin to escape the burden of their influence; then afterwards true goods may gain possession of your spirit."

Prose 2

Philosophy defines the supreme good and the perfect happiness to which all men naturally aspire. She then lists the kinds of false goods which men mistake for the true good.

Philosophy looked away for a moment, as though withdrawn into the sacred chamber of her mind; then she began to speak: "Mortal men laboriously pursue many different interests along many different paths, but all strive to reach the same goal of happiness. Now the good is defined as that which, once it is attained, relieves man of all further desires.[2] This is the supreme good and contains within itself all other lesser goods. If it lacked anything at all, it could not be the highest good, because something would be missing, and this could still be desired. Clearly, then, perfect happiness is the perfect state in which all goods are possessed. And, as I said, all men try by various means to attain this state of happiness; for there is naturally implanted in the minds of men the desire for the true good, even though foolish error draws them toward false goods.

"Some men, believing that the highest good is to have everything, exert themselves to become very rich. Others think that the highest good is to be found in the highest honors, and so they try to gain the esteem of their fellow citizens by acquiring various honors. Still others equate the highest good with the greatest personal power. Such men want to be rulers, or at least to associate themselves closely with those in power. Then there are those for whom fame seems the highest good and they labor to spread the glory of their names either in war or in practicing the arts of peace. Others measure the good in terms of gaiety and enjoyment; they think that the greatest happiness is found in pleasure. Finally, there are those who interchange the causes and results of these false goods: some desire

---

1. The Evening Star (see note 3, p. 12), but here the idea is that Hesperus becomes Lucifer, the Morning Star, and brings forth the day. *Notus*: the south wind.
2. Aristotle in *The Nicomachean Ethics*, Book 1, indicates that happiness is that for which everything else is done. See pp. 114–123, in this Norton Critical Edition.

riches in order to get power and pleasure; some desire power in order to get money or fame.

"Toward such false goods, and others like them, men direct their actions and desires; they want nobility and popularity, for example, because these seem to bring fame; or they want a wife and children because they regard them as sources of pleasure. With regard to friendship, the most sacred kind belongs to the goods of virtue, not of Fortune; all other kinds of friendship are sought out of a desire for power or pleasure. At this point it is a simple matter to evaluate the goods of the body in relation to those we have already discussed: size and strength seem to give power; beauty and speed bring fame; health gives pleasure. All this shows clearly that all men seek happiness; for whatever anyone desires beyond all else, he regards as the highest good. And, since we have defined the highest good as happiness, everyone thinks that the condition which he wants more than anything else must constitute happiness.

"You see here practically the whole range of human happiness: riches, honor, power, fame, and pleasure. Epicurus, who considered only these possibilities, held pleasure to be the highest good of them all, since the rest seem to bring joy to the soul.[3]

"But let me return now to the goals men set for themselves. In spite of its hazy memory, the human soul seeks to return to its true good; but, like the drunken man who cannot find his way home, the soul no longer knows what its good is. Should we consider those men mistaken who try to have everything? Not at all, for nothing can so surely make a man happy as being in full possession of all good things, sufficient in himself and needing no one else. Nor are they mistaken who think that the best men are most worthy of honor, for nothing which nearly all men aspire to achieve can be despised as vile. Power, too, must be considered a good thing, for it would be ridiculous to regard as trivial an asset which can accomplish more than anything else. And what of fame; should we be scornful of it? Surely we must admit that great excellence always carries with it great fame. Finally, it goes without saying that happiness excludes sadness and anguish, that it implies freedom from grief and misery, since even in small things we desire whatever brings delight and enjoyment.

"These, then, are the things which men desire to have: riches, high rank, administrative authority, glory and pleasure, because they believe that these things will give them a good standard of living, honor, power, fame and joy. And whatever men strive for in so many

---

3. Epicurus, the founder of Epicureanism, held pleasure to be the highest good. Although he probably did not equate pleasure with sensible pleasure, Lady Philosophy seems to understand him in this way.

ways must be the good. It is easy to show how strong and natural this striving is because, in spite of the variety and difference of opinion, still all men agree in loving and pursuing the goal of good.

Poem 2

"Now I will show you in graceful song, accompanied by pliant strings, how mighty Nature guides the reins of all things; how she providently governs the immense world by her laws; how she controls all things, binding them with unbreakable bonds.

"The Carthaginian lions endure their fair chains, are fed by hand, and fear the beatings they get from their masters; but if blood should smear their fierce mouths, their sluggish spirits revive, and with a roar they revert to their original nature. They shake off their chains and turn their mad fury on their masters, tearing them with bloody teeth.

"When the chattering bird, who sings in the high branches, is shut up in a narrow cage, she is not changed by the lavish care of the person who feeds her with sweet drink and tasty food. If she can escape from the cramped cage and see the cool shade of the wood, she will scatter the artificial food and fly with yearning to the trees where she will make the forest ring with her sweet voice.

"A treetop bent down by heavy pressure will bow its head to the ground; but if the pressure is released, the tree looks back to heaven again. Phoebus sets at night beneath the Hesperian waves, but returning again along his secret path he drives his chariot to the place where it always rises.

"Thus all things seek again their proper courses, and rejoice when they return to them. The only stable order in things is that which connects the beginning to the end and keeps itself on a steady course.

Prose 3

Nature inclines men toward the true good, but error deceives them with partial goods. Specifically, riches can never be wholly satisfying.

"You, too, who are creatures of earth, dream of your origin. However weak the vision of your dream may be, you have some vague idea of that goal of true happiness toward which you gaze. Nature leads you toward true good, but manifold error turns you away from it. Consider for a moment whether the things men think can give them happiness really bring them to the goal which nature planned for them. If money, or honor, or other goods of that kind really provide something which seems completely and perfectly good, then I too will admit that men can be happy by possessing them. But, if they not only cannot deliver what they promise, but are found to be gravely flawed in themselves, it is obvious that they have only the false appearance of happiness.

"First, then, since you recently were very rich, let me ask whether or not you were ever worried in spite of your abundant wealth."

"Yes," I answered, "I cannot recall a time when my mind was entirely free from worry."

"And wasn't it because you wanted something you did not have, or had something you did not want?"

"That is true," I answered.

"You wanted this, or didn't want that?"

"Yes."

"Then doesn't everyone lack something that he wants?"

"Yes, he does," I replied.

"And isn't the man who lacks something less than wholly self-sufficient?"

"That is true."

"And even you at the peak of your wealth felt this insufficiency?"

"Of course," I agreed.

"Then wealth cannot give a man everything and make him entirely self-sufficient, even though this is what money seems to promise. But I think it most important to observe that there is nothing in the nature of wealth to prevent its being taken from those who have it."

"That is quite true," I said.

"And why shouldn't you agree, since every day those who are powerful enough snatch it from those who are weaker. In fact, most lawsuits are concerned with efforts to recover money taken by violence or fraud."

I agreed that this was the case.

"Therefore, a man needs the help of others to protect his money."

"Of course."

"But he wouldn't need it, if he had no money to lose."

"There is no doubt about that."

"Well then, the situation is upside down; for riches, which are supposed to make men self-sufficient, actually make them dependent on the help of others.

"And now let us see whether riches really drive away need. Don't the wealthy become hungry and thirsty; don't they feel cold in the winter? You may argue that they have the means to satisfy their hunger and thirst, and to protect themselves against the cold. Nevertheless, the needs remain, and riches can only minimize them. For if needs are always present and making demands which must be met by spending money, clearly there will always be some need which is unsatisfied. And here I do not press the point that, although nature makes very modest demands, avarice is never satisfied. My present point is simply this: if riches cannot eliminate need, but on the contrary create new demands, what makes you suppose that they can provide satisfaction?

Poem 3

"Though the rich man has a flowing torrent of gold, his avarice can never be fully satisfied. He may decorate his neck with oriental pearls, and plow his fertile lands with a hundred oxen, but biting care will not leave him during life, and when he dies his wealth cannot go with him.

Prose 4

Honor is not the true good, nor is it the way to true happiness.

"But you may say that high public office makes the man who receives it honorable and worthy of reverence. Do you think that such offices have the power to make those who hold them virtuous and to free them from their vices? On the contrary, public honors usually reveal wickedness rather than correct it, and so we often complain that these honors are given to the worst men. Catullus, for example, called Nonius an ulcer, though he occupied high office.[4] You can see, then, the disgrace that comes to evil men who receive honors. Their unworthiness would be less obvious without the publicity of public recognition. In your own case, could any threats of danger have persuaded you to share public office with Decoratus, once you had found him to be a scoundrel and a spy?[5] We cannot judge men worthy of respect on account of the honors given them, if we find them unworthy of the honors they have received.

"But, if you found a man distinguished by his wisdom, could you think him unworthy of honor, or of the wisdom which is his?"

"Certainly not," I answered.

"For virtue has its own honor, and this honor is transferred to those who possess virtue. Since popular acclaim cannot accomplish this, clearly it does not have the beauty which is characteristic of

---

4. Catullus, a famous Roman poet of the first century B.C.E., criticized Nonius, whose identity is uncertain.
5. Decoratus was Quaestor around 508 C.E. Quaestors were elected officials of the Roman Republic who supervised the treasury and financial affairs of the State.

true honor. More attention should be paid to this point, for if public contempt makes men abject, public acclaim makes wicked men even more despised since it cannot make them worthy of honor and it exposes them to the world. But public rank itself does not escape untouched, for unworthy men tarnish the offices which they hold by infecting them with their own disease.

"And, to prove further that true honor cannot be attained through these specious dignities, think what would happen if a man who had been many times consul should go to some uncivilized foreign countries. Would the honors which he held at home make him worthy of respect in those places? But, if veneration were a natural part of public honors, it would certainly be given in every nation, just as fire always gives heat wherever it is found in the world. But, because popular respect is not a natural consequence of public office, but merely something which depends on untrustworthy public opinion, it vanishes when a man finds himself among those who do not regard his position in his home country as a special dignity.

"What I have said so far has to do with the attitudes of foreigners. Do you think that popular acclaim lasts forever among the citizens in the place where it had its origin? The office of praetor once had great power; now it is an empty name and a heavy burden on the treasury of the Senate.[6] The man who in earlier times was responsible for food supply and distribution was counted a great man; now there is no office lower in public esteem. For, as I said before, whatever does not have its own honor in itself, but depends on public whim, is sometimes valued highly, sometimes not at all. Therefore, if public honors cannot make those who have them worthy of reverence, and if, in addition, they are often tainted by the touch of wicked men, and if their value deteriorates with the passage of time, and if they are contemptible in the eyes of foreigners, what desirable beauty do they have in themselves or give to others?

Poem 4

"Although proud Nero in his raging lust adorned himself in Tyrian purple and white pearls, he was hated by all his subjects. But this wicked man once assigned the tainted seats of consulship to venerable men. Who, then, can consider those men blessed who receive their honors from evil men?

---

6. The office of Praetor changed over time. Originally, it was either a commander of an army or an elected magistrate. Around 366 C.E., the office was used to relieve the two Consuls of their judicial duties. By 395 C.E., its role was reduced to spending money on public games or public works.

Prose 5

Power is not a guarantee of happiness.

"Can royal power, of familiarity with kings, make a man truly powerful? Perhaps, you may say, as long as his happy situation endures. But both the past and the present are full of examples of kings who have fallen from happiness to misery. How wonderful is power which is found incapable even of preserving itself! And even though political power is a cause of happiness, is it not also a cause of misery when it diminishes? Although some human empires extend very widely, there are always some nations which cannot be brought under control; and at the point where power, which makes rulers happy, ends, there the impotence, which makes them miserable, begins. For this reason, rulers have always more misery than happiness. A famous tyrant, who knew the dangers of his position, symbolized the fears of kingship by hanging a drawn sword over the head of a member of his court.[7]

"What, then, is the nature of this power which cannot rid a man of gnawing anxieties nor save him from fear? Those who brag of their power want to live in security, but cannot. Do you consider a person powerful whom you see unable to have what he wants? Do you think a person mighty who is always surrounded by bodyguards, who is more afraid than those whom he intimidates, who puts himself in the hands of his servants in order to seem powerful?

"And what shall I say about the followers of men in power, when the power they attach themselves to is obviously so weak? They can be destroyed by the fall of their leader, or even by his whim while he is still in power. Nero forced his friend and teacher, Seneca, to choose his own manner of execution; Antoninus had Papinianus cut down by the swords of the soldiers, even though he had long been a power among the courtiers. Both of these unfortunate men wanted to give up their power; indeed, Seneca tried to give his wealth to Nero and retire.[8] But both were destroyed by their very greatness and neither could have what he wanted.

"What, then, is the value of power which frightens those who have it, endangers those who want it, and irrevocably traps those who have it? Are those true friends whom we acquire by fortune rather

---

7. The reference is to the Sword of Damocles. Dionysius the Elder of Syracuse illustrated to Damocles, a court sycophant, the life of a ruler by surrounding Damocles with luxury and suspending a sword from a horsehair over his neck. Cicero presents this story in *Tusculan Disputations*, 5, 21.

8. Aemilius Papinianus, a famous lawyer, was executed in 212 C.E. by the Roman Emperor Caracalla (Marcus Aurelius Antoninus), son of the Emperor Severus, for declining to excuse Caracalla's murder of his brother Geta and his friends to secure the title of Emperor. On Seneca, see note 6, p. 7.

than virtue? Misfortune will make an enemy of the man whom good fortune made a friend. And what scoundrel is more deadly than one who has been a friend?

Poem 5

"The man who wishes to be powerful must check his desires; he must not permit himself to be overcome by lust, or submit to its foul reins. For even though your rule extends so far that India trembles before you and Ultima Thule[9] serves you, if you cannot withstand black care, and live without wretched moaning, you have no power.

Prose 6

True happiness is not found in fame.

"As for glory, how deceptive it often is, and how shameful! The tragic playwright justly cries: 'Oh Fame, Fame, how many lives of worthless men you have exalted!'[1] For many men have achieved a great name based on the false opinion of the masses; and what is more disgraceful than that? Those who are falsely praised must blush when they hear the applause. And, even if the praise is merited, what does it matter to the wise man who measures his virtue by the truth of his conscience, not by popular esteem. And if it seems a good thing to have widened one's fame, it follows that it must seem a bad thing not to have done so. But since, as I explained earlier, there will always be some countries to which a man's fame does not extend, it follows that the person you think famous will be unknown in some other part of the world.

"In this discussion of fame, I do not think mere popularity even worth mentioning since it does not rest on good judgment, nor has it any lasting life. Moreover, everyone knows that to be called noble is a stupid and worthless thing. If it has anything to do with fame, the fame belongs to others; for nobility appears to be a kind of praise which is really merited by parents. If praise makes a person famous, then those who receive praise are famous; therefore, the praise of others (in this case, of your parents) will not make you famous if you have no fame of your own. In my opinion, therefore, if there is anything to be said for nobility, it lies only in the necessity imposed on the nobility to carry on the virtues of their ancestors.

9. The name of the most northern region of the world.
1. Euripides, *Andromache* 319f. [Translator's note.]

Poem 6

"The whole race of men on this earth springs from one stock. There is one Father of all things; One alone provides for all. He gave Phoebus his rays, the moon its horns. To the earth He gave men, to the sky the stars. He clothed with bodies the souls He brought from heaven.[2]

"Thus, all men come from noble origin. Why then boast of your ancestors? If you consider your beginning, and God your Maker, no one is base unless he deserts his birthright and makes himself a slave to vice.

Prose 7

Bodily pleasure cannot make men happy.

"What now shall I say about bodily pleasures? The appetite for them is full of worry, and the fulfillment full of remorse. What dreadful disease and intolerable sorrow, the fruits of wickedness, they bring to the bodies of those who enjoy them! What pleasure there may be in these appetites I do not know, but they end in misery as anyone knows who is willing to recall his own lusts. If they can produce happiness, then there is no reason why beasts should not be called happy, since their whole life is devoted to the fulfillment of bodily needs. The pleasure one finds in his wife and children ought to be a most wholesome thing, but the man who protested that he found his sons to be his torturers spoke what may too often be true. How terrible such a condition can be you must learn from me, since you have never experienced it at first hand, nor do you now suffer from it. In this matter I commend the opinion of Euripides who said that the childless man is happy by his misfortune.

Poem 7

"It is the nature of all bodily pleasure to punish those who enjoy it. Like the bee after its honey is given, it flies away, leaving its lingering sting in the hearts it has struck.

---

2. Lady Philosophy blends Roman mythology with Christianity by proclaiming God to be the source of all.

Prose 8

Philosophy concludes that these limited goods are transitory and cannot bring happiness. On the contrary, they are often positively harmful.

"There is no doubt, therefore, that these are the wrong roads to happiness; they cannot take anyone to the destination which they promise. Let me briefly show you the evils within them. If you try to accumulate money, you must deprive someone else of it. If you want to cover yourself with honors, you will become indebted to those who can bestow them; and, by wishing to outdo others in honor, you will humiliate yourself by begging.

"If you want power, you risk the danger of your subjects' treachery. If you seek fame, you will become involved in difficulties and lose your security. If you seek a life of pleasure—but who would not spurn and avoid subjection to so vile and fragile a thing as his body? Indeed, those who boast of bodily goods are relying on weak and uncertain possessions. For you are not bigger than an elephant, nor stronger than a bull, nor as quick as a tiger.

"Fix your gaze on the extent, the stability, the swift motion of the heavens, and stop admiring base things. The heavens are not more remarkable in these qualities than in the reason by which they are governed. The beauty of your person passes swiftly away; it is more fleeting than spring flowers. And if, as Aristotle says, men had the eyes of Lynceus and could see through stone walls, would they not find the superficially beautiful body of Alcibiades[3] to be most vile upon seeing his entrails? It is not your nature which makes you seem fair but the weak eyes of those who look at you. You may esteem your bodily qualities as highly as you like as long as you admit that these things you admire so much can be destroyed by the trifling heat of a three-day fever.

"All these arguments can be summed up in the truth that these limited goods, which cannot achieve what they promise, and are not perfect in embracing all that is good, are not man's path to happiness, nor can they make him happy in themselves.

Poem 8

"Alas, what ignorance drives miserable men along crooked paths! You do not look for gold in the green trees, nor for jewels hanging on the vine; you do not set your nets in the high mountains when you want a

---

3. An Athenian soldier and statesman who plays an important role in Plato's *Symposium*; considered very handsome. *Lynceus*: an Argonaut (men who accompanied Jason in his quest for the Golden Fleece) whose sight was so sharp he could see objects at great distances.

fish for dinner; nor, if you want to hunt deer, do you seek them along the Tyrenean seas. On the contrary, men are skilled in knowing the hidden caves in the sea, and in knowing where white pearls and scarlet dye are found; they know what beaches are rich in various kinds of fish.

"But, when it comes to the location of the good which they desire, they are blind and ignorant. They dig the earth in search of the good which soars above the star-filled heavens. What can I say to show what fools they are? Let them pursue their riches and honors and, when they have painfully accumulated their false goods, then they may come to recognize the true.

Prose 9

Philosophy completes her discussion of false happiness and its causes. She then takes up the subject of true happiness and the supreme good.

"Up to this point," said Philosophy, "I have shown clearly enough the nature of false happiness, and, if you have understood it, I can now go on to speak of true happiness."

"I understand well enough," I answered, "that sufficiency is not attained by riches, nor power by ruling others, nor honor by public recognition, nor fame by public acclaim, nor joy by pleasures."

"But have you understood the reasons why this is so?"

"I think I have a vague idea," I said, "but I wish you would show me more plainly."

"The reasons are clear enough. What nature has made simple and indivisible, human error has divided and changed from true and perfect to false and imperfect. Would you say that one who lacks nothing stands in need of power?"

"Of course not."

"You are quite right; for whoever is deficient in any way needs outside help."

"That is true," I said.

"Therefore, sufficiency and power have one and the same nature."

"That seems to be true."

"And would you say that a thing which is perfectly self-sufficient and completely powerful should be scorned, or is it, on the contrary, worthy of honor?"

"Undoubtedly it is most worthy of honor."

"Then we may add reverence to sufficiency and power, and conclude that all three are really one."[4]

---

4. This is an important claim: what is self-sufficient and all powerful is worthy of reverence. This claim justifies worshipping a perfect being.

"That is true."

"Next, would you think such a thing obscure and base, or rather, famous and renowned? Now think for a moment whether that which is conceded to be self-sufficient, all powerful, and worthy of great reverence can stand in need of any fame which it cannot give to itself, and therefore seem in some way defective."

"I confess that being what it is it must also be famous."

"It follows, then, that fame cannot be separated from the other three."

"That is true."

"Therefore, that which is self-sufficient, which can do everything by its own power, which is honored and famous, is not this also most pleasant and joyful?"

"I cannot imagine how anyone possessing all these attributes could be sad; and so, if the argument thus far is sound, I must confess that this thing must also be joyful."

"Then," Philosophy went on, "it must be granted that, although the names of sufficiency, power, fame, reverence, and joy are different, in substance all are one and the same thing."

"That must be granted," I agreed.

"Human depravity, then, has broken into fragments that which is by nature one and simple; men try to grasp part of a thing which has no parts and so get neither the part, which does not exist, nor the whole, which they do not seek."

"How is this?" I asked.

"The man who seeks wealth in order to avoid poverty is not interested in power; he would rather be obscure and weak and will even deprive himself of many natural pleasures so that he won't lose the money he has collected. But such a man does not even acquire sufficiency; he is powerless, plagued by trouble, held in contempt, and hidden in obscurity. Similarly, the man who seeks only power wastes his money, scorns pleasures and honors that carry with them no power, and thinks nothing of fame. But see how much he is missing: sometimes he is without the necessities of life, he is plagued by anxieties, and when he cannot overcome them he loses that which he wants most—he ceases to be powerful. Honors, fame, and pleasure can be shown to be equally defective; for each is connected with the others, and whoever seeks one without the others cannot get even the one he wants."

"What happens when someone tries to get them all at the same time?" I asked.

"He, indeed, reaches for the height of happiness, but can he find it in these things which, as I have shown, cannot deliver what they promise?"

"Of course not," I said.

"Happiness, then, is by no means to be sought in these things which are commonly thought to offer the parts of what is sought for."

"Nothing can be truer than this," I agreed.

"Now you have grasped the nature of false happiness and its causes. Now turn your mind's eye in the opposite direction and there you will see the true happiness which I promised to show you."

"But this is clear even to a blind man," I said, "and you revealed it a little while ago when you tried to explain the causes of false happiness. For, unless I am mistaken, true and perfect happiness is that which makes a man self-sufficient, powerful, worthy of reverence and renown, and joyful. And, to show that I have understood you, I acknowledge that whatever can truly provide any one of these must be true and perfect happiness, since all are one and the same."

"O, my scholar," Philosophy answered, "your observation is a happy one if you add just one thing."

"What is that?" I asked.

"Do you imagine that there is any mortal and frail thing which can bring about a condition of this kind?"

"Not at all," I said, "but I think you have proved that beyond any need for further discussion."

"Then these false causes of happiness are mere appearances of the true good and merely seem to give certain imperfect goods to mortal men; but they cannot give true and perfect good."

"I agree," I said.

"Now then, since you know what true happiness is, and the things that falsely seem to offer it, you must now learn where to look for true happiness."

"This," I answered, "is what I have eagerly looked forward to."

"But since, as Plato says in his *Timaeus*, we ought to implore divine help even in small things, what do you think is called for now if we are to gain access to the throne of the highest good?"

"We must invoke the Father of all things without whose aid no beginning can be properly made."

"You are right," said Philosophy, and she began to sing this song:

Poem 9[5]

"Oh God, Maker of heaven and earth, Who govern the world with eternal reason, at your command time passes from the beginning. You place all things in motion, though You are yourself without

---

5. The influence of Plato's *Timaeus* on this section of the work is great. See the supplemental text from *The Timaeus* on pp. 107–14 of this volume. This excerpt explains the three-fold action of the World Soul that Plato uses to explain the creation of the world.

change. No external causes impelled You to make this work from chaotic matter. Rather it was the form of the highest good, existing within You without envy, which caused You to fashion all things according to the eternal exemplar. You who are most beautiful produce the beautiful world from your divine mind and, forming it in your image, You order the perfect parts in a perfect whole.

"You bind the elements in harmony so that cold and heat, dry and wet are joined, and the purer fire does not fly up through the air, nor the earth sink beneath the weight of water.

"You release the world-soul throughout the harmonious parts of the universe as your surrogate, threefold in its operations, to give motion to all things. That soul, thus divided, pursues its revolving course in two circles, and, returning to itself, embraces the profound mind and transforms heaven to its own image.

"In like manner You create souls and lesser living forms and, adapting them to their high flight in swift chariots, You scatter them through the earth and sky. And when they have turned again toward You, by your gracious law, You call them back like leaping flames.

"Grant, Oh Father, that my mind may rise to Thy sacred throne. Let it see the fountain of good; let it find light, so that the clear light of my soul may fix itself in Thee. Burn off the fogs and clouds of earth and shine through in Thy splendor. For Thou art the serenity, the tranquil peace of virtuous men. The sight of Thee is beginning and end; one guide, leader, path, and goal.

Prose 10

Philosophy teaches Boethius that the supreme good and highest happiness are found in God and are God.

"Since you have seen the forms of imperfect and perfect good, I think it is now time to show where this perfection of happiness resides. First, we must ask whether a good of the kind you defined a short while ago can exist at all, so that we may not be deceived by an empty shadow of thought and thus be prevented from reaching the truth of our problem. Now, no one can deny that something exists which is a kind of fountain of all goodness; for everything which is found to be imperfect shows its imperfection by the lack of some perfection. It follows that if something is found to be imperfect in its kind, there must necessarily be something of that same kind which is perfect.[6] For without a standard of perfection we cannot judge

---

6. This argument for the existence of perfection will show up in Aquinas's Fourth Way of proving God's existence. It is drawn from Platonic and Neoplatonic sources.

anything to be imperfect. Nature did not have its origins in the defective and incomplete but in the integral and absolute; it fell from such beginnings to its present meanness and weakness.

"But if, as I have just pointed out, there is a certain imperfect happiness in transitory goods, no one can doubt that there is a perfect and enduring happiness."

"That is firmly and truly established," I said.

"Now consider where this perfect happiness has its dwelling place. It is the common conception of the human mind that God, the ruler of all things, is good. For, since nothing can be thought of better than God, who can doubt that He is the good, other than whom nothing is better. And that God is good is demonstrated by reason in such a way as to convince us that He is the perfect good. If He were not, He could not be the ruler of all things; for there would be something better than He, something possessing perfect good, which would seem to be older and greater than He. For all perfect things have been shown to come before less perfect ones. And so, if we are to avoid progression *ad infinitum*, we must agree that the most high God is full of the highest and most perfect good. But we have already established that perfect good is true happiness; therefore it follows that true happiness has its dwelling in the most high God."

"I agree," I said. "Your argument cannot be contradicted."

"But observe," Philosophy continued, "how you may prove scrupulously and inviolably what I have just said, namely, that the most high God is full of the highest good."

"How?" I asked.

"By avoiding the notion that the Father of all things has received from others the highest good with which He is filled, or that He has it naturally in such a way that He and the happiness which He has may be said to differ in essence. For, if you should suppose that He receives it from someone else, you could think that the one who gives it is greater than the one who receives it; but we worthily confess that God is the most excellent of all beings. And if He has this happiness by nature, but differs from it, then someone else who can will have to explain how these diverse things are joined together, since we are speaking of God the Creator of all things. Finally, that which is different from anything cannot be the thing from which it differs; therefore, that which according to its nature differs from the highest good cannot be the highest good. But it is blasphemous to think this about One other than whom, as we know, nothing is greater. And surely there can be nothing better by nature than its source; therefore, I may conclude with certainty that whatever is the source of all things must be, in its substance, the highest good."

"I agree."

"And do you also agree that the highest good is happiness?"

"Yes."

"Then," said Philosophy, "you must agree that God is happiness."[7]

"I found your earlier arguments unassailable, and I see that this conclusion follows from them."

"Then consider whether the same conclusion is not even more firmly established by this, that there cannot exist two highest goods which differ from one another. Clearly, when two goods differ, one cannot be the other; therefore, neither can be perfect since it lacks the other. But that which is not perfect certainly cannot be the highest good; therefore, those things which are the highest good cannot be diverse. But I have proved that happiness and God are the highest good; therefore, that must be the highest happiness which is the highest divinity."

"I can think of nothing truer, or more reasonable, or worthier of God," I said.

"From this conclusion, then, I will give you a kind of corollary, just as the geometricians infer from their demonstrated propositions things which they call deductions. Since men become happy by acquiring happiness, and since happiness is divinity itself, it follows that men become happy by acquiring divinity. For as men become just by acquiring integrity, and wise by acquiring wisdom, so they must in a similar way become gods by acquiring divinity. Thus everyone who is happy is a god and, although it is true that God is one by nature, still there may be many gods by participation."

"This is a beautiful and precious idea," I said, "whether you call it a corollary or a deduction."

"And there is nothing more beautiful," Philosophy went on, "than the truth which reason persuades us to add to this."

"What is that?" I asked.

"Since happiness seems composed of many things, would you say that all these are joined together in happiness, as a variety of parts in one body, or does one of the parts constitute the essence of happiness with all the rest complementing it?"

"I wish you would explain this point by recalling what is involved."

Philosophy then continued. "Do we not agree that happiness is good?"

---

7. That God is happiness seems an odd claim since we do not attribute states like happiness to God. Perhaps Boethius is thinking that because God lacks nothing and unhappiness is a result of some lack, God is not unhappy and thus happy. Clearly, the thrust of the *Consolation* leads one to think that Boethius wants to claim that the highest happiness for a human being is eternal association with God in the next life.

"Indeed, it is the highest good," I replied.

"Then we must add this good to all the others; for happiness is considered the fullest sufficiency, the greatest power, honor, fame, and pleasure. Now are all these to be regarded as good in the sense that they are members or parts of happiness, or are they simply related to the good as to their crown?"

"I understand the problem now and am eager to have your answer."

"Here then is the solution. If all these goods were constituent parts of happiness, each would differ from the others; for it is the nature of parts to be different things constituting one body. But I have proved that all these goods are one and the same thing; therefore they cannot be parts. Otherwise, happiness would seem to be constituted of one part, which is a contradiction in terms."[8]

"There is no doubt about that," I said, "but you have not yet given me the solution."

"Clearly, all the rest must be related to the good. For riches are sought because they are thought good, power because it is believed to be good, and the same is true of honor, fame, and pleasure. Therefore, the good is the cause and sum of all that is sought for; for if a thing has in it neither the substance nor the appearance of good, it is not sought or desired by men. On the other hand, things which are not truly good, but only seem to be, are sought after as if they were good. It follows, then, that goodness is rightly considered the sum, pivot, and cause of all that men desire.[9] The most important object of desire is that for the sake of which something else is sought as a means; as, for example, if a person wishes to ride horseback in order to improve his health, he desires the effect of health more than the exercise of riding.

"Since, therefore, all things are sought on account of the good, it is the good itself, not the other things, which is desired by everyone. But, as we agreed earlier, all those other things are sought for the sake of happiness; therefore, happiness alone is the object of men's desires. It follows clearly from this that the good and happiness are one and the same thing."

"I cannot see how any one could disagree."

"But we have also proved that God and true happiness are one and the same."

"That is so."

"We can, therefore, safely conclude that the essence of God is to be found in the good, and nowhere else.

---

8. This argument bears a striking similarity to Socrates' claims in the dialogue called *The Protagoras* that all virtues are the same and not simply part of what is called Virtue.
9. Again, the structure of the argument bears a close connection to Aristotle's claims in *The Nicomachean Ethics* that activities and objects are sought for the sake of happiness. See the supplemental text from Aristotle's *Ethics* on pp. 114–23 of this volume.

Poem 10

"Come, all you who are trapped and bound by the foul chains of that deceiving lust which occupies earth-bound souls. Here you will find rest from your labors, a haven of steady quiet, a refuge from misery.

"Nothing that the river Tagus with its golden shores can give, nor the Hermus with its jeweled banks, the Indus of the torrid zone, gleaming with green and white stones, none of these can clear man's vision. Instead, they hide blind souls in their shadows.[1]

"Whatever pleases and excites your mind here, Earth has prepared in her deep caves. The shining light which rules and animates the heavens avoids the dark ruins of the soul. Whoever can see this light will discount even the bright rays of Phoebus."

Prose 11

Philosophy shows that God is One and that He is the goal toward which all things tend.

"I must agree, since your entire argument is established by sound reasons."

"Then," Philosophy continued, "how highly would you value it, if you could know what the absolute good is?"

"Such knowledge would be of infinite value," I said, "if I were also able to know God who is the absolute good."

"Well, I will show you this with certainty, if the conclusions we have arrived at so far are correct."

"They are indeed," I said.

"I have already proved that the things which most people want are not the true and perfect good since they differ from one another; and, since one or the other is always missing, they cannot provide full and perfect good. But I have also shown that they become the true good when they are gathered together as it were into a single form and operation, so that sufficiency becomes the same as power, honor, fame, and pleasure. And I have further shown that unless they are all one and the same, there is no reason to consider them desirable."

"You have proved this beyond doubt."

"Therefore, if these partial goods cannot be truly good if they are different, but are good if they become one, then clearly they become good by acquiring unity."

---

1. The river Tagus is the longest river of the Iberian Peninsula. It rises in eastern Spain and empties into the Atlantic Ocean near Lisbon, Portugal. The river Hermus (Hermos) flows through Lydia (modern Turkey) and into the Aegean Sea. The Indus River of India and Pakistan flows from the Himalayas and empties into the Arabian Sea.

"This seems to be true," I said.

"But, if you also grant that every good is good by participating in the perfect good, then you should concede by a similar line of reasoning that the good and the one are the same. For things are of the same essence if their effects are of the same nature."

"I cannot deny that."

"And do you also understand that everything that is remains and subsists in being as long as it is one; but that when it ceases to be one it dies and corrupts?"

"How is this?"

"In the case of animals, when body and spirit are joined together in one being and remain so, that being is called a living thing; but when this unity is dissolved by the separation of body and soul, the being dies and is no longer a living animal. Even the body seems to be human as long as it remains one form in the union of its members; but, if this unity is broken by the separation and scattering of the body's members, it ceases to be what it was before. If we go on to examine other things we will see that each has its being as long as it is one, but when it begins to lose that oneness, it dies."

"On further consideration, I see that this is so."

"Is there anything, then, which acting naturally, gives up its desire to live and chooses to die and decay?"

"When I consider animals whose natures give them some choice, I know of none which gives up the will to live and of its own accord seeks death as long as it is free of external pressure. For every living being acts to preserve its life and to avoid death and injury. But, about plants and trees and inanimate objects, I simply do not know."

"You should not be in doubt about them, since you observe that trees and plants take root in suitable places and, to the extent made possible by their natures, do not wither and die. Some grow in the fields, some in the mountains, some in marshland, some in rocky places, some flourish in the sterile sands; but if any of these should be transplanted to some other place, they would die. Nature gives all things what they need and takes care that they live as long as they can. Why do all plants get their nourishment from roots, like a mouth drinking from the ground, and build up rugged bark over the pith? Why is the soft substance on the inside, while on the outside is the firm wood, and covering all is the bark, a rugged defender against harm, protecting the plant against storms? Note, too how diligent nature is in propagating every species by multiplying the seed. Everyone knows that these natural processes are designed for the permanent preservation of the species as well as for the present life of individual plants.

"Even things believed to be inanimate do what is proper to their natures in much the same way. Why does lightness cause flames to rise and weight cause earth to settle, if not that these phenomena are appropriate to the things concerned? In addition, each thing is kept in being by that which is naturally proper to it, just as each thing is corrupted by that which is naturally opposed to it. Hard things, such as stones, resist fragmentation by the tough cohesion of their parts; but fluid things, such as air and water, are easily parted, but then quickly flow together again; fire, however, cannot be cut at all. We are not concerned here with the voluntary motions of the intelligent soul, but only of those natural operations of which we are unconscious, such as, for example, digestion of food and breathing during sleep. Indeed, even in living beings, the desire to live comes not from the wishes of the will but from the principles of nature. For often the will is driven by powerful causes to seek death, though nature draws back from it. On the other hand, the work of generation, by which alone the continuation of mortal things is achieved, is sometimes restrained by the will, even though nature always desires it. Thus, this love for the self clearly comes from natural instinct and not from voluntary activity. Providence gave to his creatures this great urge for survival so that they would desire to live as long as they naturally could. Therefore you cannot possibly doubt that everything which exists naturally desires to continue in existence and to avoid harm."

"I now see clearly," I said, "what up to now seemed uncertain."

"Furthermore," Philosophy went on, "whatever seeks to exist and endure also desires to be one; for without unity existence itself cannot be sustained."

"That is true," I said.

"Then all things desire unity."

I agreed.

"But I have already shown that unity is the same as goodness."

"True," I said.

"Therefore, all things desire the good, so that we can define the good as that which is desired by all."

"That is perfectly correct," I agreed. "For either there is no one thing to which all other things are related, and therefore they wander without direction or goal, or, if there is something toward which all things hasten, it is the highest of all goods."

"I am greatly pleased with you, my pupil, for you have found the key to truth. And you also see clearly what a while ago you said you did not understand."

"What is that?" I asked.

"The end, or goal, of all things. For surely it is that which is desired by all; and, since we have identified that as the good, we must conclude that the good is the end toward which all things tend.[2]

2. Plato claims that all men desire the good. Aristotle claims that all things desire the good.

Poem 11

"The man who searches deeply for the truth, and wishes to avoid being deceived by false leads, must turn the light of his inner vision upon himself. He must guide his soaring thoughts back again and teach his spirit that it possesses hidden among its own treasures whatever it seeks outside itself.

"Then all that was hidden by the dark cloud of error will shine more clearly than Phoebus; for the body, with its burden of forgetfulness, cannot drive all light from his mind. The seed of truth grows deep within and is roused to life by the breath of learning. For how can you answer questions truly unless the spark of truth glows deep in your heart? If Plato's Muse speaks truly, whatever is learned is a recollection of something forgotten."[3]

Prose 12

Philosophy shows that God rules the universe by his goodness and that all created things obey him.

"I agree fully with Plato," I said, "for this is the second time I have been reminded of these truths. I forgot them first under the oppressive influence of my body, then later when I was depressed by grief."

Philosophy replied, "If you consider carefully the conclusions you have so far granted, you will quickly remember something else which you said a while ago that you did not know."

"What is that?"

"The way the world is governed," she said.

"I do remember confessing my ignorance about that," I answered, "and, even though I can now anticipate your answer, I want to hear it plainly from you."

"Earlier in our discussion," Philosophy said, "you affirmed without any doubt that the world is ruled by God."

"I still have no doubt about it, and never will, for these reasons: this world could never have achieved its unity of form from such different and contrary parts unless there were One who could bring together such diverse things. And, once this union was effected, the very diversity of discordant and opposed natures would have ripped it apart and destroyed it, if there were not One who could sustain what He had made. Nor could the stable order of nature continue, nor its motions be so regular in place, time, causality, space and

---

3. Plato claims in *The Meno* and *The Phaedo* that all knowledge is recollection. That is, all knowledge is already in the soul but we forget these truths when the soul is joined to the body. When we learn, we are merely rediscovering the truths that are in our soul.

quality, unless there were One who could govern this variety of change while remaining immutable Himself. This power, whatever it may be, by which created things are sustained and kept in motion, I call by the name which all men use, God."

Philosophy answered, "Since this is your conviction, I think it will be easy to restore your happiness and bring you back safely to your own country. Now let us return to our task. Have we not already shown that sufficiency is among the attributes of happiness, and are we not agreed that God is absolute happiness?"

"That is right," I said.

"Then He needs no outside help in ruling the world; otherwise, if He were in need of anything He would not be completely self-sufficient."

"That is necessarily true," I said.

"Therefore He disposes all things by himself alone."

"I agree."

"Moreover, I have proved that God is absolute good."

"I remember that," I said.

"Then if He, whom we have agreed to be the good, rules all things by himself, He must dispose everything according to the good. He is, in a manner of speaking, the wheel and rudder by which the vessel of the world is kept stable and undamaged."

"I fully agree," I said, "and I saw in advance, though somewhat vaguely, that this is what you would say."

"I don't doubt it," Philosophy replied, "for I think that you are now looking more sharply for the truth. But what I am now going to tell you is equally clear."

"What is that?" I asked.

"Since God is rightly believed to govern all things with the rudder of goodness, and since all these things naturally move toward the good, as I said earlier, can you doubt that they willingly accept His rule and submit freely to His pleasure as subjects who are agreeable and obedient to their leader?"

"This must be so," I answered, "for no rule could be called happy if it were a bondage of willing slaves rather than one designed for the welfare of compliant citizens."

"Then there is nothing which, by following nature, strives to oppose God?"

"Nothing," I agreed.

"And, if anything should try to oppose Him, could it be at all successful against the One we have rightly shown to be the supreme power of happiness?"

"It would have no chance whatever," I said.

"Then there is nothing which has either the desire or the power to oppose this highest good?"

"Nothing."

"Then it is the supreme good which rules all things firmly and disposes all sweetly."

"I am delighted," I said, "not only by your powerful argument and its conclusion, but even more by the words you have used. And I am at last ashamed of the folly that so profoundly depressed me."

"You have read in the fables of the poets how giants made war on heaven; but this benign power overthrew them as they deserved. But now let us set our arguments against each other and perhaps from their opposition some special truth will emerge."

"As you wish," I said.

"No one can doubt that God is almighty," Philosophy began.

"Certainly not, unless he is mad," I answered.

"But nothing is impossible for one who is almighty."

"Nothing."

"Then can God do evil?"

"No, of course not."

"Then evil is nothing, since God, who can do all things, cannot do evil."[4]

"You are playing with me," I said, "by weaving a labyrinthine argument from which I cannot escape. You seem to begin where you ended and to end where you began. Are you perhaps making a marvelous circle of the divine simplicity? A little while ago you began with happiness, declared it to be the highest good, and located its dwelling in almighty God. You said that God himself is the highest good and perfect happiness. From this you inferred that no one could be happy unless he too were a god. Then you went on to say that the very form of the good is the essence of God and of happiness; and you said further that unity is identical with the good which is sought by everything in nature. You also affirmed that God rules the universe by the exercise of His goodness, that all things willingly obey Him, and that there is no evil in nature. And you proved all this without outside assumptions and used only internal proofs which draw their force from one another."

Philosophy answered, "I have not mocked you at all. With the help of God whose aid we invoked we have reached the most important point of all. For it is the nature of the divine essence neither to pass to things outside itself nor to take any external thing to itself. As Parmenides puts it, the divine essence is 'in body like a sphere, perfectly rounded on all sides';[5] it rotates the moving orb of the universe while it remains unmoved itself. You ought not to be surprised that I have sought no outside proofs, but have used only those within the scope of our subject,

---

4. Augustine claims that evil is nothing in a variety of works, e.g., *The Confessions, On Free Choice of the Will.* The idea that evil is nothing is also held by Abelard and Anselm, among others.

5. Parmenides was an Eleatic philosopher. When claiming that the Infinite is a sphere, he was trying to indicate that the Infinite is without limits of any type; he was not trying to say that it was literally spherical.

since you have learned, on Plato's authority, that the language we use ought to be related to the subject of our discourse.

Poem 12

"Happy is he who can look into the shining spring of good; happy is he who can break the heavy chains of earth.

"Long ago the Thracian poet, Orpheus, mourned for his dead wife. With his sorrowful music he made the woodland dance and the rivers stand still. He made the fearful deer lie down bravely with the fierce lions; the rabbit no longer feared the dog quieted by his song.[6]

"But as the sorrow within his breast burned more fiercely, that music which calmed all nature could not console its maker. Finding the gods unbending, he went to the regions of hell. There he sang sweet songs to the music of his harp, songs drawn from the noble fountains of his goddess mother, songs inspired by his powerless grief and the love which doubled his grief.

"Hell is moved to pity when, with his melodious prayer, he begs the favor of those shades. The three-headed guardian of the gate is paralyzed by that new song; and the Furies, avengers of crimes who torture guilty souls with fear, are touched and weep in pity. Ixion's head is not tormented by the swift wheel, and Tantalus, long maddened by his thirst, ignores the waters he now might drink. The vulture is filled by the melody and ignores the liver of Tityus.

"At last, the judge of souls, moved by pity, declares, 'We are conquered. We return to this man his wife, his companion, purchased by his song. But our gift is bound by the condition that he must not look back until he has left hell.' But who can give lovers a law? Love is a stronger law unto itself. As they approached the edge of night, Orpheus looked back at Eurydice, lost her, and died.

"This fable applies to all of you who seek to raise your minds to sovereign day. For whoever is conquered and turns his eyes to the pit of hell, looking into the inferno, loses all the excellence he has gained."

---

6. Boethius is telling the story of Orpheus (the greatest musician and poet of Greek myth) and his trip to the Underworld to bring back his dead wife, Eurydice. Through his music, Orpheus charms Cerberus, the three-headed dog who guards Hades, as well as Hades (Pluto) himself. Hades releases Eurydice on the condition that Orpheus not look at her before they are out of the Underworld. Orpheus, however, looks at her and loses her a second time.

The Furies, daughters of Uranus and Gaea, were goddesses who punished all crimes. Ixion was the first human being to shed the blood of a relative. He tried to seduce Hera, Zeus's wife, and Zeus punished him by binding him to a flying, blazing wheel. Tantalus is the son of Zeus as well as King of Sipylos. For some crime—either giving ambrosia to human beings or killing and serving his son Pelops to the gods—he was put in the Underworld. Whenever he tried to drink, the water would recede, and, whenever he reached for food, it would be pulled out of his grasp.

Tityus was a giant god who was asked by Hera to attack Leto. Leto's children, Apollo and Artemis, heard her screams and killed Tityus. He was punished in the Underworld by being stretched out on a large area and having his liver continuously eaten by vultures.

Book 4

Prose I

Boethius wonders about the existence, and apparent success, of evil in the world created and ruled by God.

Philosophy told the story of Orpheus softly and sweetly, with her customary dignity. When she had finished, and seemed about to continue her discourse, I broke in, still depressed by my personal grief.

"O guide to true light, all that you have so far told me is divine in itself and perfectly convincing by virtue of your argument. But, although the sorrow caused by my misfortunes had made me forget these truths, I had not always been ignorant of them. Here, though, is the greatest cause of my sadness: since there is a good governor of all things, how can there be evil, and how can it go unpunished.[1] Think how astonishing this is. But it is even more amazing that with wickedness in full control, virtue not only goes unrewarded, but is trampled underfoot by the wicked and is punished instead of vice. That this can happen in the realm of an all-knowing and all-powerful God who desires only good must be a cause of surprise and sorrow to everyone."

Philosophy answered, "It would indeed be a monstrous thing and astonishing to everyone if, as you suppose, in the well-ordered house of so great a father the vilest objects were cherished and the most precious were regarded with contempt. But this is not the case. For if our previous conclusions are valid, and with the help of Him whose kingdom we are now speaking of, you will discover that the good are always powerful and the evil always weak and futile, that vice never goes unpunished nor virtue unrewarded, that the good prosper and the evil suffer misfortune, and much else which will remove the causes of your complaint and strengthen your convictions.[2] And

---

1. Once again, a statement of the problem of evil: if there is a good, omnipotent God, how can there be evil?
2. Lady Philosophy answers the problem of evil by claiming that ultimately God does, in fact, reward good and punish evil.

since under my guidance you have understood the essence of true happiness, and have found out where it resides, I shall now run through the steps in my explanation which I think necessary and show you the path which will take you home. And I shall give wings to your mind which can carry you aloft, so that, without further anxiety, you may return safely to your own country under my direction, along my path, and by my means.

Poem 1

"My wings are swift, able to soar beyond the heavens. The quick mind which wears them scorns the hateful earth and climbs above the globe of the immense sky, leaving the clouds below. It soars beyond the point of fire caused by the swift motion of the upper air until it reaches the house of stars. There it joins Phoebus in his path, or rides with cold, old Saturn, companion of that flashing sphere, running along the starry circle where sparkling night is made. When it has seen enough, it flies beyond the farthest sphere to mount the top of the swift heaven and share the holy light.

"There the Lord of kings holds His scepter, governing the reins of the world. With sure control He drives the swift chariot, the shining judge of all things.

"If the road which you have forgotten, but now search for, brings you here, you will cry out: 'This I remember, this is my own country, here I was born and here I shall hold my place.' Then if you wish to look down upon the night of earthly things which you have left, you will see those much feared tyrants dwelling in exile here."

Prose 2

Philosophy shows that the good have true power and the vicious do not.

Hearing this I said, "What wonderful things you promise! And I have no doubt that you can do them. But do not hold me in suspense now that you have made me so eager."

"First," Philosophy answered, "you will agree that the good always have power and the wicked do not. Each of these propositions proves the other: for, since good and evil are contraries, if good is shown to be powerful, the weakness of evil necessarily follows. Conversely, if evil is shown to be weak, the strength of good is clear. But, in order to demonstrate this truth fully, I will prove my point in both ways one after the other.

"The success of any human action depends upon two things: will and power.[3] If either is lacking nothing can be done. If the will is absent, nothing is attempted; if power is lacking, the will is frustrated. Therefore, if you find someone wanting something and not getting it, you must conclude that he is without the power to obtain what he wants."

"That is quite clear," I said, "and no one can deny it."

"On the other hand, you will agree that the man who gets what he wants had the power to get it."

"That is equally clear."

"Moreover, whatever a man can do, he has the power to do; but what he cannot do shows lack of power."

"That is true," I agreed.

"Then do you recall that earlier in our discussion we found that every intention of the human will is directed toward happiness, however various its inclinations may be?"

"I remember that to have been proved."

"And do you also recall that happiness is the good, so that everyone who seeks happiness also desires the good?"

"I have not forgotten," I said. "Indeed, I hold it fast in my memory."

"Therefore, all men, good and bad, have the same purpose in striving to obtain the good."

"That follows," I agreed.

"But it is also true that men become good by obtaining the good."

"Yes."

"So good men obtain what they desire."

"That seems to be true."

"But evil men would not be evil if they obtained the good they seek."

"That is true."

"Therefore, since both seek the good, but good men obtain it and evil men do not, it follows that good men have power but evil men are impotent."

"To doubt that would be to disregard the nature of things and the force of argument."

"Next," Philosophy continued, "suppose that there are two persons to whom the same natural function is assigned: one of them accomplishes the action by natural means, but the other is unable to do so and uses unnatural means, not indeed to accomplish the action but to pretend to do so. Which of these two would you consider the more powerful?"

---

3. Power is the capacity to perform actions. The will is one of the three parts of the soul. (Intellect and memory are the other two.) The will is regarded by Boethius and other medieval thinkers as the source for all actions. When the will desires (wills) something, it acts.

"I think I see what you are driving at, but please explain more fully."

"Well, you will agree that the act of walking is natural for men, and that the feet are the natural means of accomplishing the action."

"Quite so."

"Then if one man is able to walk on his feet, and another, who is deprived of this natural capability, tries to walk by crawling on his hands, which of the two must rightly be thought the stronger?"

"That goes without saying," I answered, "for everyone knows that the man who can use his natural capacities is stronger than one who cannot."

"Well then," she continued, "the highest good is proposed equally to good and bad men. Good men seek it by the natural means of the virtues; evil men, however, try to achieve the same goal by a variety of concupiscences, and that is surely an unnatural way of seeking the good. Don't you agree?"

"I do, indeed. And I see clearly the consequence of your line of reasoning. For it follows that the good are powerful and the wicked are impotent."

"Your deduction is correct and indicates to your physician an improving state of health and resistance. But since I see that you are so quick to understand, I will condense my demonstration. Consider how great is the weakness of vicious men who are unable to achieve that goal toward which their nature leads, even forces, them. What would happen if they were deprived of this great and nearly irresistible natural tendency? Think how grave is this impotence of wicked men. For the goal which they are pursuing is not a trivial or frivolous thing; they fail in the race for the very summit of all things; they fail miserably to achieve even the things for which they struggle night and day. And just here the powers of good men are clearly seen. For, as you would consider an effective walker one who could go on foot as far as it is possible to go, so you must consider him to be most powerful who achieves the goal of all human desires, the good beyond which there is nothing. An obvious conclusion follows from this: the wicked are wholly deprived of strength. For why do they neglect virtue and pursue vice? Is it because they are ignorant of the good? Well, what greater weakness is there than the blindness of ignorance? Or do they know what they should seek, but are driven astray by lust? If so, they are made weak by intemperance and cannot overcome their vices. Or, do they knowingly and willfully desert the good and turn to vice? Anyone acting that way loses not only his strength but his very being, since to forsake the common goal of all existence is to forsake existence itself.

"Perhaps it may strike some as strange to say that evil men do not exist, especially since they are so numerous; but it is not so strange. For I do not deny that those who are evil are *evil*; but I do deny that they *are*, in the pure and simple sense of the term. For just as you may call a cadaver a dead man, but cannot call it simply a man, so I would concede that vicious men are evil, but I cannot say, in an absolute sense, that they exist.[4] For a thing is which maintains its place in nature and acts in accord with its nature. Whatever fails to do this loses the existence which is proper to its nature. But you may argue that evil men are capable of action. I will not deny it, but such capability is the product of weakness, not of strength. For they can do evil acts which they could not have done if they had been able to remain capable of good. And that possibility of doing evil shows clearly that they can do nothing. For, if our earlier conclusion that evil is nothing still stands, it is clear that the wicked can do nothing since they can do only evil."

"That is evident," I agreed.

"And, so that you may understand what the nature of this power is, let me remind you what we have already proved that there is nothing more powerful than the Supreme Good."

"That is true."

"But," Philosophy went on, "the sovereign Good cannot do evil."

"Certainly not."

"And does anyone think that men can do all things?"

"No one in his right mind could think so."

"But men can do evil."

"Unfortunately, they can."

"Therefore, since He who can only do good can do all things, and those who can do evil cannot do all things, it is obvious that those who can do evil are less powerful. Moreover, we have already shown that every kind of power is included among the things which men desire, and that all objects of human desire are related to the good as the goal of their natures. But the ability to commit crime is not related to the good, and so it is not desirable. And, since every power should be desired, it follows that the power to do evil is not a power at all. From all this it is clear that good men have power, but evil men are weak. Likewise, the truth of Plato's doctrine is evident; only the wise can do what they want to do; the wicked can follow their desires, but they cannot accomplish what they want. For they do what they feel like doing, and they suppose that they will find among their pleasures the good they are really looking for. But they are bound to fail, since shameful behavior does not bring happiness.

---

4. Boethius is extending the notion that evil is nothing in interesting ways. Clearly, an evil man exists as a man. But if evil is nothing, his being evil must be nothing. So, as an evil man, a man does not exist. Rather, he is a man who departs from the nature that men should have.

Poem 2

"Those high and mighty kings you see sitting on high in glory, dressed in purple, surrounded by armed guards, can breathe cruel fury, threaten with fierce words. But if you strip off the coverings of vain honor from those proud men, you will see underneath the tight chains they wear. Lust rules their hearts with greedy poisons, rage whips them, vexing their minds to stormy wrath. Sometimes they are slaves to sorrow, sometimes to delusive hope. This is the picture of individual man with all his tyrant passions; enslaved by these evil powers, he cannot do what he wishes.

Prose 3

The good are always rewarded and the wicked always punished.

"Do you see now the mire in which vice wallows, and the light in which probity shines? This shows clearly that the good are always rewarded and the wicked always punished. The aim or goal of an action may justly be said to be the reward of that action; as in a race, the prize a man competes for is said to be the reward. We have demonstrated that happiness is the good for which all things are done. Absolute good, therefore, is set up as a kind of common prize for all human activity. Now this prize is always achieved by good men, and further, no one who lacks the good may rightly be called a good man. Therefore, men of moral probity always achieve their reward. No matter how the wicked rave, the wise man never loses his prize; nor does it ever diminish.

"The wickedness of others does not deprive virtuous men of their glory. But if a man should find his happiness in a reward received from someone else, then either the one who gave it, or some other person, could take it away. But since a man's own probity confers this reward, he can lose the reward only by ceasing to be virtuous. Finally, since every reward is desired precisely because it is believed to be good, who can think that one who possesses good is without his reward?

"And what a reward it is, the greater and best of all! For recall the corollary I showed you before and make this inference: since the good is happiness, all good men are made happy by the very fact that they are good. And we have already shown that those who are happy are gods. Therefore, the reward of good men, which time cannot lessen, nor power diminish, nor the wickedness of any man tarnish, is to become gods.

"Since this is so, the wise man can be certain of the punishment of the wicked. For, since good and evil, reward and punishment, are opposites, the rewards of the good necessarily indicate the opposite—the punishment of the wicked. Therefore, just as virtue is the reward of virtuous men, so wickedness itself is the punishment of the wicked. Certainly, when a man is punished he knows that he suffers evil. And, if they think about their condition, can those who are not only tainted, but even infected by vice, the worst of all evils, consider themselves free from punishment? Consider the punishment which afflicts the evil as compared with the rewards of the good. You learned earlier that whatever is, is one, and that whatever is one, is good; it follows then that whatever is must also be good. And it follows from this that whatever loses its goodness ceases to be. Thus wicked men cease to be what they were; but the appearance of their human bodies, which they keep, shows that they once were men. To give oneself to evil, therefore, is to lose one's human nature. Just as virtue can raise a person above human nature, so vice lowers those whom it has seduced from the condition of men beneath human nature. For this reason, anyone whom you find transformed by vice cannot be counted a man.[5]

"You will say that the man who is driven by avarice to seize what belongs to others is like a wolf; the restless, angry man who spends his life in quarrels you will compare to a dog. The treacherous conspirator who steals by fraud may be likened to a fox; the man who is ruled by intemperate anger is thought to have the soul of a lion. The fearful and timid man who trembles without reason is like a deer; the lazy, stupid fellow is like an ass. The volatile, inconstant man who continually changes direction is like a bird; the man who is sunk in foul lust is trapped in the pleasures of a filthy sow. In this way, anyone who abandons virtue ceases to be a man, since he cannot share in the divine nature, and instead becomes a beast.

Poem 3

"Eurus, the east wind, caught the sails of Ulysses' wandering ships and drove them to the island where lived the fair goddess Circe, daughter of the Sun.[6] She mixed for her new guests a drink tainted

---

5. Unity, goodness, and being were often held to be identical qualities. Thus, to the degree that one lacks goodness, one lacks existence. So an evil man exists less than a good man since the evil man lacks goodness.

6. Lady Philosophy is recounting Ulysses' encounter with Circe from Homer's *Odyssey*. She emphasizes the control over bodies Circe has while having no control over minds, as indicated by their mental mourning of their physical changes.

by her magic, and by her skillful use of herbs she changed the sailors into different shapes. Some grew the faces of wild boars, others became African lions with sharp teeth and claws; some were turned into wolves, and when they tried to cry they howled; others wandered meekly about the house like Indian tigers.

"But, in spite of so many misfortunes, Mercury, the winged God of Arcady, had mercy on Ulysses and saved him from the poison of his hostess. Nevertheless, his sailors greedily drank the evil cups; they were changed into swine and turned from food to husks and acorns. No part of them remained unchanged—they lost both voice and body; only the mind remained to mourn the monstrous change they had suffered.

"But see how weak was the power of the goddess and her impotent herbs. She had power over the bodies of men, but could not change their hearts. The strength of man is within, hidden in the remote tower of the heart. Poisons which can make him forget himself are more potent and deadly than Circe's because they corrupt the inner man. They do not harm the body, but they horribly wound the mind."

Prose 4

Philosophy argues that, in spite of appearances, the wicked are impotent and miserably unhappy.

When she had finished, I said, "I see that you are right in saying that; although vicious men keep the appearance of their human bodies, they are nevertheless changed into beasts as far as the character of their souls is concerned. Still, I wish that these cruel and wicked minds were not permitted to ruin good men."

"They are not permitted to do that, as I shall show you at the proper time. If, however, the power which they are thought to have were taken from them, their punishment would be greatly diminished. For, though this may seem incredible to some, the wicked are necessarily more unhappy when they have their way than they would be if they could not do what they wanted to do.[7] If it is bad to desire evil, it is worse to be able to accomplish it; for if it were not accomplished, the disordered will would be ineffectual. So, when you

---

7. Plato argues this position in *The Gorgias* (see pp. 97–106 in this volume) as well as *The Republic*. According to him, one should seek a balanced soul. Wicked men pursue ends that cause imbalance in their souls if they achieve their desires. In fact, the wicked are benefited by punishment—a point Lady Philosophy makes a few paragraphs later.

see someone with the will and the power to commit crime actually commit it, you know that he is necessarily the victim of a threefold misfortune; for each of those three things—the will, the power, and the act itself—contains its own punishment."

"I grant that," I answered. "But I hope that they may quickly be relieved of this misfortune by losing their power to commit crime."

"They will lose it sooner than you may wish, perhaps, and sooner than they think. For nothing happens so slowly in the brief span of this life that the immortal spirit finds it long to wait for; the high hopes and well-laid plots of the wicked are often quickly and unexpectedly destroyed, and this does, indeed, limit their misery.

"If wickedness makes men miserable, the longer they are wicked the more wretched they must be. And I would consider most unhappy those who did not finally find an end to their wickedness in death. If, then, we have found out the truth about the misery of wickedness, it is clear that unhappiness which lasts forever must be infinite."

"That is a strange and difficult conclusion," I said, "but I recognize that it follows from that which I have already conceded to be true."

"You are right," Philosophy answered, "but anyone who finds it hard to accept a conclusion ought either to point out a false step in the argument or show that the series of propositions does not indicate a necessary conclusion. Otherwise he must grant the inference if he has granted the premises.

"What I am now about to say may seem equally surprising, yet it follows with equal certainty from my argument."

"What is it?" I asked.

"That the wicked are happier when they are punished than when they evade justice. I am not now suggesting the argument that might occur to anyone, that vicious men are corrected by punishment or led to reform by the fear of it, or that such punishment sets an example to others so that they will avoid involvement in crime. In addition to the possibility of correcting and the power of example, there is still another way in which the wicked who avoid punishment can be shown to be more unhappy than those who are punished."

"What is that?" I asked.

"We have shown, have we not, that the good are happy and the wicked unhappy?"

"Yes."

"If, then, an unhappy man achieves some good, is he not happier than the man whose unhappiness is complete and unmixed with the slightest good?"

"I should think so," I said.

"And, if the misery of the man who has no good at all is increased by additional evils, isn't he much unhappier than the man who is relieved by acquiring some good?"

"Yes, of course."

"Therefore, the wicked receive some good when they are punished, because the punishment itself is good inasmuch as it is just; conversely, when the wicked avoid punishment, they become more evil, because you have already admitted that such impunity is evil because it is unjust."

"I cannot deny that."

"Therefore, the wicked who unjustly escape punishment are more unhappy than those who are justly punished."

"I agree that this follows from what has already been proved. But," I asked, "do you leave no room for the punishment of souls after the death of the body?"

"I do, indeed," Philosophy answered, "and such punishments are severe. Some are imposed as bitter penalties, others as merciful purgation. But it is not now my intention to speak of these. So far I have tried to make you see that the power of evil men, which you find intolerable, does not exist, and that those same men, whom you think go unpunished, really never escape the penalties of their wickedness. Further, I have shown that their apparent impunity is short-lived, that the longer it goes on the unhappier they become, and that if it were eternal they would be absolutely wretched. Finally, I have proved that wicked men who unjustly escape punishment are more miserable than those who are justly punished. And it follows from this that when they seem to escape chastisement, they are in reality undergoing more severe punishment."

"When I consider your argument," I said, "I find that nothing could be more true. But, if we consider the ordinary judgment of men, who is likely to find these ideas credible, or who will even listen to them?"

"That is true," Philosophy answered, "because men cannot raise eyes accustomed to darkness to the light of clear truth. They are like those birds who can see at night but are blind in the daylight. For as long as they fix their attention on their own feelings, rather than on the true nature of things, they think that the license of passion and immunity from punishment bring happiness. But think of the sanctions of eternal law. If you conform your spirit to better things, you have no need of human approval and reward; you have placed yourself among the more excellent. But, if you turn to what is cheap and low, do not expect someone else to punish you; you will have lowered yourself to a condition of squalor. It is as if you were to look by turns at the sordid earth and at the heavens, compelled by the power of sight—and nothing else—to be now in the dirt, now among the stars. Just because thoughtless men do not understand this, should we lower ourselves to those whom we have shown to be like beasts? If a man who had completely lost his sight should forget that he had ever been able to see, and be quite unaware of any natural disability, would we too think that this blind man could see?

"Most thoughtless people will not even grant another equally strong argument to the effect that those who injure others are more unhappy than those whom they injure."

"I would like to hear your explanation of that."

"Would you deny that every wicked man deserves to be punished?"

"No."

"And is it absolutely clear that the wicked are unhappy?"

"Yes."

"Then you agree that those who deserve punishment are miserable."

"That follows," I agreed.

"Then, if you were the judge, whom would you punish: the one who did the injury, or the one who suffered it?"

"Without any hesitation I would satisfy the injured party by punishing the one who hurt him."

"Then you must be convinced that the one who does evil is more miserable than the one to whom evil is done."

"That follows."

"From this, then, and for other reasons based on the principle that wickedness by its very nature makes men miserable, we see that an injury done to another causes unhappiness in the doer rather than in the recipient. But at present, lawyers take the opposite tack. They try to arouse sympathy in the judges for those who have suffered grave injury, when those who have harmed them are much more deserving of pity. Such criminals ought to be brought to justice by kind and compassionate accusers, as sick men are taken to the doctor, so that their disease of guilt might be cured by punishment. In this way, defense attorneys could be dispensed with, or, if they wanted to help their clients, they would become accusers. And, if the wicked themselves could somehow see the virtue they had abandoned, and could be convinced that they could free themselves from the strain of vice and acquire virtue by undergoing punishment, they would ignore the pain, dismiss their lawyers, and give themselves up entirely to their accusers and judges.

"In this way, wise men could abolish hatred; for no one but a fool would hate good men, and hating evil men would make no sense. Viciousness is a kind of disease of the soul, like illness in the body. And if sickness of the body is not something we hate, but rather regard with sympathy, we have much more reason to pity those whose minds are afflicted with wickedness, a thing worse than any sickness.

Poem 4

"Why do you whip yourselves to frenzy, and ever seek your fate by self-destruction? If you look for death, she stands nearby of her own accord; she does not restrain her swift horses. Those whom snakes, lions, tigers, bears, and boars are poised to kill raise their weapons against each other. Do men raise unjust quarrels and fierce wars because their lands and customs are different? Is this why they seek death from each other? Surely this is not just cause for such cruelty. If you would give every man what he deserves, then love the good and pity those who are evil."

Prose 5

Boethius continues to wonder why an all-powerful God seems sometimes to reward the wicked with happiness and to afflict the good with sorrow.

Then I said, "I understand that happiness and misery come to good and wicked men according to their merits. Still, I find that there is a mixture of some good and some evil in every man's fortune, as that term is popularly understood. Surely no wise man wants to live in exile, poverty, and ignominy; he would rather live prosperously in his own country, and enjoy riches, honors, and the exercise of power. The operation of wisdom is manifested more effectively and recognized more clearly when the happiness of those who govern is shared by the people; and this is especially true when imprisonment and other consequences of legal punishment are imposed on the criminals for whom they were intended. Therefore I am amazed and shocked to find this ideal turned upside down, so that punishments designed for the wicked are imposed on good men, and the rewards of virtue are seized by the wicked. I wish you would tell me how such unjust confusion can possibly be explained. For I would be less surprised if I could believe that all things happened as the result of accidental chance. But my belief in God and his governing power increases my amazement. Since He often gives joy to the good and bitterness to the wicked, but on the other hand often reverses this dispensation, how can all this be distinguished from accidental chance unless we understand the cause of it?"

"It is no wonder," Philosophy answered, "that a situation should seem random and confused when its principle of order is not understood. But, although you do not know why things are as they are, still you cannot doubt that in a world ruled by a good Governor all things do happen justly.

Poem 5

"The man who does not know why the stars of Arcturus turn near the highest pole, nor why slow Boötes[8] drives his chariot to dip his flames into the sea, yet rises again so quickly, must be amazed by the laws of celestial bodies. When the horns of the full moon grow pale, dimmed by the darkness of night, and the stars which Phoebe had obscured with her shining face are now uncovered, popular error excites the people and they beat brazen cymbals with rapid blows.[9]

"No one wonders why the storms of Corus beat the shore with pounding waves, nor why the frozen drifts of snow are melted by the hot rays of the sun. The causes of such natural phenomena are quickly understood; but those others are obscure and disturb the mind. All sudden and rare events bewilder the unstable and the uninformed. But if the cloudy error of ignorance is swept away, such things will seem strange no longer."

Prose 6

Philosophy discourses on Providence and Fate. She shows that what may seem unjust confusion in the affairs of men is directed by Providence toward the good.

"That is true," I said. "But, since you can reveal the hidden cause of things and throw light on reasons that are veiled in darkness, I beg you to tell me what you know about this apparent injustice which I find so inexplicable and troublesome."

Then she smiled a little and said, "You are asking about the greatest of all mysteries, one which can hardly be fully explained. This problem is such that when one doubt is cleared up many more arise like the heads of the Hydra, and continue to spring up unless they are checked by the most active fire of the mind. Among the many questions raised by this problem are these: the simplicity of Providence, the course of Fate, unforeseeable chance, divine knowledge and predestination, and free will.[1] You yourself know how difficult these questions are, but since it is part of your medicine to know

---

8. The Boötes constellation is one of the forty-eight constellations listed by Ptolemy. It is often referred to as the "Bear Watcher" since it appears to be watching over the constellations Ursa Major and Ursa Minor. *Arcturus*: the brightest star in the constellation Boötes. One finds Arcturus by following the arc of the handle of the Big Dipper.
9. There are ancient superstitions that regard an eclipse of the Moon as the beginning of its disappearance. It was thought that the noise of the crashing of cymbals would prevent the Moon from disappearing. Corus is the northwest wind; see page 6, n.1.
1. These topics form the bulk of the remaining sections of the *Consolation*.

these things, I shall try to say something about them even though
our time is short. But you will have to do without the pleasure of
verse for a while as I put together the pattern of my argument."

"As you wish," I said.

Then, as though she were making a new beginning, Philosophy
explained: "The generation of all things, and the whole course of
mutable natures and of whatever is in any way subject to change, take
their causes, order, and forms from the unchanging mind of God. This
divine mind established the manifold rules by which all things are
governed while it remained in the secure castle of its own simplicity.
When this government is regarded as belonging to the purity of the
divine mind, it is called Providence; but when it is considered with
reference to the things which it moves and governs, it has from very
early times been called Fate.[2] It is easy to see that Providence and
Fate are different if we consider the power of each. Providence is the
divine reason itself which belongs to the most high ruler of all things
and which governs all things; Fate, however, belongs to all mutable
things and is the disposition by which Providence joins all things in
their own order. For Providence embraces all things equally, however
diverse they are, however infinite. Fate, on the other hand, sets particular things in motion once they have been given their own forms,
places, and times. Thus Providence is the unfolding of temporal
events as this is present to the vision of the divine mind; but this
same unfolding of events as it is worked out in time is called Fate.
Although the two are different things, one depends upon the other,
for the process of Fate derives from the simplicity of Providence. Just
as the craftsman conceives in his mind the form of the thing he
intends to make, and then sets about making it by producing in successive temporal acts that which was simply present in his mind, so
God by his Providence simply and unchangeably disposes all things
that are to be done, even though the things themselves are worked
out by Fate in many ways and in the process of time.

"Therefore, whether Fate is carried out by divine spirits in the
service of Providence, or by a soul, or by the whole activity of nature,
by the heavenly motions of the stars, by angelic virtue or diabolical
cleverness, or by some or all of these agents, one thing is certain: Providence is the immovable and simple form of all things which come
into being, while Fate is the moving connection and temporal order of
all things which the divine simplicity has decided to bring into being.
It follows then, that everything which is subject to Fate is also subject
to Providence, and that Fate itself is also subject to Providence.

2. The distinction between Providence (government according to the Divine Mind) and Fate
(events as they occur in time in the world) is very important for the work as a whole.
Boethius uses the distinction to offer a solution to the problem of evil and to reconcile
God's knowledge with the freedom of human actions.

"Some things, however, which are subject to Providence are above the force of Fate and ungoverned by it. Consider the example of a number of spheres in orbit around the same central point: the innermost moves toward the simplicity of the center and becomes a kind of hinge about which the outer spheres circle; whereas the outermost, whirling in a wider orbit, tends to increase its orbit in space the farther it moves from the indivisible midpoint of the center. If, however, it is connected to the center, it is confined by the simplicity of the center and no longer tends to stray into space. In like manner, whatever strays farthest from the divine mind is most entangled in the nets of Fate; conversely, the freer a thing is from Fate, the nearer it approaches the center of all things. And if it adheres firmly to the divine mind, it is free from motion and overcomes the necessity of Fate. Therefore, the changing course of Fate is to the simple stability of Providence as reasoning is to intellect, as that which is generated is to that which *is*, as time is to eternity, as a circle to its center. Fate moves the heavens and the stars, governs the elements in their mixture, and transforms them by mutual change; it renews all things that are born and die by the reproduction of similar offspring and seeds. This same power binds the actions and fortunes of men in an unbreakable chain of causes and, since these causes have their origins in an unchangeable Providence, they too must necessarily be unchangeable. In this way things are governed perfectly when the simplicity residing in the divine mind produces an unchangeable order of causes.[3] This order, by its own unchanging nature, controls mutable things which otherwise would be disordered and confused.

"Therefore, even though things may seem confused and discordant to you, because you cannot discern the order that governs them, nevertheless everything is governed by its own proper order directing all things toward the good. Nothing is done for the sake of evil, even by wicked men who, as I have proved, are actually seeking the good when they are perverted by wretched error, since the order which flows from the center of the highest good does not turn anyone aside from his original course.

"But, you ask, what worse confusion can there be than for the good to enjoy prosperity and suffer adversity, and for the wicked also to get both what they want and what they cannot bear? But is human judgment so infallible that those who are thought to be good and evil are necessarily what they seem to be? If so, why are men's judgments so often in conflict, so that the same men are thought by some to deserve reward and by others punishment? And, even granting that someone can distinguish between good and evil persons, can he, like the doctor examining the body of his patient, look into

3. A determined world is emphasized.

the inner temper of the soul? The problems of such judgments are similar: for it is a mystery to the layman why some healthy persons find sweet foods agreeable, others sour foods, and why some sick persons are helped by gentle treatment, others by harsh medicines. The physician, however, does not find such things at all strange because he understands the nature of sickness and health. Now, what is the health of souls but virtue, and what is their sickness but vice? And who, indeed, is the preserver of the good and the corrector of the wicked but God, the governor and physician of men's minds, who looks into the great mirror of his providence and, knowing what is best for each one, causes it to happen? Here, then, is the great miracle of the order of Fate: divine wisdom does what the ignorant cannot understand.

"I shall limit my discussion of the divine judgment to a few things which human reason can comprehend. The man whom you think most just and honorable may seem quite otherwise to the Providence which knows all things. Thus my disciple Lucan observed that, although Cato[4] favored the side of those who were conquered, the gods favored the conquerors. Therefore, when you see something happen here contrary to your ideas of what is right, it is your opinion and expectation which is confused, while the order in things themselves is right. Take, for example, the man so fortunate as to seem approved by both God and men; he may actually be so weak in character that if he were to suffer adversity he would forsake virtue on the grounds that it seemed not to bring him good fortune. Therefore God in his wise dispensation spares the man whom adversity might ruin, so that he may not suffer who cannot stand suffering. Another man who is perfect in all virtues, holy, and dear to God, may be spared even bodily sickness because Providence judges it wrong for him to be touched by any adversity at all. As one who is better than I put it: 'the body of the holy man is made of pure ether.'[5] It often happens that supreme rule is given to good men so that infectious evil may be held in check. To others, Providence gives a mixture of prosperity and adversity according to the disposition of their souls: she gives trouble to some whom too much luxury might spoil; others she tests with hardships in order to strengthen their virtues by the exercise of patience. Some people fear to undertake burdens they could easily bear, while others treat too lightly those they are unable to handle; both types are led on by Providence to find themselves by trials. Some have earned worldly fame at the price of glorious death; others, by not breaking under torture, have proved to the world that

---

4. A Roman Stoic philosopher, who in 46 B.C.E. committed suicide after Julius Caesar's victory at Thapsus; Caesar's victory led to the ruin of the Roman Republic. *Lucan*: a Roman poet of the first century, who deals with the Caesar's rise in the Roman Civil War.
5. The passage is in Greek but the source is unknown.

virtue cannot be conquered by evil. No one can doubt that such trials are good and just and beneficial to those who suffer them.

"Moreover, the lot of the wicked, which is sometimes painful and sometimes easy, comes from the same source and for the same reasons. No one wonders at the troubles they undergo, since everyone thinks that is just what they deserve. Such punishment both deters others from crime and prompts those who suffer it to reform. On the other hand, the prosperity of the wicked is a powerful argument for the good, because they see how they ought to evaluate the kind of good fortune which the wicked so often enjoy. Still another good purpose may be served by the prosperity of the wicked man: if his nature is so reckless and violent that poverty might drive him to crime, Providence may cure this morbid tendency by making him wealthy. When such a man recognizes his viciousness and contrasts his guilt with his fortune, he may perhaps become alarmed at the painful consequences of losing what he enjoys so much. He will then change his ways and behave himself as long as he fears the loss of his wealth. Some who have achieved prosperity unworthily have been driven by it to well deserved ruin. Some have been given the right to punish so that the good might be tested and the evil punished. For just as there is no agreement between the just and the unjust, so the unjust themselves cannot get along together. And why not, since such men are at odds with themselves and their vicious consciences, and often regret their own foolish actions. From this condition the highest Providence often brings about the miracle by which the wicked make other wicked men good. For, when they find themselves unjustly persecuted by vicious men, they burn with hatred against them and return to the practice of virtue because they cannot bear to be like those whom they hate. Only to divine power are evil things good, when it uses them so as to draw good effects from them.[6] All things are part of a certain order, so that when something moves away from its assigned place, it falls into a new order of things. Nothing in the realm of Providence is left to chance.

"But it is hard for me to recount all this as if I were a God, for it is not fitting for men to understand intellectually or to explain verbally all the dispositions of the divine work. It is enough to have understood only that God, the Creator of all things in nature, also governs all things, directing them to good. And, since He carefully preserves everything which He made in his own likeness, He excludes by fatal necessity all evil from the bounds of his state. Therefore, if you fix your attention on Providence as the governor of all things, you will find that the evil which is thought to abound in the world is really

6. Boethius is affirming God's governance of the world. Through his determined plan, which governs all by necessity, God can draw good out of evil, and thus the evil God permits is justified.

nonexistent. But I see that you are weary from listening so long to this extended and difficult discourse and want to be refreshed by poetry. Listen then, and gather your strength for what is yet to be explained.

Poem 6

"If you wish to discern the laws of the high and mighty God, the high thunderer, with an unclouded mind, look up to the roof of highest heaven. There the stars, united by just agreement, keep the ancient peace. The sun, driven by red fire, does not impede the cold circle of Phoebe. Nor does the Great Bear driving its course at the world's top hide itself in the western ocean; it never wants to drown its flames in the sea, though it sees other stars plunge beneath the waves. The faithful Hesperus announces the approach of night at the assigned time; then, as Lucifer, it brings back the warming day.[7]

"Thus mutual love governs their eternal movement and the war of discord is excluded from the bounds of heaven. Concord rules the elements with fair restraint: moist things yield place to dry, cold and hot combine in friendship; flickering fire rises on high, and gross earth sinks down. Impelled by the same causes, the flowering year breathes out its odors in warm spring; hot summer dries the grain and autumn comes in burdened with fruit; then falling rain brings in wet winter.

"This ordered change nourishes and sustains all that lives on earth; then snatches away and buries all that was born, hiding it in final death. Meanwhile, the Creator sits on high, governing and guiding the course of things. King and lord, source and origin, law and wise judge of right. All things which He placed in motion, He draws back and holds in check; He makes firm whatever tends to stray. If He did not recall them to their true paths and set them again on their circling courses, all things that the stable order now contains would be wrenched from their source and perish.

"This is the common bond of love by which all things seek to be held to the goal of good. Only thus can things endure: drawn by love they turn again to the Cause which gave them being.

Prose 7

Philosophy, at the request of Boethius, restates in popular form her thesis that all fortune is good.

"And now," said Philosophy, "do you understand the implications of what I have told you?"

7. See notes 3, p. 12; 1, p. 32; and 8, p. 70.

"What do you mean?" I asked.

"That all fortune is good."

"But how can that be?" I said.

"Look here," Philosophy answered. "Since all fortune whether sweet or bitter, has as its purpose the reward or trial of good men or the correction and punishment of the wicked, it must be good because it is clearly either just or useful."

"Your reasoning is true," I said, "and your explanation is sound, especially when I consider what you have taught me about Providence and Fate. But if you don't mind, we ought to put this among the doctrines which you not long ago called surprising."

"Why so?" Philosophy asked.

"Because people ordinarily hold that some men suffer bad fortune."

"You mean that you want to accommodate our discourse to the common speech so that we will not move too far from ordinary human ways?"

"Yes, if you don't mind."

"Well; then, do you agree that whatever is profitable is good?"

"Yes."

"And that whatever tests or corrects is profitable?"

"Yes."

"And therefore good?"

"Yes."

"This, then, is the situation of the virtuous who struggle courageously against misfortune, or of those who are trying to reform and become virtuous."

"That is quite true," I said.

"And what about the prosperity which is given to good men as a reward; do ordinary people think that bad?"

"No. They rightly consider it to be very good."

"Well then, what about the adversity which restrains the wicked by punishing them justly?"

"Quite the contrary," I answered. "They consider that the worst fate that can be imagined."

"Then notice that by following the popular opinion of the people we have arrived at a most surprising conclusion."

"How so?" I asked.

"Our argument so far has proved that the fortune of the virtuous, or of those who are advancing toward virtue, is good, whatever it may be; but the fortune of those who continue in wickedness is bad."

"That is true," I said, "but no one would dare say so."

"A wise man ought not to regret his struggles with fortune any more than a brave soldier should be intimidated by the noise of battle; for difficulty is the natural lot of each. For the soldier it is the source of increasing glory; for the wise man it is the means of confirming his wisdom. Indeed, virtue gets its name from that virile strength which is not overcome by adversity. And you, who are advancing in virtue, should not expect to be weakened by ease or softened by pleasure. You fight manfully against any fortune, neither despairing in the face of misfortune nor becoming corrupt in the enjoyment of prosperity. Hold fast to the middle ground with courage. Those who fall short or go too far are scornful of happiness and are deprived of the reward of labor. You can make of your fortune what you will; for any fortune which seems difficult either tests virtue or corrects and punishes vice.

Poem 7

"Agamemnon, the avenging son of Atreus, waged war for ten years until, by devastating Troy, he purged the dishonor done his brother's marriage.[8] When he wished to fill the sails of the Greek fleet, and bring back the winds by a bloody sacrifice, he put off the role of father and, as a sorrowing priest, cut the throat of his daughter.

"Ulysses mourned his lost comrades whom fierce Polyphemus, lying in his dark cave, had devoured into his vast belly; but the monster, driven mad by his blinded eye, repaid those former tears with joy.[9]

"Hercules is famous for his hard labors.[1] He tamed the proud Centaurs; won the spoils of the fierce Nemean lion; shot down the Stymphalian birds with his sure arrows; stole the golden apples from the watchful dragon; and shackled Cerberus with a triple chain. He conquered Diomede and fed the savage mares their cruel master's flesh. He burned the Hydra's poison heads, shamed the river Achelous by breaking his horns and made him bury his face in his banks. He killed Antaeus on the Libyan beach, and slew Cacus to slake the wrath of Evander. The boar marked with foam those shoulders which were to bear the weight of heaven. For his last labor he bore heaven on his strong neck, and for this he won again the prize of heaven.

"Go now, strong men! Follow the high road of great example. Why slack off and turn your backs? When you overcome the earth, the stars will be yours."

---

8. Agamemnon was the leader of the Greeks in the Trojan War. He led the expedition to avenge the insult that Paris, son of Priam who was king of Troy, gave to Menelaus, Agamemnon's brother, when Paris stole Menelaus's wife, Helen of Troy. The goddess Diana sent winds to prevent the sailing of the Greek ships and was appeased only when Agamemnon sacrificed his own daughter, Iphigenia, to her.
9. Ulysses in Homer's *Odyssey* put out the eye of the cyclops, Polyphemus, after he ate five of Ulysses' men.
1. Hercules was subject to Eurystheus, King of Mycenae, for twelve years. He performed the twelve labors that Boethius recounts and was made divine for his achievements.

Book 5

Prose 1

Philosophy discusses the question of chance.

When Philosophy had finished her song and was about to turn to the discussion of other matters, I interrupted saying, "Your exhortation is a worthy one and your authority is great, but I know from experience that you are right in saying that the question of Providence involves many other problems. I should like to know whether there is any such thing as chance, and, if so, what it may be."

"I have been trying, as quickly as possible, to carry out my promise to show you the way back to your true country. These other questions are somewhat beside the main point of my argument, even though they are quite important in themselves. I shouldn't want you to become so wearied by side trips that you would not be able to complete the main journey."

"Please do not worry about that," I said. "For it would comfort me to understand the things in which I take the greatest pleasure. When every part of your argument is convincingly established, none of its implications will cause any doubt."

"I will do as you ask," she replied, and took up her explanation again.

"If chance is defined as an event produced by random motion and without any sequence of causes, then I say that there is no such thing as chance; apart from its use in the present context, I consider it an empty word. For what room can there be for random events since God keeps all things in order? The commonplace that nothing can come from nothing is true; and the old philosophers never denied it, though they did not apply it to the effective cause of things but only to the material subject as a kind of foundation of all their reasoning about nature. But if anything should happen without cause, it would seem to come from nothing. And if this cannot be, chance as we defined it a moment ago is impossible."

"Then is there nothing which can rightly be called chance?" I asked. "Does nothing happen fortuitously? Or is there something to

which those words refer, even if it is not rightly understood b
nary people?"

"My true follower, Aristotle, gave a brief and sound definition of
chance in his *Physics*."[1]

"What did he say?" I asked.

"Whenever anything is done for one reason, but something other
than what was intended happens on account of other reasons, it is
called chance. For example, when a man digs the earth with the
intention of cultivating it, and finds a treasure of buried gold, this is
thought to happen by chance. But it does not come from nothing
since the event has its own causes whose unforeseen and unexpected concurrence seems to have produced an effect by chance.
For, if the farmer had not dug the ground, and if someone had not
buried his gold in that spot, the treasure would not have been found.
These are the causes of the fortunate accident which is brought
about by the coincidence of causes and not by the intention of the
one performing the action. For neither the man who buried the gold,
nor the man who was cultivating the field, intended that the money
should be found; but, as I said, it happened coincidentally that the
farmer dug where the other had buried the money.

"Therefore, we can define chance as an unexpected event brought
about by a concurrence of causes which had other purposes in view.
These causes come together because of that order which proceeds
from inevitable connection of things, the order which flows from the
source which is Providence and which disposes all things, each in its
proper time and place.[2]

Poem 1

"The Tigris and Euphrates flow from a single source in the
Achaemenian rocks, where the Parthian warrior turns in his flight to
shoot his arrows into the pursuing enemy, but they quickly flow apart
in separate streams.[3] If they should join their waters again in one
channel, all that each stream carries would come together; the boats
that sail on each, the floating trees torn up by floods, and the waters

---

1. In *Physics* 2, 4–5 and *Metaphysics* 4, 30, Aristotle presents this view of chance Lady
   Philosophy offers: an event causally determined that is unexpected.
2. Boethius, through Lady Philosophy, claims that there is an inevitable order to events in
   the world and that it comes from Providence.
3. The Tigris and Euphrates rivers, found in modern-day Iraq, rise in Armenia. They join
   and become the Shatt al-Arab waterway and empty into the Persian Gulf. Parthian war-
   riors (originating in northern Iran) were famous for their ability to shoot arrows while
   retreating.

too would mingle by chance. But steep channels and the downward flow of the current govern these seemingly random events. Chance, too, which seems to rush along with slack reins, is bridled and governed by law."

Prose 2

Philosophy argues that rational natures must necessarily have free will.

"I have listened carefully and agree that chance is as you say. But, within this series of connected causes, does our will have any freedom, or are the motions of human souls also bound by the fatal chain?"

"There is free will," Philosophy answered, "and no rational nature can exist which does not have it. For any being, which by its nature has the use of reason, must also have the power of judgment by which it can make decisions and, by its own resources, distinguish between things which should be desired and things which should be avoided. Now everyone seeks that which he judges to be desirable, but rejects whatever he thinks should be avoided. Therefore, in rational creatures there is also freedom of desiring and shunning.

"But I do not say that this freedom is the same in all beings. In supreme and divine substances there is clear judgment, uncorrupted will, and effective power to obtain what they desire. Human souls, however, are more free while they are engaged in contemplation of the divine mind, and less free when they are joined to bodies, and still less free when they are bound by earthly fetters.[4] They are in utter slavery when they lose possession of their reason and give themselves wholly to vice. For when they turn away their eyes from the light of supreme truth to mean and dark things, they are blinded by a cloud of ignorance and obsessed by vicious passions. By yielding and consenting to these passions, they worsen the slavery to which they have brought themselves and are, as it were, the captives of their own freedom. Nevertheless, God, who beholds all things from eternity, foresees all these things in his providence and disposes each according to its predestined merits.[5]

---

4. Boethius, through Lady Philosophy, links freedom with rationality. He seems to say that rational agents are more free to the degree that they imitate the power and judgment of God.
5. Through Lady Philosophy, Boethius maintains that God determines all, even the free acts of rational beings.

Poem 2

" 'He sees all things and hears all things.'[6] Sweet-voiced Homer sings of the clear light of bright Phoebus; but the sun's weak rays cannot pierce the bowels of the earth nor the depths of the sea. It is not so with the Creator of this great sphere. No mass of earth, no dark and clouded night can resist his vision which looks down on all things. He sees at once, in a single glance, all things that are, or were, or are to come. Since He is sole observer of all things, you may call Him the true Sun."

Prose 3

Boethius contends that divine foreknowledge and freedom of the human will are incompatible.

"Now I am confused by an even greater difficulty," I said.

"What is it?" Philosophy answered, "though I think I know what is bothering you."

"There seems to be a hopeless conflict between divine foreknowledge of all things and freedom of the human will. For if God sees everything in advance and cannot be deceived in any way, whatever his Providence foresees will happen, must happen.[7] Therefore, if God foreknows eternally not only all the acts of men, but also their plans and wishes, there cannot be freedom of will; for nothing whatever can be done or even desired without its being known beforehand by the infallible Providence of God. If things could somehow be accomplished in some way other than that which God foresaw, his foreknowledge of the future would no longer be certain. Indeed, it would be merely uncertain opinion, and it would be wrong to think that of God.

"I cannot agree with the argument by which some people believe that they can solve this problem. They say that things do not happen because Providence foresees that they will happen, but, on the contrary, that Providence foresees what is to come because it will happen, and in this way they find the necessity to be in things, not in Providence. For, they say, it is not necessary that things should happen because they are foreseen, but only that things which will happen be foreseen—as though the problem were whether divine

---

6. God knows all, and God's knowledge occurs all at once. Boethius will soon elaborate on what he means.
7. Boethius in his own voice claims that there seems to be a conflict between God's knowledge and the freedom of the human will.

Providence is the cause of the necessity of future events, or the necessity of future events is the cause of divine Providence. But our concern is to prove that the fulfillment of things which God has foreseen is necessary, whatever the order of causes, even if the divine foreknowledge does not seem to make the occurrence of future events necessary. For example, if a man sits down, the opinion that he is sitting must be true; and conversely, if the opinion that someone is sitting be true, then that person must necessarily be sitting. Therefore, there is necessity in both cases: the man must be sitting and the opinion must be true. But the man is not sitting because the opinion is true; the opinion is true because the sitting came before the opinion about it. Therefore, even though the cause of truth came from one side, necessity is common to both.

"A similar line of reasoning applies to divine foreknowledge and future events. For even though the events are foreseen because they will happen, they do not happen because they are foreseen. Nevertheless, it is necessary either that things which are going to happen be foreseen by God, or that what God foresees will in fact happen; and either way the freedom of the human will is destroyed. But of course it is preposterous to say that the outcome of temporal things is the cause of eternal foreknowledge. Yet to suppose that God foresees future events because they are going to happen is the same as supposing that things which happened long ago are the cause of divine Providence. Furthermore, just as when I know that a thing is, that thing must necessarily be; so when I know that something will happen, it is necessary that it happen. It follows, then, that the outcome of something known in advance must necessarily take place.

"Finally, if anyone thinks that a thing is other than it actually is, he does not have knowledge but merely a fallible opinion, and that is quite different from the truth of knowledge. So, if the outcome of some future event is either uncertain or unnecessary, no one can know in advance whether or not it will happen. For just as true knowledge is not tainted by falsity, so that which is known by it cannot be otherwise than as it is known. And that is the reason why knowledge never deceives; things must necessarily be as true knowledge knows them to be. If this is so, how does God foreknow future possibilities whose existence is uncertain? If He thinks that things will inevitably happen which possibly will not happen, He is deceived. But it is wrong to say that, or even to think it. And if He merely knows that they may or may not happen, that is, if He knows only their contingent possibilities, what is such knowledge worth, since it does not know with certainty? Such knowledge is no better than that expressed by the ridiculous prophecy of Tiresias: 'Whatever I say will either be or not be.'[8] Divine Providence would be no better than human opinion if God judges as men do and knows only that uncertain events are doubtful. But if nothing can be uncertain to Him who is the most certain source of all things, the outcome is certain of all things which He knows with certainty shall be.

"Therefore, there can be no freedom in human decisions and actions, since the divine mind, foreseeing everything without possibility of error, determines and forces the outcome of everything that is to happen. Once this is granted, it is clear that the structure of all human affairs must collapse. For it is pointless to assign rewards and punishment to the good and wicked since neither are deserved if the actions of men are not free and voluntary. Punishment of the wicked and recognition of the good, which are now considered just, will seem quite unjust since neither the good nor the wicked are governed by their own will but are forced by the inevitability of predetermination. Vice and virtue will be without meaning, and in their place there will be utter confusion about what is deserved. Finally, and this is the most blasphemous thought of all, it follows that the Author of all good must be made responsible for all human vice since the entire order of human events depends on Providence and nothing on man's intention.

"There is no use in hoping or praying for anything, for what is the point in hope or prayer when everything that man desires is determined by unalterable process? Thus man's only bonds with God, hope and prayer, are destroyed. We believe that our just humility may earn the priceless reward of divine grace, for this is the only way in which men seem able to communicate with God; we are joined to that inaccessible light by supplication before receiving what we ask. But if we hold that all future events are governed by necessity, and therefore that prayer has no value, what will be left to unite us to the sovereign Lord of all things? And so mankind must, as you said earlier, be cut off from its source and dwindle into nothing.

Poem 3

"What cause of discord breaks the ties which ought to bind this union of things? What God has set such conflict between these two truths? Separately each is certain, but put together they cannot be reconciled. Is there no discord between them? Can they exist side by side and be equally true?

---

8. Tiresias, the blind prophet of Thebes, was the most famous soothsayer of Ancient Greece. This prophecy is a statement of the obvious: either something is or it is not.

"The human mind, overcome by the body's blindness, cannot discern by its dim light the delicate connections between things. But why does the mind burn with such desire to discover the hidden aspects of truth? Does it know what it is so eager to know? Then why does it go on laboriously trying to discover what it already knows? And if it does not know, why does it blindly continue the search? For who would want something of which he is unaware, or run after something he does not know? How can such a thing be found, or, if found, how would it be recognized by someone ignorant of its form?

"When the human mind knew the mind of God, did it know the whole and all its parts? Now the mind is shrouded in the clouds of the body, but it has not wholly forgotten itself; and, although it has lost its grasp of particulars, it still holds fast to the general truth. Therefore, whoever seeks the truth knows something: he is neither completely informed nor completely ignorant. He works with what he remembers of the highest truth, using what he saw on high in order to fill in the forgotten parts."

Prose 4

Philosophy begins her argument that divine Providence does not preclude freedom of the will by stressing the difference between divine and human knowledge.

"This is an old difficulty about Providence," Philosophy answered. "It was raised by Cicero in his book on divination, and has for a long time been a subject of your own investigation, but so far none of you has treated it with enough care and conviction.[9] The cause of the obscurity which still surrounds the problem is that the process of human reason cannot comprehend the simplicity of divine foreknowledge. If in any way we could understand that, no further doubt would remain. I shall try to make this clear after I have explained the things which trouble you.

"First, let me ask why you regard as inconclusive the reasoning of those who think that foreknowledge is no hindrance to free will because it is not the cause of the necessity of future things. For do you have any argument for the necessity of future events other than the principle that things which are known beforehand must happen? If, as you have just now conceded, foreknowledge does not impose necessity on future events, why must the voluntary outcome of things be bound to predetermined results? For the sake of argument,

---

9. Boethius, through Lady Philosophy, credits Cicero with articulating the problem of the relationship between God's knowledge and human freedom in his *On Divination*, 2, 8f.

so that you may consider what follows from it, let us suppose that there is no foreknowledge. Then would the things which are done by free will be bound by necessity in this respect?"

"Not at all."

"Then, let us suppose that foreknowledge exists but imposes no necessity on things. The same independence and absolute freedom of will would remain.

"But you will say that even though foreknowledge does not impose necessity on future events, it is still a sign that they will necessarily happen. It must follow then that even if there were no foreknowledge the outcome of these future things would be necessary. For signs only show what is, they do not cause the things they point to. Therefore we must first prove that nothing happens other than by necessity, in order to demonstrate that foreknowledge is a sign of this necessity. Otherwise, if there is no necessity, then foreknowledge cannot be a sign of something that does not exist. Moreover, it is clear that firmly based proof does not rest on signs and extrinsic arguments but is deduced from suitable and necessary causes. But how can it be that things which are foreseen should not happen? We do not suppose that things will not happen, if Providence has foreknowledge that they will; rather we judge that, although they will happen, they have nothing in their natures which makes it necessary that they should happen. For we see many things in the process of happening before our eyes, just as the chariot driver sees the results of his actions as he guides his chariot; and this is true in many of our activities. Do you think that such things are compelled by necessity to happen as they do?"

"No. For the results of art would be vain if they were all brought about by compulsion."[1]

"Then, since they come into being without necessity, these same things were not determined by necessity before they actually happened. Therefore, there are some things destined to happen in the future whose outcome is free of any necessity. For everyone, I think, would say that things which are now happening were going to happen before they actually came to pass. Thus, these things happen without necessity even though they were known in advance. For just as knowledge of things happening now does not imply necessity in their outcomes, so foreknowledge of future things imposes no necessity on their outcomes in the future.

"But, you will say, the point at issue is whether there can be any foreknowledge of things whose outcomes are not necessary. For

---

1. The notion of compulsion is introduced as contrary to freedom. If a person's action is compelled by external forces (e.g., wind causes someone to fall from a cliff), the action is not free.

these things seem opposed to each other, and you think that if things can be foreseen they must necessarily happen, and that if the necessity is absent they cannot be foreseen, and that nothing can be fully known unless it is certain.[2] If uncertain things are foreseen as certain, that is the weakness of opinion, not the truth of knowledge. You believe that to judge that a thing is other than it is departs from the integrity of knowledge. Now the cause of this error lies in your assumption that whatever is known, is known only by the force and nature of the things which are known; but the opposite is true. Everything which is known is known not according to its own power but rather according to the capacity of the knower.[3]

"Let me illustrate with a brief example: the roundness of a body is known in one way by the sense of touch and in another by the sight. The sight, remaining at a distance, takes in the whole body at once by its reflected rays; but the touch makes direct contact with the sphere and comprehends it piecemeal by moving around its surface. A man himself is comprehended in different ways by the senses, imagination, reason, and intelligence. The senses grasp the figure of the thing as it is constituted in matter; the imagination, however, grasps the figure alone without the matter. Reason, on the other hand, goes beyond this and investigates by universal consideration the species itself which is in particular things. The vision of intelligence is higher yet, and it goes beyond the bounds of the universe and sees with the clear eye of the mind the pure form itself.

"In all this we chiefly observe that the higher power of knowing includes the lower, but the lower can in no way rise to the higher. For the senses achieve nothing beyond the material, the imagination cannot grasp universal species, reason cannot know simple forms; but the intelligence, as though looking down from on high, conceives the underlying forms and distinguishes among them all, but in the same way in which it comprehends the form itself which cannot be known to any other power. The intelligence knows the objects of the lower kinds of knowledge: the universals of the reason, the figures of the imagination, the matter of the senses, but not by using reason, or imagination, or senses. With a single glance of the mind it formally, as it were, sees all things. Similarly, when reason knows a universal nature, it comprehends all the objects of imagination and the senses without using either. For reason defines the general nature of her conception as follows: man is a biped, rational animal. This is a universal idea, but no one ignores the fact that man is also an imaginable

2. "Necessity" has various senses. In one sense, events happen by necessity if they are compelled. In another sense, they happen by necessity if they follow from necessary causes. In another sense, they follow necessarily from certain conditions. Boethius has not here clarified what sense of necessity is at issue.
3. "Everything which is known is known not according to its own power but rather according to the capacity of the knower." This is a key claim in Boethius's solution to the conflict between God's knowledge and human freedom.

and sensible object which reason knows by rational conception rather than by the imagination and senses. Similarly, although the imagination begins by seeing and forming figures with the senses, nevertheless it can, without the aid of the senses, behold sensible objects by an imaginative rather than a sensory mode of knowing.

"Do you see, then, how all these use their own power in knowing rather than the powers of the objects which are known? And this is proper, for since all judgment is in the act of the one judging, it is necessary that everyone should accomplish his own action by his own power, not by the power of something other than himself.

Poem 4

"Long ago the philosophers of the Porch at Athens, old men who saw things dimly, believed that sense impressions and images were impressed on the mind by external objects, just as then they used to mark letters on a blank page of wax with their quick pens.[4] But, if the active mind can discover nothing by its own powers, and merely remains passively subject to the impressions of external bodies, like a mirror reflecting the empty shapes of other things, where does that power come from which dwells in souls and sees all things? What is that power which perceives individual things and, by knowing them, can distinguish among them? What is the power which puts together again the parts it has separated and, pursuing its due course, lifts its gaze to the highest things, then descends again to the lowest, then returns to itself to refute false ideas with truth?

"This is a more effective, and a much more powerful cause than any which merely receives impressions from material things. Still, the sense impression comes first, arousing and moving the powers of the soul in the living body. When light strikes the eyes, or sound the ears, the aroused power of the mind calls into action the corresponding species which it holds within, joining them to the outward signs and mixing images with the forms it has hidden in itself.

Prose 5

To understand this mystery, human reason must contemplate the power of the divine intelligence.

"Thus, in the case of sentient bodies external stimuli affect the sense organs, and a physical sensation precedes the activity of the

---

4. The reference is to the Stoic school of philosophy, founded by Zeno (see note 4, p. 7). They held that the external world impresses itself on the senses and mind. We are, however, able to assent to what affects us or not assent to it.

mind, calling the mind to act upon itself and in this way to activate the interior forms which before were inactive. Now if, as I say, in sentient bodies the soul is affected by external bodies but judges these stimuli presented to the body not passively, but by virtue of its own power, how much more do intelligences which are wholly free from all bodily affections use the power of the mind rather than objects extrinsic to themselves in arriving at judgments. According to this principle, various and different substances have different ways of knowing. There are certain immobile living things which are without any means of knowing other than by sense impressions. Shellfish and other forms of marine life which are nourished as they stick to rocks are creatures of this kind. Beasts which have the power of motion, on the other hand, have the impulse to seek and avoid certain things, and they have imagination. But reason is characteristic of the human race alone, just as pure intelligence belongs to God alone.

"It follows, then, that the most excellent knowledge is that which by its own nature knows not only its own proper object but also the objects of all lower kinds of knowledge. What, then, should we think if the senses and imagination were to oppose reason by arguing that the universal, which reason claims to know, is nothing? Suppose they were to argue that whatever can be sensed or imagined cannot be universal; and that therefore either the judgment of reason is true, and there are no objects of sense knowledge, or, since everyone knows that many things can be known by the senses and the imagination, that the conception of reason, which regards whatever is sensible and singular as if it were universal, is vain and empty. And suppose, further, that reason should answer that it conceives sensible and imaginable objects under the aspect of universality, but that the senses and imagination cannot aspire to the knowledge of universality because their knowledge cannot go beyond corporeal figures. Moreover, reason might continue, in matters of knowledge we ought to trust the stronger and more perfect judgment. In such a controversy we who possess the power of reason, as well as of imagination and sense perception, ought to take the side of reason.

"The situation is much the same when human reason supposes that the divine intelligence beholds future events only as reason herself sees them. For you argue that if some things seem not to have certain and necessary outcomes, they cannot be foreknown as certainly about to happen. Therefore, you say that there can be no foreknowledge of these things, or, if we believe that there is such foreknowledge, that the outcome of all things is controlled by necessity. But if we, who are endowed with reason, could possess the intelligence of the divine mind, we would judge that just as the senses and imagination should accede to reason, so human reason ought justly to submit itself to the divine mind. Let us rise, if we can, to the summit of the highest intelligence; for there reason will see what in itself it cannot see: that a certain and definite foreknowledge can behold even those things which have no certain outcome. And this foreknowledge is not mere conjecture but the unrestricted simplicity of supreme knowledge.

Poem 5

"How varied are the shapes of living things on earth! Some there are with bodies stretched out, crawling through the dust, spending their strength in an unbroken furrow; some soar in the air, beating the wind with light wings, floating in easy flight along tracks of air. Some walk along the ground through woods and across green fields. All these, you observe, differ in their varied forms, but their faces look down and cause their senses to grow sluggish.

"The human race alone lifts its head to heaven and stands erect, despising the earth. Man's figure teaches, unless folly has bound you to the earth, that you who look upward with your head held high should also raise your soul to sublime things, lest while your body is raised above the earth, your mind should sink to the ground under its burden.

Prose 6

Philosophy solves the problem of Providence and free will by distinguishing between simple and conditional necessity.

"Since, as we have shown, whatever is known is known according to the nature of the knower, and not according to its own nature, let us now consider as far as is lawful the nature of the Divine Being, so that we may discover what its knowledge is. The common judgment of all rational creatures holds that God is eternal. Therefore let us consider what eternity is, for this will reveal both the divine nature and the divine knowledge.

"Eternity is the whole, perfect, and simultaneous possession of endless life.[5] The meaning of this can be made clearer by comparison with temporal things. For whatever lives in time lives in the present, proceeding from past to future, and nothing is so constituted in time that it can embrace the whole span of its life at once. It has not yet arrived at tomorrow, and it has already lost yesterday; even the

---

5. A very influential definition. It indicates that what is eternal happens all at once.

life of this day is lived only in each moving, passing moment. Therefore, whatever is subject to the condition of time, even that which—as Aristotle conceived the world to be[6]—has no beginning and will have no end in a life coextensive with the infinity of time, is such that it cannot rightly be thought eternal. For it does not comprehend and include the whole of infinite life all at once, since it does not embrace the future which is yet to come. Therefore, only that which comprehends and possesses the whole plenitude of endless life together; from which no future thing nor any past thing is absent, can justly be called eternal. Moreover, it is necessary that such a being be in full possession of itself, always present to itself, and hold the infinity of moving time present before itself.

"Therefore, they are wrong who, having heard that Plato held that this world did not have a beginning in time and would never come to an end,[7] suppose that the created world is coeternal with its Creator. For it is one thing to live an endless life, which is what Plato ascribed to the world, and another for the whole of unending life to be embraced all at once as present, which is clearly proper to the divine mind. Nor should God be thought of as older than His creation in extent of time, but rather as prior to it by virtue of the simplicity of His nature. For the infinite motion of temporal things imitates the immediate present of His changeless life and, since it cannot reproduce or equal life, it sinks from immobility to motion and declines from the simplicity of the present into the infinite duration of future and past. And, since it cannot possess the whole fullness of its life at once, it seems to imitate to some extent that which it cannot completely express, and it does this by somehow never ceasing to be. It binds itself to a kind of present in this short and transitory period which, because it has a certain likeness to that abiding, unchanging present, gives everything it touches a semblance of existence. But, since this imitation cannot remain still, it hastens along the infinite road of time, and so it extends by movement the life whose completeness it could not achieve by standing still. Therefore, if we wish to call things by their proper names, we should follow Plato in saying that God indeed is eternal, but the world is perpetual.

"Since, then, every judgment comprehends the subjects presented to it according to its own nature, and since God lives in the eternal present, His knowledge transcends all movement of time and abides in the simplicity of its immediate present. It encompasses the

---

6. Aristotle thought the world was perpetual, meaning it has existed at every instant of time and will exist for every instant of time.
7. Boethius, through Lady Philosophy, ascribes to Plato (in *The Timaeus*) a view very similar to Aristotle's that the world is in time and perpetual. God, however, is eternal since God is outside of time and (logically) prior to it.

infinite sweep of past and future, and regards all things in its simple comprehension as if they were now taking place. Thus, if you will think about the foreknowledge by which God distinguishes all things, you will rightly consider it to be not a foreknowledge of future events, but knowledge of a never changing present. For this reason, divine knowledge is called providence, rather than prevision, because it resides above all inferior things and looks out on all things from their summit.

"Why then do you imagine that things are necessary which are illuminated by this divine light, since even men do not impose necessity on the things they see? Does your vision impose any necessity upon things which you see present before you?"

"Not at all," I answered.

"Then," Philosophy went on, "if we may aptly compare God's present vision with man's, He sees all things in his eternal present as you see some things in your temporal present. Therefore, this divine foreknowledge does not change the nature and properties of things; it simply sees things present before it as they will later turn out to be in what we regard as the future. His judgment is not confused; with a single intuition of his mind He knows all things that are to come, whether necessarily or not. Just as, when you happen to see simultaneously a man walking on the street and the sun shining in the sky, even though you see both at once, you can distinguish between them and realize that one action is voluntary, the other necessary; so the divine mind, looking down on all things, does not disturb the nature of the things which are present before it but are future with respect to time. Therefore, when God knows that something will happen in the future, and at the same time knows that it will not happen through necessity, this is not opinion but knowledge based on truth.

"If you should reply that whatever God foresees as happening cannot help but happen, and that whatever must happen is bound by necessity—if you pin me down to this word 'necessity'—I grant that you state a solid truth, but one which only a profound theologian can grasp. I would answer that the same future event is necessary with respect to God's knowledge of it, but free and undetermined if considered in its own nature. For there are two kinds of necessity: one is simple, as the necessity by which all men are mortals; the other is conditional, as is the case when, if you know that someone is walking, he must necessarily be walking.[8] For whatever is known,

---

8. Simple necessity is contrasted with conditional necessity. Something has simple necessity if it is the way it is no matter what else is the case. Something is conditionally necessary if it is the way it is only because a certain condition obtains. For example, it is necessary that a bachelor be an unmarried male for this is what the term 'bachelor' means. However, any particular male might or might not be a bachelor. Yet, it is necessarily the case that if a male is unmarried, he is a bachelor.

must be as it is known to be; but this condition does not involve that other, simple necessity. It is not caused by the peculiar nature of the person in question, but by an added condition. No necessity forces the man who is voluntarily walking to move forward; but as long as he is walking, he is necessarily moving forward. In the same way, if Providence sees anything as present, that thing must necessarily be, even though it may have no necessity by its nature. But God sees as present those future things which result from free will. Therefore, from the standpoint of divine knowledge these things are necessary because of the condition of their being known by God; but, considered only in themselves, they lose nothing of the absolute freedom of their own natures.

"There is no doubt, then, that all things will happen which God knows will happen; but some of them happen as a result of free will. And, although they happen, they do not, by their existence, lose their proper natures by which, before they happened, they were able not to happen.[9] But, you may ask, what does it mean to say that these events are not necessary, since by reason of the condition of divine knowledge they happen just as if they were necessary? The meaning is the same as in the example I used a while ago of the sun rising and the man walking. At the time they are happening, they must necessarily be happening; but the sun's rising is governed by necessity even before it happens, while the man's walking is not. Similarly, all the things God sees as present will undoubtedly come to pass; but some will happen by the necessity of their natures, others by the power of those who make them happen.[1] Therefore, we quite properly said that these things are necessary if viewed from the standpoint of divine knowledge, but if they are considered in themselves, they are free of the bonds of necessity. In somewhat the same way, whatever is known by the senses is singular in itself, but universal as far as the reason is concerned.

"But, you may say, if I can change my mind about doing something, I can frustrate Providence, since by chance I may change something which Providence foresaw. My answer is this: you can indeed alter what you propose to do, but, because the present truth of Providence sees that you can, and whether or not you will, you cannot frustrate the divine knowledge any more than you can escape the eye of someone who is present and watching you, even though you may, by your free will, vary your actions. You may still wonder,

---

9. Boethius, through Lady Philosophy, indicates that, for free actions, what occurs could not occur. How this "ability to be otherwise" is to be interpreted, however, is not clear from the text.
1. The contrast here seems to be between agents that act by necessity, called natural agents (like the sun), and agents that act by power of their nature to act, called voluntary agents (like human beings).

however, whether God's knowledge is changed by your decisions, so that when you wish now one thing, now another, the divine knowledge undergoes corresponding changes. This is not the case. For divine Providence anticipates every future action and converts it to its own present knowledge. It does not change, as you imagine, foreknowing this or that in succession, but in a single instant, without being changed itself, anticipates and grasps your changes. God has this present comprehension and immediate vision of all things not from the outcome of future events, but from the simplicity of his own nature. In this way, the problem you raised a moment ago is settled. You observed that it would be unworthy of God if our future acts were said to be the cause of divine knowledge. Now you see that this power of divine knowledge, comprehending all things as present before it, itself constitutes the measure of all things and is in no way dependent on things that happen later.[2]

"Since this is true, the freedom of the human will remains inviolate, and laws are just since they provide rewards and punishments to human wills which are not controlled by necessity. God looks down from above, knowing all things, and the eternal present of his vision concurs with the future character of our actions, distributing rewards to the good and punishments to the evil. Our hopes and prayers are not directed to God in vain, for if they are just they cannot fail. Therefore, stand firm against vice and cultivate virtue. Lift up your soul to worthy hopes, and offer humble prayers to heaven. If you will face it, the necessity of virtuous action imposed upon you is very great, since all your actions are done in the sight of a Judge who sees all things."

2. Boethius, through Lady Philosophy, claims that God's providing knowledge (Providence) is the measure of all things. God's knowledge does not rely on the existence of events in the world; rather, events in the world follow God's eternal knowledge of them. The passage seems to bring us to acknowledge the causal efficacy of God's knowledge and move Boethius's discussion of the relationship between God's knowledge and human freedom from the purely logical order it has seemed to follow for the most part of Book 5.

CONTEXTS

PLATO

From The Gorgias[†]

* * *

SOCRATES But in my opinion, Polus, the unjust or doer of unjust actions is miserable in any case,—more miserable, however, if he be not punished and does not meet with retribution, and less miserable if he be punished and meets with retribution at the hands of gods and men.

POLUS You are maintaining a strange doctrine, Socrates.

SOC. I shall try to make you agree with me, O my friend, for as a friend I regard you. Then these are the points at issue between us— are they not? I was saying that to do is worse than to suffer injustice?

POL. Exactly so.

SOC. And you said the opposite?

POL. Yes.

SOC. I said also that the wicked are miserable, and you refuted me?

POL. By Zeus I did.

SOC. In your own opinion, Polus.

POL. Yes, and I rather suspect that I was in the right.

SOC. You further said that the wrong-doer is happy if he be unpunished?

POL. Certainly.

SOC. And I affirm that he is most miserable, and that those who are punished are less miserable—are you going to refute this proposition also?

POL. A proposition which is harder of refutation than the other, Socrates.

SOC. Say rather, Polus, impossible; for who can refute the truth?

POL. What do you mean? If a man is detected in an unjust attempt to make himself a tyrant, and when detected is racked, mutilated, has his eyes burned out, and after having had all sorts of great injuries inflicted on him, and having seen his wife and children suffer the like, is at last impaled or tarred and burned alive, will he be happier than if he escape and become a tyrant, and continue all through life doing what he likes and holding the reins of government, the envy and admiration both of citizens and strangers? Is that the paradox which, as you say, cannot be refuted?

---

† From *The Dialogues of Plato*, trans. Benjamin Jowett (New York: Oxford UP, 1892). The translator's footnote has been omitted.

SOC. There again, noble Polus, you are raising hobgoblins instead of refuting me; just now you were calling witnesses against me. But please to refresh my memory a little; did you say—'in an unjust attempt to make himself a tyrant'?

POL. Yes, I did.

SOC. Then I say that neither of them will be happier than the other,—neither he who unjustly acquires a tyranny, nor he who suffers in the attempt, for of two miserables one cannot be the happier, but that he who escapes and becomes a tyrant is the more miserable of the two. Do you laugh, Polus? Well, this is a new kind of refutation,—when any one says anything, instead of refuting him to laugh at him.

POL. But do you not think, Socrates, that you have been sufficiently refuted, when you say that which no human being will allow? Ask the company.

SOC. O Polus, I am not a public man, and only last year, when my tribe were serving as Prytanes, and it became my duty as their president to take the votes, there was a laugh at me, because I was unable to take them. And as I failed then, you must not ask me to count the suffrages of the company now; but if, as I was saying, you have no better argument than numbers, let me have a turn, and do you make trial of the sort of proof which, as I think, is required; for I shall produce one witness only of the truth of my words, and he is the person with whom I am arguing; his suffrage I know how to take; but with the many I have nothing to do, and do not even address myself to them. May I ask then whether you will answer in turn and have your words put to the proof? For I certainly think that I and you and every man do really believe, that to do is a greater evil than to suffer injustice: and not to be punished than to be punished.

POL. And I should say neither I, nor any man: would you yourself, for example, suffer rather than do injustice?

SOC. Yes, and you, too; I or any man would.

POL. Quite the reverse; neither you, nor I, nor any man.

SOC. But will you answer?

POL. To be sure, I will; for I am curious to hear what you can have to say.

SOC. Tell me, then, and you will know, and let us suppose that I am beginning at the beginning: which of the two, Polus, in your opinion, is the worst?—to do injustice or to suffer?

POL. I should say that suffering was worst.

SOC. And which is the greater disgrace?—Answer.

POL. To do.

SOC. And the greater disgrace is the greater evil?

POL. Certainly not.

Soc. I understand you to say, if I am not mistaken, that the honourable is not the same as the good, or the disgraceful as the evil?

Pol. Certainly not.

Soc. Let me ask a question of you: When you speak of beautiful things, such as bodies, colours, figures, sounds, institutions, do you not call them beautiful in reference to some standard: bodies, for example, are beautiful in proportion as they are useful, or as the sight of them gives pleasure to the spectators; can you give any other account of personal beauty?

Pol. I cannot.

Soc. And you would say of figures or colours generally that they were beautiful, either by reason of the pleasure which they give, or of their use, or of both?

Pol. Yes, I should.

Soc. And you would call sounds and music beautiful for the same reason?

Pol. I should.

Soc. Laws and institutions also have no beauty in them except in so far as they are useful or pleasant or both?

Pol. I think not.

Soc. And may not the same be said of the beauty of knowledge?

Pol. To be sure, Socrates; and I very much approve of your measuring beauty by the standard of pleasure and utility.

Soc. And deformity or disgrace may be equally measured by the opposite standard of pain and evil?

Pol. Certainly.

Soc. Then when of two beautiful things one exceeds in beauty, the measure of the excess is to be taken in one or both of these; that is to say, in pleasure or utility or both?

Pol. Very true.

Soc. And of two deformed things, that which exceeds in deformity or disgrace, exceeds either in pain or evil—must it not be so?

Pol. Yes.

Soc. But then again, what was the observation which you just now made, about doing and suffering wrong? Did you not say, that suffering wrong was more evil, and doing wrong more disgraceful?

Pol. I did.

Soc. Then, if doing wrong is more disgraceful than suffering, the more disgraceful must be more painful and must exceed in pain or in evil or both: does not that also follow?

Pol. Of course.

Soc. First, then, let us consider whether the doing of injustice exceeds the suffering in the consequent pain: Do the injurers suffer more than the injured?

POL. No, Socrates; certainly not.

SOC. Then they do not exceed in pain?

POL. No.

SOC. But if not in pain, then not in both?

POL. Certainly not.

SOC. Then they can only exceed in the other?

POL. Yes.

SOC. That is to say, in evil?

POL. True.

SOC. Then doing injustice will have an excess of evil, and will therefore be a greater evil than suffering injustice?

POL. Clearly.

SOC. But have not you and the world already agreed that to do injustice is more disgraceful than to suffer?

POL. Yes.

SOC. And that is now discovered to be more evil?

POL. True.

SOC. And would you prefer a greater evil or a greater dishonour to a less one? Answer, Polus, and fear not; for you will come to no harm if you nobly resign yourself into the healing hand of the argument as to a physician without shrinking, and either say 'Yes' or 'No' to me.

POL. I should say 'No.'

SOC. Would any other man prefer a greater to a less evil?

POL. No, not according to this way of putting the case, Socrates.

SOC. Then I said truly, Polus, that neither you, nor I, nor any man, would rather do than suffer injustice; for to do injustice is the greater evil of the two.

POL. That is the conclusion.

SOC. You see, Polus, when you compare the two kinds of refutations, how unlike they are. All men, with the exception of myself, are of your way of thinking; but your single assent and witness are enough for me,—I have no need of any other; I take your suffrage, and am regardless of the rest. Enough of this, and now let us proceed to the next question; which is, Whether the greatest of evils to a guilty man is to suffer punishment, as you supposed, or whether to escape punishment is not a greater evil, as I supposed. Consider:— You would say that to suffer punishment is another name for being justly corrected when you do wrong?

POL. I should.

SOC. And would you not allow that all just things are honourable in so far as they are just? Please to reflect, and tell me your opinion.

POL. Yes, Socrates, I think that they are.

SOC. Consider again:—Where there is an agent, must there not also be a patient?

POL. I should say so.

SOC. And will not the patient suffer that which the agent does, and will not the suffering have the quality of the action? I mean, for example, that if a man strikes, there must be something which is stricken?

POL. Yes.

SOC. And if the striker strikes violently or quickly, that which is struck will be struck violently or quickly?

POL. True.

SOC. And the suffering to him who is stricken is of the same nature as the act of him who strikes?

POL. Yes.

SOC. And if a man burns, there is something which is burned?

POL. Certainly.

SOC. And if he burns in excess or so as to cause pain, the thing burned will be burned in the same way?

POL. Truly.

SOC. And if he cuts, the same argument holds—there will be something cut?

POL. Yes.

SOC. And if the cutting be great or deep or such as will cause pain, the cut will be of the same nature?

POL. That is evident.

SOC. Then you would agree generally to the universal proposition which I was just now asserting: that the affection of the patient answers to the act of the agent?

POL. I agree.

SOC. Then, as this is admitted, let me ask whether being punished is suffering or acting?

POL. Suffering, Socrates; there can be no doubt of that.

SOC. And suffering implies an agent?

POL. Certainly, Socrates; and he is the punisher.

SOC. And he who punishes rightly, punishes justly?

POL. Yes.

SOC. And therefore he acts justly?

POL. Justly.

SOC. Then he who is punished and suffers retribution, suffers justly?

POL. That is evident.

SOC. And that which is just has been admitted to be honourable?

POL. Certainly.

SOC. Then the punisher does what is honourable, and the punished suffers what is honourable?

POL. True.

SOC. And if what is honourable, then what is good, for the honourable is either pleasant or useful?

POL. Certainly.

SOC. Then he who is punished suffers what is good?

POL. That is true.

SOC. Then he is benefited?

POL. Yes.

SOC. Do I understand you to mean what I mean by the term 'benefited'? I mean, that if he be justly punished his soul is improved.

POL. Surely.

SOC. Then he who is punished is delivered from the evil of his soul?

POL. Yes.

SOC. And is he not then delivered from the greatest evil? Look at the matter in this way:—In respect of a man's estate, do you see any greater evil than poverty?

POL. There is no greater evil.

SOC. Again, in a man's bodily frame, you would say that the evil is weakness and disease and deformity?

POL. I should.

SOC. And do you not imagine that the soul likewise has some evil of her own?

POL. Of course.

SOC. And this you would call injustice and ignorance and cowardice, and the like?

POL. Certainly.

SOC. So then, in mind, body, and estate, which are three, you have pointed out three corresponding evils—injustice, disease, poverty?

POL. True.

SOC. And which of the evils is the most disgraceful?—Is not the most disgraceful of them injustice, and in general the evil of the soul?

POL. By far the most.

SOC. And if the most disgraceful, then also the worst?

POL. What do you mean, Socrates?

SOC. I mean to say, that what is most disgraceful has been already admitted to be most painful or hurtful, or both.

POL. Certainly.

SOC. And now injustice and all evil in the soul has been admitted by us to be most disgraceful?

POL. It has been admitted.

SOC. And most disgraceful either because most painful and causing excessive pain, or most hurtful, or both?

POL. Certainly.

SOC. And therefore to be unjust and intemperate, and cowardly and ignorant, is more painful than to be poor and sick?

POL. Nay, Socrates; the painfulness does not appear to me to follow from your premises.

SOC. Then, if, as you would argue, not more painful, the evil of the soul is of all evils the most disgraceful; and the excess of disgrace must be caused by some preternatural greatness, or extraordinary hurtfulness of the evil.

POL. Clearly.

SOC. And that which exceeds most in hurtfulness will be the greatest of evils?

POL. Yes.

SOC. Then injustice and intemperance, and in general the depravity of the soul, are the greatest of evils?

POL. That is evident.

SOC. Now, what art is there which delivers us from poverty? Does not the art of making money?

POL. Yes.

SOC. And what art frees us from disease? Does not the art of medicine?

POL. Very true.

SOC. And what from vice and injustice? If you are not able to answer at once, ask yourself whither we go with the sick, and to whom we take them.

POL. To the physicians, Socrates.

SOC. And to whom do we go with the unjust and intemperate?

POL. To the judges, you mean.

SOC. —Who are to punish them?

POL. Yes.

SOC. And do not those who rightly punish others, punish them in accordance with a certain rule of justice?

POL. Clearly.

SOC. Then the art of money-making frees a man from poverty; medicine from disease; and justice from intemperance and injustice?

POL. That is evident.

SOC. Which, then, is the best of these three?

POL. Will you enumerate them?

SOC. Money-making, medicine, and justice.

POL. Justice, Socrates, far excels the two others.

SOC. And justice, if the best, gives the greatest pleasure or advantage or both?

POL. Yes.

SOC. But is the being healed a pleasant thing, and are those who are being healed pleased?

POL. I think not.

SOC. A useful thing, then?

POL. Yes.

SOC. Yes, because the patient is delivered from a great evil; and this is the advantage of enduring the pain—that you get well?

POL. Certainly.

SOC. And would he be the happier man in his bodily condition, who is healed, or who never was out of health?

POL. Clearly he who was never out of health.

SOC. Yes; for happiness surely does not consist in being delivered from evils, but in never having had them.

POL. True.

SOC. And suppose the case of two persons who have some evil in their bodies, and that one of them is healed and delivered from evil, and another is not healed, but retains the evil—which of them is the most miserable?

POL. Clearly he who is not healed.

SOC. And was not punishment said by us to be a deliverance from the greatest of evils, which is vice?

POL. True.

SOC. And justice punishes us, and makes us more just, and is the medicine of our vice?

POL. True.

SOC. He, then, has the first place in the scale of happiness who has never had vice in his soul; for this has been shown to be the greatest of evils.

POL. Clearly.

SOC. And he has the second place, who is delivered from vice?

POL. True.

SOC. That is to say, he who receives admonition and rebuke and punishment?

POL. Yes.

SOC. Then he lives worst, who, having been unjust, has no deliverance from injustice?

POL. Certainly.

SOC. That is, he lives worst who commits the greatest crimes, and who, being the most unjust of men, succeeds in escaping rebuke or correction or punishment; and this, as you say, has been accomplished by Archelaus and other tyrants and rhetoricians and potentates?

POL. True.

SOC. May not their way of proceeding, my friend, be compared to the conduct of a person who is afflicted with the worst of diseases and yet contrives not to pay the penalty to the physician for his sins against his constitution, and will not be cured, because, like a

child, he is afraid of the pain of being burned or cut:—Is not that a
parallel case?

POL. Yes, truly.

SOC. He would seem as if he did not know the nature of health
and bodily vigour; and if we are right, Polus, in our previous conclusions, they are in a like case who strive to evade justice, which they
see to be painful, but are blind to the advantage which ensues from
it, not knowing how far more miserable a companion a diseased soul
is than a diseased body; a soul, I say, which is corrupt and unright-
eous and unholy. And hence they do all that they can to avoid punishment and to avoid being released from the greatest of evils; they
provide themselves with money and friends, and cultivate to the
utmost their powers of persuasion. But if we, Polus, are right, do you
see what follows, or shall we draw out the consequences in form?

POL. If you please.

SOC. Is it not a fact that injustice, and the doing of injustice, is
the greatest of evils?

POL. That is quite clear.

SOC. And further, that to suffer punishment is the way to be
released from this evil?

POL. True.

SOC. And not to suffer, is to perpetuate the evil?

POL. Yes.

SOC. To do wrong, then, is second only in the scale of evils; but
to do wrong and not to be punished, is first and greatest of all?

POL. That is true.

SOC. Well, and was not this the point in dispute, my friend? You
deemed Archelaus happy, because he was a very great criminal and
unpunished: I, on the other hand, maintained that he or any other
who like him has done wrong and has not been punished, is, and
ought to be, the most miserable of all men; and that the doer of
injustice is more miserable than the sufferer; and he who escapes
punishment, more miserable than he who suffers.—Was not that
what I said?

POL. Yes.

SOC. And it has been proved to be true?

POL. Certainly.

SOC. Well, Polus, but if this is true, where is the great use of
rhetoric? If we admit what has been just now said, every man ought
in every way to guard himself against doing wrong, for he will
thereby suffer great evil?

POL. True.

SOC. And if he, or any one about whom he cares, does wrong, he
ought of his own accord to go where he will be immediately punished; he will run to the judge, as he would to the physician, in order

that the disease of injustice may not be rendered chronic and become the incurable cancer of the soul; must we not allow this consequence, Polus, if our former admissions are to stand:—is any other inference consistent with them?

POL.   To that, Socrates, there can be but one answer.

SOC.   Then rhetoric is of no use to us, Polus, in helping a man to excuse his own injustice, or that of his parents or friends, or children or country; but may be of use to any one who holds that instead of excusing he ought to accuse—himself above all, and in the next degree his family or any of his friends who may be doing wrong; he should bring to light the iniquity and not conceal it, that so the wrong-doer may suffer and be made whole; and he should even force himself and others not to shrink, but with closed eyes like brave men to let the physician operate with knife or searing iron, not regarding the pain, in the hope of attaining the good and the hon-ourable; let him who has done things worthy of stripes, allow him-self to be scourged, if of bonds, to be bound, if of a fine, to be fined, if of exile, to be exiled, if of death, to die, himself being the first to accuse himself and his own relations, and using rhetoric to this end, that his and their unjust actions may be made manifest, and that they themselves may be delivered from injustice, which is the great-est evil. Then, Polus, rhetoric would indeed be useful. Do you say 'Yes' or 'No' to that?

POL.   To me, Socrates, what you are saying appears very strange, though probably in agreement with your premises.

SOC.   Is not this the conclusion, if the premises are not dis-proven?

POL.   Yes; it certainly is.

SOC.   And from the opposite point of view, if indeed it be our duty to harm another, whether an enemy or not—I except the case of self-defence—then I have to be upon my guard—but if my enemy injures a third person, then in every sort of way, by word as well as deed, I should try to prevent his being punished, or appearing before the judge; and if he appears, I should contrive that he should escape, and not suffer punishment: if he has stolen a sum of money, let him keep what he has stolen and spend it on him and his, regardless of religion and justice; and if he have done things worthy of death, let him not die, but rather be immortal in his wickedness; or, if this is not possible, let him at any rate be allowed to live as long as he can. For such purposes, Polus, rhetoric may be useful, but is of small if of any use to him who is not intending to commit injustice; at least, there was no such use discovered by us in the previous discussion.

* * *

PLATO

From The Timaeus[†]

* * *

TIMAEUS All men, Socrates, who have any degree of right feeling, at the beginning of every enterprise, whether small or great, always call upon God. And we, too, who are going to discourse of the nature of the universe, how created or how existing without creation, if we be not altogether out of our wits, must invoke the aid of Gods and Goddesses and pray that our words may be acceptable to them and consistent with themselves. Let this, then, be our invocation of the Gods, to which I add an exhortation of myself to speak in such manner as will be most intelligible to you, and will most accord with my own intent.

First then, in my judgment, we must make a distinction and ask, What is that which always is and has no becoming; and what is that which is always becoming and never is? That which is apprehended by intelligence and reason is always in the same state; but that which is conceived by opinion with the help of sensation and without reason, is always in a process of becoming and perishing and never really is. Now everything that becomes or is created must of necessity be created by some cause, for without a cause nothing can be created. The work of the creator, whenever he looks to the unchangeable and fashions the form and nature of his work after an unchangeable pattern, must necessarily be made fair and perfect; but when he looks to the created only, and uses a created pattern, it is not fair or perfect. Was the heaven then or the world, whether called by this or by any other more appropriate name—assuming the name, I am asking a question which has to be asked at the beginning of an enquiry about anything—was the world, I say, always in existence and without beginning? or created, and had it a beginning? Created, I reply, being visible and tangible and having a body, and therefore sensible; and all sensible things are apprehended by opinion and sense and are in a process of creation and created. Now that which is created must, as we affirm, of necessity be created by a cause. But the father and maker of all this universe is past finding out; and even if we found him, to tell of him to all men would be impossible. And there is still a question to be asked about him: Which of the patterns had the artificer in view when he made the world,—the pattern of the unchangeable, or of that which is created?

[†] From *The Dialogues of Plato*, trans. Benjamin Jowett (New York: Oxford UP, 1892). The footnotes are the translator's, except as indicated. One of the translator's notes has been omitted.

If the world be indeed fair and the artificer good, it is manifest that he must have looked to that which is eternal; but if what cannot be said without blasphemy is true, then to the created pattern. Every one will see that he must have looked to the eternal; for the world is the fairest of creations and he is the best of causes. And having been created in this way, the world has been framed in the likeness of that which is apprehended by reason and mind and is unchangeable, and must therefore of necessity, if this is admitted, be a copy of something. Now it is all-important that the beginning of everything should be according to nature. And in speaking of the copy and the original we may assume that words are akin to the matter which they describe; when they relate to the lasting and permanent and intelligible, they ought to be lasting and unalterable, and, as far as their nature allows, irrefutable and immovable—nothing less. But when they express only the copy or likeness and not the eternal things themselves, they need only be likely and analogous to the real words. As being is to becoming, so is truth to belief. If then, Socrates, amid the many opinions about the gods and the generation of the universe, we are not able to give notions which are altogether and in every respect exact and consistent with one another, do not be surprised. Enough, if we adduce probabilities as likely as any others; for we must remember that I who am the speaker, and you who are the judges, are only mortal men, and we ought to accept the tale which is probable and enquire no further.

Socrates　Excellent, Timaeus; and we will do precisely as you bid us. The prelude is charming, and is already accepted by us—may we beg of you to proceed to the strain?

Tim.　Let me tell you then why the creator made this world of generation. He was good, and the good can never have any jealousy of anything. And being free from jealousy, he desired that all things should be as like himself as they could be. This is in the truest sense the origin of creation and of the world, as we shall do well in believing on the testimony of wise men: God desired that all things should be good and nothing bad, so far as this was attainable. Wherefore also finding the whole visible sphere not at rest, but moving in an irregular and disorderly fashion, out of disorder he brought order, considering that this was in every way better than the other. Now the deeds of the best could never be or have been other than the fairest; and the creator, reflecting on the things which are by nature visible, found that no unintelligent creature taken as a whole was fairer than the intelligent taken as a whole; and that intelligence could not be present in anything which was devoid of soul. For which reason, when he was framing the universe, he put intelligence in soul, and soul in body, that he might be the creator of a work which was by nature fairest and best. Wherefore, using the language of probability, we may say that the world became a living creature truly endowed with soul and intelligence by the providence of God.

This being supposed, let us proceed to the next stage: In the likeness of what animal did the Creator make the world? It would be an unworthy thing to liken it to any nature which exists as a part only; for nothing can be beautiful which is like any imperfect thing; but let us suppose the world to be the very image of that whole of which all other animals both individually and in their tribes are portions. For the original of the universe contains in itself all intelligible beings, just as this world comprehends us and all other visible creatures. For the Deity, intending to make this world like the fairest and most perfect of intelligible beings, framed one visible animal comprehending within itself all other animals of a kindred nature. Are we right in saying that there is one world, or that they are many and infinite? There must be one only, if the created copy is to accord with the original. For that which includes all other intelligible creatures cannot have a second or companion; in that case there would be need of another living being which would include both, and of which they would be parts, and the likeness would be more truly said to resemble not them, but that other which included them. In order then that the world might be solitary, like the perfect animal, the creator made not two worlds or an infinite number of them; but there is and ever will be one only-begotten and created heaven.

Now that which is created is of necessity corporeal, and also visible and tangible. And nothing is visible where there is no fire, or tangible which has no solidity, and nothing is solid without earth. Wherefore also God in the beginning of creation made the body of the universe to consist of fire and earth. But two things cannot be rightly put together without a third; there must be some bond of union between them. And the fairest bond is that which makes the most complete fusion of itself and the things which it combines; and proportion is best adapted to effect such a union. For whenever in any three numbers, whether cube or square, there is a mean, which is to the last term what the first term is to it; and again, when the mean is to the first term as the last term is to the means,—then the mean becoming first and last, and the first and last both becoming means, they will all of them of necessity come to be the same, and having become the same with one another will be all one. If the universal frame had been created a surface only and having no depth, a single mean would have sufficed to bind together itself and the other terms; but now, as the world must be solid, and solid bodies are always compacted not by one mean but by two, God placed water and air in the mean between fire and earth, and made them to have the same proportion so far as was possible (as fire is to air so is air to water, and as air is to water so is water to earth); and thus he bound and put together a visible and tangible heaven. And for these reasons, and out of such elements which are in number four, the body of the world was created, and it was harmonized by proportion, and therefore has the spirit of friendship; and having been reconciled to itself, it was indissoluble by the hand of any other than the framer.

Now the creation took up the whole of each of the four elements; for the Creator compounded the world out of all the fire and all the water and all the air and all the earth, leaving no part of any of them nor any power of them outside. His intention was, in the first place, that the animal should be as far as possible a perfect whole and of perfect parts: secondly, that it should be one, leaving no remnants out of which another such world might be created: and also that it should be free from old age and unaffected by disease. Considering that if heat and cold and other powerful forces which unite bodies surround and attack them from without when they are unprepared, they decompose them, and by bringing diseases and old age upon them, make them waste away—for this cause and on these grounds he made the world one whole, having every part entire, and being therefore perfect and not liable to old age and disease. And he gave to the world the figure which was suitable and also natural. Now to the animal which was to comprehend all animals, that figure was suitable which comprehends within itself all other figures. Wherefore he made the world in the form of a globe, round as from a lathe, having its extremes in every direction equidistant from the centre, the most perfect and the most like itself of all figures; for he considered that the like is infinitely fairer than the unlike. This he finished off, making the surface smooth all around for many reasons; in the first place, because the living being had no need of eyes when there was nothing remaining outside him to be seen; nor of ears when there was nothing to be heard; and there was no surrounding atmosphere to be breathed; nor would there have been any use of organs by the help of which he might receive his food or get rid of what he had already digested, since there was nothing which went from him or came into him: for there was nothing beside him. Of design he was created thus, his own waste providing his own food, and all that he did or suffered taking place in and by himself. For the Creator conceived that a being which was self-sufficient would be far more excellent than one which lacked anything; and, as he had no need to take anything or defend himself against any one, the Creator did not think it necessary to bestow upon him hands: nor had he any need of feet, nor of the whole apparatus of walking; but the movement suited to his spherical form was assigned to him, being of all the seven that which is most appropriate to mind and intelligence; and he was made to move in the same manner and on the same spot, within his own limits revolving in a circle. All the other six motions were taken away from him, and he was made not to partake of their deviations. And as this circular movement required no feet, the universe was created without legs and without feet.

Such was the whole plan of the eternal God about the god that was to be, to whom for this reason he gave a body, smooth and even, having a surface in every direction equidistant from the centre, a body entire and perfect, and formed out of perfect bodies. And in the centre he put the soul, which he diffused throughout the body, making it also to be the exterior environment of it; and he made the universe a circle moving in a circle, one and solitary, yet by reason of its excellence able to converse with itself, and needing no other friendship or acquaintance. Having these purposes in view he created the world a blessed god.

Now God did not make the soul after the body, although we are speaking of them in this order; for having brought them together he would never have allowed that the elder should be ruled by the younger; but this is a random manner of speaking which we have, because somehow we ourselves too are very much under the dominion of chance. Whereas he made the soul in origin and excellence prior to and older than the body, to be the ruler and mistress, of whom the body was to be the subject. And he made her out of the following elements and on this wise: Out of the indivisible and unchangeable, and also out of that which is divisible and has to do with material bodies, he compounded a third and intermediate kind of essence, partaking of the nature of the same[1] and of the other, and this compound he placed accordingly in a mean between the indivisible, and the divisible and material. He took the three elements of the same, the other, and the essence, and mingled them into one form, compressing by force the reluctant and unsociable nature of the other into the same. When he had mingled them with the essence and out of three made one, he again divided this whole into as many portions as was fitting, each portion being a compound of the same, the other, and the essence. And he proceeded to divide after this manner:—First of all, he took away one part of the whole [1], and then he separated a second part which was double the first [2], and then he took away a third part which was half as much again as the second and three times as much as the first [3], and then he took a fourth part which was twice as much as the second [4], and a fifth part which was three times the third [9], and a sixth part which was eight times the first [8], and a seventh part which was twenty-seven times the first [27]. After this he filled up the double

---

1. Omitting αὖ πέρι

intervals [i. e. between 1, 2, 4, 8] and the triple [i. e. between 1, 3, 9, 27], cutting off yet other portions from the mixture and placing them in the intervals, so that in each interval there were two kinds of means, the one exceeding and exceeded by equal parts of its extremes [as for example 1, $\frac{4}{3}$, 2, in which the mean $\frac{4}{3}$ is one-third of 1 more than 1, and one-third of 2 less than 2], the other being that kind of mean which exceeds and is exceeded by an equal number.[2] Where there were intervals of $\frac{3}{2}$ and of $\frac{4}{3}$ and of $\frac{9}{8}$, made by the connecting terms in the former intervals, he filled up all the intervals of $\frac{4}{3}$ with the interval of $\frac{9}{8}$, leaving a fraction over; and the interval which this fraction expressed was in the ratio of 256 to 243.[3] And thus the whole mixture out of which he cut these portions was all exhausted by him. This entire compound he divided lengthways into two parts, which he joined to one another at the centre like the letter X, and bent them into a circular form, connecting them with themselves and each other at the point opposite to their original meeting-point; and, comprehending them in a uniform revolution upon the same axis, he made the one the outer and the other the inner circle. Now the motion of the outer circle he called the motion of the same, and the motion of the inner circle the motion of the other or diverse. The motion of the same he carried round by the side[4] to the right, and the motion of the diverse diagonally[5] to the left. And he gave dominion to the motion of the same and like, for that he left single and undivided; but the inner motion he divided in six places and made seven unequal circles having their intervals in ratios of two and three, three of each, and bade the orbits proceed in a direction opposite to one another; and three [Sun, Mercury, Venus] he made to move with equal swiftness, and the remaining four [Moon, Saturn, Mars, Jupiter] to move with unequal swiftness to the three and to one another, but in due proportion.

Now when the Creator had framed the soul according to his will, he formed within her the corporeal universe, and brought the two together, and united them centre to centre. The soul, interfused everywhere from the centre to the circumference of heaven, of which also she is the external envelopment, herself turning in herself, began a divine beginning of never-ceasing and rational life

2. E.g. $\bar{1}$, $\frac{4}{3}$, $\frac{3}{2}$, $\bar{2}$, $\frac{8}{3}$, 3, $\bar{4}$, $\frac{16}{8}$, 6, $\bar{8}$ and

$\bar{1}$, $\frac{3}{2}$, 2, $\bar{3}$, $\frac{9}{2}$, 6, $\bar{9}$, $\frac{27}{2}$, 18, $\overline{27}$

3. E.g. 243 : 256 :: $\frac{81}{64}$: $\frac{4}{5}$ :: $\frac{143}{128}$: 2 :: $\frac{81}{22}$: $\frac{8}{2}$ :: $\frac{248}{64}$: 4 :: $\frac{61}{16}$: $\frac{16}{8}$ :: $\frac{242}{32}$: 8.

(MARTIN.)

[In 1841, Thomas Henri Martin published an edition of *The Timaeus* called *Études sur Le Timée de Platon.* —Editor.]

4. I.e. of the rectangular figure supposed to be inscribed in the circle of the Same.
5. I. e. across the rectangular figure from corner to corner.

enduring throughout all time. The body of heaven is visible, but the soul is invisible, and partakes of reason and harmony, and being made by the best of intellectual and everlasting natures, is the best of things created. And because she is composed of the same and of the other and of the essence, these three, and is divided and united in due proportion, and in her revolutions returns upon herself, the soul, when touching anything which has essence, whether dispersed in parts or undivided, is stirred through all her powers, to declare the sameness or difference of that thing and some other; and to what individuals are related, and by what affected, and in what way and how and when, both in the world of generation and in the world of immutable being. And when reason, which works with equal truth, whether she be in the circle of the diverse or of the same— in voiceless silence holding her onward course in the sphere of the self-moved—when reason, I say, is hovering around the sensible world and when the circle of the diverse also moving truly imparts the intimations of sense to the whole soul, then arise opinions and beliefs sure and certain. But when reason is concerned with the rational, and the circle of the same moving smoothly declares it, then intelligence and knowledge are necessarily perfected. And if any one affirms that in which these two are found to be other than the soul, he will say the very opposite of the truth.

When the father and creator saw the creature which he had made moving and living, the created image of the eternal gods, he rejoiced, and in his joy determined to make the copy still more like the original; and as this was eternal, he sought to make the universe eternal, so far as might be. Now the nature of the ideal being was everlasting, but to bestow this attribute in its fulness upon a creature was impossible. Wherefore he resolved to have a moving image of eternity, and when he set in order the heaven, he made this image eternal but moving according to number, while eternity itself rests in unity; and this image we call time. For there were no days and nights and months and years before the heaven was created, but when he constructed the heaven he created them also. They are all parts of time, and the past and future are created species of time, which we unconsciously but wrongly transfer to the eternal essence; for we say that he 'was,' he 'is,' he 'will be,' but the truth is that 'is' alone is properly attributed to him, and that 'was' and 'will be' are only to be spoken of becoming in time, for they are motions, but that which is immovably the same cannot become older or younger by time, nor ever did or has become, or hereafter will be, older or younger, nor is subject at all to any of those states which affect moving and sensible things and of which generation is the cause. These are the forms of time, which imitates eternity and revolves according to a law of number. Moreover, when we say that what has become *is* become and what becomes *is* becoming, and that what will become *is* about to become and that the non-existent *is* non-existent,—all these are inaccurate modes of expression. But perhaps this whole subject will be more suitably discussed on some other occasion.

Time, then, and the heaven came into being at the same instant in order that, having been created together, if ever there was to be a dissolution of them, they might be dissolved together. It was framed after the pattern of the eternal nature, that it might resemble this as far as was possible; for the pattern exists from eternity, and the created heaven has been, and is, and will be, in all time. Such was the mind and thought of God in the creation of time. The sun and moon and five other stars, which are called the planets, were created by him in order to distinguish and preserve the numbers of time; and when he had made their several bodies, he placed them in the orbits in which the circle of the other was revolving ✱✱✱,—in seven orbits seven stars. First, there was the moon in the orbit nearest the earth, and next the sun, in the second orbit above the earth; then came the morning star and the star sacred to Hermes, moving in orbits which have an equal swiftness with the sun, but in an opposite direction; and this is the reason why the sun and Hermes and Lucifer overtake and are overtaken by each other. To enumerate the places which he assigned to the other stars, and to give all the reasons why he assigned them, although a secondary matter, would give more trouble than the primary. These things at some future time, when we are at leisure, may have the consideration which they deserve, but not at present.

✱ ✱ ✱

ARISTOTLE

From The Nicomachean Ethics, Book 1[†]

Every art and every scientific inquiry, and similarly every action and purpose, may be said to aim at some good. Hence the good has been well defined as that at which all things aim. But it is clear that there is a difference in the ends; for the ends are sometimes activities, and sometimes results beyond the mere activities. Also, where there are certain ends beyond the actions, the results are naturally superior to the activities.

As there are various actions, arts, and sciences, it follows that the ends are also various. Thus health is the end of medicine, a vessel of

---

[†] Aristotle, *The Nicomachean Ethics*, Book 1, trans. J. E. C. Welldon (New York: Macmillan, 1892). The footnotes are the translator's.

shipbuilding, victory of strategy, and wealth of domestic economy. It often happens that there are a number of such arts or sciences which fall under a single faculty, as the art of making bridles, and all such other arts as make the instruments of horsemanship, under horsemanship, and this again as well as every military action under strategy, and in the same way other arts or sciences under other faculties. But in all these cases the ends of the architectonic arts or sciences, whatever they may be, are more desirable than those of the subordinate arts or sciences, as it is for the sake of the former that the latter are themselves sought after. It makes no difference to the argument whether the activities themselves are the ends of the actions, or something else beyond the activities as in the above mentioned sciences.

If it is true that in the sphere of action there is an end which we wish for its own sake, and for the sake of which we wish everything else, and that we do not desire all things for the sake of something else (for, if that is so, the process will go on *ad infinitum*, and our desire will be idle and futile) it is clear that this will be the good or the supreme good. Does it not follow then that the knowledge of this supreme good is of great importance for the conduct of life, and that, *if we know it*, we shall be like archers who have a mark at which to aim, we shall have a better chance of attaining what we want? But, if this is the case, we must endeavour to comprehend, at least in outline, its nature, and the science or faculty to which it belongs.

It would seem that this is the most authoritative or architectonic science or faculty, and such is evidently the political; for it is the political science or faculty which determines what sciences are necessary in states, and what kind of sciences should be learnt, and how far they should be learnt by particular people. We perceive too that the faculties which are held in the highest esteem, e.g. strategy, domestic economy, and rhetoric, are subordinate to it. But as it makes use of the other practical sciences, and also legislates upon the things to be done and the things to be left undone, it follows that its end will comprehend the ends of all the other sciences, and will therefore be the true good of mankind. For although the good of an individual is identical with the good of a state, yet the good of the state, whether in attainment or in preservation, is evidently greater and more perfect. For while in an individual by himself it is something to be thankful for, it is nobler and more divine in a nation or state.

These then are the objects at which the present inquiry aims, and it is in a sense a political[1] inquiry. But our statement of the case will be

---

1. It is characteristic of Aristotle's philosophy to treat Ethics as a branch or department of Politics.

adequate, if it be made with all such clearness as the subject-matter admits; for it would be as wrong to expect the same degree of accuracy in all reasonings as in all manufactures. Things noble and just, which are the subjects of investigation in political science, exhibit so great a diversity and uncertainty that they are sometimes thought to have only a conventional, and not a natural, existence. There is the same sort of uncertainty in regard to good things, as it often happens that injuries result from them; thus there have been cases in which people were ruined by wealth, or again by courage. As our subjects then and our premises are of this nature, we must be content to indicate the truth roughly and in outline; and as our subjects and premises are true generally *but not universally*, we must be content to arrive at conclusions which are only generally true. It is right to receive the particular statements which are made in the same spirit; for an educated person will expect accuracy in each subject only so far as the nature of the subject allows; he might as well accept probable reasoning from a mathematician as require demonstrative proofs from a rhetorician. But everybody is competent to judge the subjects which he understands, and is a good judge of them. It follows that in particular subjects it is a person of *special* education, and in general a person of universal education, who is a good judge. Hence the young[2] are not proper students of political science, as they have no experience of the actions of life which form the premises and subjects of the reasonings. Also it may be added that from their tendency to follow their emotions they will not study the subject to any purpose or profit, as its end is not knowledge but action. It makes no difference whether a person is young in years or youthful in character; for the defect *of which I speak* is not one of time but is due to the emotional character of his life and pursuits. Knowledge is as useless to such a person as it is to an intemperate person. But where the desires and actions of people are regulated by reason the knowledge of these subjects will be extremely valuable.

But having said so much by way of preface as to the students of political science, the spirit in which it should be studied, and the object which we set before ourselves, let us resume our argument as follows:

As every knowledge and moral purpose aspires to some good, what is in our view the good at which the political science aims, and what is the highest of all practical goods? As to its name there is, I may say, a general agreement. The masses and the cultured classes agree in

---

2. This is believed to be the passage which Shakespeare had in mind, though the reference to it is put in Hector's mouth,

   "young men, whom Aristotle thought
   Unfit to hear moral philosophy."
   Troilus and Cressida, Act ii Scene 2

calling it happiness, and conceive that "to live well" or "to do well" is the same thing as "to be happy." But as to the nature of happiness they do not agree, nor do the masses give the same account of it as the philosophers. The former define it as something visible and palpable, e.g. pleasure, wealth, or honour; different people give different definitions of it, and often the same person gives different definitions at different times; for when a person has been ill, it is health, when he is poor, it is wealth, and, if he is conscious of his own ignorance, he envies people who use grand language above his own comprehension. Some *philosophers*[3] on the other hand have held that, besides these various goods, there is an absolute good which is the cause of goodness in them all. It would perhaps be a waste of time to examine all these opinions, it will be enough to examine such as are most popular or as seem to be more or less reasonable.

But we must not fail to observe the distinction between the reasonings which proceed from first principles and the reasonings which lead up to first principles. For Plato[4] was right in raising the difficult question whether the *true* way was from first principles or to first principles, as in the race-course from the judges to the goal, or *vice versa*. We must begin then with such facts as are known. But facts may be known in two ways, i.e. either relatively to ourselves or absolutely. It is probable then that *we* must begin with such facts as are known to us, *i.e. relatively*. It is necessary therefore, if a person is to be a competent student of what is noble and just and of politics in general, that he should have received a good moral training. For the fact that a thing is so is a first principle or starting-point,[5] and, if the fact is sufficiently clear, it will not be necessary to go on to ask the reason of it. But a person who has received a good moral training either possesses first principles, or will have no difficulty in acquiring them. But if he does not possess them, and cannot acquire them, he had better lay to heart Hesiod's lines:[6]

> "Far best is he who is himself all-wise,
> And he, too, good who listens to wise words;
> But whoso is not wise nor lays to heart
> Another's wisdom is a useless man."

But to return from our digression: It seems not unreasonable that people should derive their conception of the good or of happiness from men's lives. Thus ordinary or vulgar people conceive it to be

---

3. Aristotle is thinking of the Platonic "ideas."
4. The reference is probably not to any special passage in the dialogues of Plato, but to the general drift or scope of the Socratic dialectics.
5. Aristotle's reasoning depends in part on the double meaning of ἀρχή viz. (1) starting-point or beginning, (2) first principle or axiomatic truth.
6. *Ἔργα καὶ Ἡμέραι 291–295.

pleasure, and accordingly approve a life of enjoyment. For there are practically three prominent lives, the sensual, the political, and, thirdly, the speculative. Now the mass of men present an absolutely slavish appearance, as choosing the life of brute beasts, but they meet with consideration because so many persons in authority share the tastes of Sardanapalus.[7] Cultivated and practical people, on the other hand, identify happiness with honour, as honour is the general end of political life. But this appears too superficial for our present purpose; for honour seems to depend more upon the people who pay it than upon the person to whom it is paid, and we have an intuitive feeling that the good is something which is proper to a man himself and cannot easily be taken away from him. It seems too that the reason why men seek honour is that they may be confident of their own goodness. Accordingly they seek it at the hands of the wise and of those who know them well, and they seek it on the ground of virtue ; hence it is clear that in their judgment at any rate virtue is superior to honour. It would perhaps be right then to look upon virtue rather than honour as being the end of the political life. Yet virtue again, it appears, lacks completeness; for it seems that a man may possess virtue and yet be asleep or inactive throughout life, and, not only so but he may experience the greatest calamities and misfortunes. But nobody would call such a life a life of happiness, unless he were maintaining a paradox. It is not necessary to dwell further on this subject, as it is sufficiently discussed in the popular philosophical treatises.[8] The third life is the speculative which we will investigate hereafter.[9]

The life of money-making is in a sense a life of constraint, and it is clear that wealth is not the good of which we are in quest; for it is useful in part as a means to something else. It would be a more reasonable view therefore that the things mentioned before, viz. *sensual pleasure, honour and virtue,* are ends than that wealth is, as they are things which are desired on their own account. Yet these too are apparently not ends, although much argument has been employed[1] to show that they are.

We may now dismiss this subject; but it will perhaps be best to consider the universal *good,* and to discuss the meaning in which the phrase is used, although there is this difficulty in such an enquiry, that the *doctrine of* ideas has been introduced by our friends.[2] Yet it

---

7. The most luxurious, and the last, Assyrian monarch.
8. The "popular philosophical treatises" τὰ ἐγκύκλια φιλοσοφήματα as they are called περὶ οὐρανοῦ i. ch. 9, p. 279 A₃₀ represent, as I suppose, the discussions and conclusions of thinkers outside the Aristotelian school and are in fact the same as the ἐξωτερικοὶ λόγοι.
9. The investigation of the speculative life occurs in Book x.
1. The usage of Aristotle is in favour of taking καταβέβληνται to mean "has been employed" rather than "has been wasted"; see especially περὶ Κόσμον ch. 6, p. 397 B₁₉.
2. In reference, of course, to Plato.

will perhaps seem the best, and indeed the right course, at least when
the truth is at stake, to go so far as to sacrifice what is near and dear
to us, especially as we are philosophers. For friends and truth are
both dear to us, but it is a sacred duty to prefer the truth.

Now the authors of this theory did not make ideas of things in
which they predicated priority and posteriority. Hence they did not
constitute an idea of numbers. But good is predicated equally of
substance, quality and relation, and the absolute or essential, *i.e.
substance*, is in its nature prior to the relative, as relativity is like an
offshoot or accident of existence; hence there cannot be an idea
which is common to them both. Again, there are as many ways of
predicating good as of predicating existence; for it is predicated of
substance as e.g. of God or the mind, or of quality as of the virtues,
or of quantity as of the mean, or of relativity as of the useful, or of
time as of opportunity, or of place as of a habitation, and so on. It is
clear then that it cannot be a common universal idea or a unity;
otherwise it would not be predicated in all the categories[3] but only
in one. Thirdly, as there is a single science of all such things as fall
under a single idea, there would have been a single science of all
good things, *if the idea of "good" were single*; but in fact there are
many sciences even of such good things as fall under a single cate-
gory, strategy, e.g. being the science of opportunity in war, and medicine the science of opportunity in disease, medicine again being the
science of the mean in respect of food, and gymnastic the science of
the mean in respect of exercise. It would be difficult, too, to say what
is meant by the "absolute" in anything, if in "absolute man" and in
"man" there is one and the same conception of man. For there will
be no difference between them in respect of manhood, and, if so,
neither will there be any difference between "absolute good" and
"good" in respect of goodness. Nor again will good be more good if it
is eternal, since a white thing which lasts for a long time is not
whiter than that which lasts for a single day. There seems to be more
plausibility in the doctrine of the Pythagoreans[4] who place unity in
the catalogue of goods, and Speusippus[5] apparently agrees with
them. However these are questions which may be deferred to
another occasion; but there is an objection to my arguments which
suggests itself, viz. that the *Platonic* theory does not apply to every
good, that the things which in themselves are sought after and wel-
comed are reckoned as one species and the things which tend to
produce or in any sense preserve these or to prevent their opposites

---

3. For the "categories", see Κατηγορίαι ch. 4.
4. The point is that it is apparently more reasonable to describe unity as a good than to
   describe good as a unity. The Pythagoreans, or some of them, drew up catalogues of opposites (συστοιχίαι) as Aristotle explains *Metaph.* i. ch. 5.
5. Plato's nephew and successor in the Academy.

are reckoned as goods in a secondary sense as being means to these. It is clear then that there will be two kinds of goods, some being absolute goods, and others secondary. Let us then separate goods which are merely serviceable from absolute goods and consider if they are conceived as falling under a single idea. But what kind of things is it that may be defined as absolute goods? Will it be all such as are sought after independently of their consequences, e.g. wisdom, sight, and certain pleasures and honours? For granting that we seek after these sometimes as means to something else, still we may define them as absolute goods. Or is none of these things an absolute good, nor anything else except the idea? But then the type *or idea* will be purposeless, *i.e. it will not comprise any particulars.* If, on the other hand, these things too are absolute goods, the conception of the good will necessarily appear the same in them all, as the conception of whiteness appears the same in snow and in white lead. But the conception of honour, wisdom and pleasure, are distinct and different in respect of goodness. "Good" then is not a common term falling under one idea. But in what sense is the term used? For it does not seem to be an accidental homonymy.[6] Is it because all goods issue from one source or all tend to one end; or is it rather a case of analogy? for as the sight is to the body, so is the mind to the soul, *i.e. the mind may be called the eye of the soul, and so on.* But it will perhaps be well to leave this subject for the present, as an exact discussion of it would belong rather to a different branch of philosophy. But the same is true of the idea; for even if there is some one good which is predicated of all these things, or some abstract and absolute good, it will plainly not be such as a man finds practicable and attainable, and therefore will not be such a good as we are in search of. It will possibly be held, however, that it is worth while to apprehend this *universal good*, as having a relation to the goods which are attainable and practicable; for if we have this as a model, we shall be better able to know the things which are good relatively to ourselves, and, knowing them, to acquire them. Now although there is a certain plausibility in this theory, it seems not to harmonize with scientific experience; for while all sciences aim at a certain good and seek to supply a deficiency, they omit the knowledge of the universal good. Yet it is not reasonable to suppose that what would be so extremely helpful is ignored, and not sought at all by artists generally. But it is difficult to see what benefit a cobbler or carpenter will get in reference to his art by knowing the absolute good, or how the contemplation of the absolute idea will make a person a better physician or general. For it appears that a physician

---

6. What is meant by an "accidental homonymy" or equivocation is easily seen in the various senses of a single English word such as *bull.*

does not regard health abstractedly, but regards the health of man or rather perhaps of a particular man, as he gives his medicine to individuals.

But leaving this subject for the present let us revert to the good of which we are in quest and consider what its nature may be. For it is clearly different in different actions or arts; it is one thing in medicine, another in strategy, and so on. What then is the good in each of these instances? It is presumably that for the sake of which all else is done. This in medicine is health, in strategy, victory, in domestic architecture, a house, and so on. But in every action and purpose it is the end, as it is for the sake of the end that people all do everything else. If then there is a certain end of all action, it will be this which is the practicable good, and if there are several such ends it will be these.

Our argument has arrived by a different path at the same conclusion as before; but we must endeavour to elucidate it still further. As it appears that there are more ends than one and some of these, e.g. wealth, flutes, and instruments generally we desire as means to something else, it is evident that they are not all final ends. But the highest good is clearly something final. Hence if there is only one final end, this will be the object of which we are in search, and if there are more than one, it will be the most final of them. We speak of that which is sought after for its own sake as more final than that which is sought after as a means to something else; we speak of that which is never desired as a means to something else as more final than the things which are desired both in themselves and as means to something else; and we speak of a thing as absolutely final, if it is always desired in itself and never as a means to something else.

It seems that happiness preeminently answers to this description, as we always desire happiness for its own sake and never as a means to something else, whereas we desire honour, pleasure, intellect, and every virtue, partly for their own sakes (for we should desire them independently of what might result from them) but partly also as being means to happiness, because we suppose they will prove the instruments of happiness. Happiness, on the other hand, nobody desires for the sake of these things, nor indeed as a means to anything else at all.

We come to the same conclusion if we start from the consideration of self-sufficiency, if it may be assumed that the final good is self-sufficient. But when we speak of self-sufficiency, we do not mean that a person leads a solitary life all by himself, but that he has parents, children, wife, and friends, and fellow-citizens in general, as man is naturally a social being. But here it is necessary to prescribe some limit; for if the circle be extended so as to include parents, descendants, and friends' friends, it will go on indefinitely.

Leaving this point, however, for future investigation, we define the self-sufficient as that which, taken by itself, makes life desirable, and wholly free from want, and this is our conception of happiness.

Again, we conceive happiness to be the most desirable of all things, and that not merely as one among other good things. If it were one among other good things, the addition of the smallest good would increase its desirableness; for the accession makes a superiority of goods, and the greater of two goods is always the more desirable. It seems then that happiness is something final and self-sufficient, being the end of all action.

Perhaps, however, it seems a truth which is generally admitted, that happiness is the supreme good; what is wanted is to define its nature a little more clearly. The best way of arriving as such a definition will probably be to ascertain the function of Man. For, as with a flute-player, a statuary, or any artisan, or in fact anybody who has a definite function and action, his goodness, or excellence seems to lie in his function, so it would seem to be with Man, if indeed he has a definite function. Can it be said then that, while a carpenter and a cobbler have definite functions and actions, Man, unlike them, is naturally functionless? The reasonable view is that, as the eye, the hand, the foot, and similarly each several part of the body has a definite function, so Man may be regarded as having a definite function apart from all these. What then, can this function be? It is not life; for life is apparently something which man shares with the plants; and it is something peculiar to him that we are looking for. We must exclude therefore the life of nutrition and increase. There is next what may be called the life of sensation. But this too, is apparently shared by Man with horses, cattle, and all other animals. There remains what I may call the practical life of the rational part *of Man's being*. But the rational part is twofold; it is rational partly in the sense of being obedient to reason, and partly in the sense of possessing reason and intelligence. The practical life too is conceived of in two ways,[7] *viz, either as a moral state or as a moral activity*: but we must understand by it the life of activity, as this seems to be the truer form of the conception.

The function of Man then is an activity of soul in accordance with reason, or not independently of reason. Again the functions of a person of a certain kind, and of such a person who is good of his kind e.g. of a harpist and a good harpist, are in our view generically the same, and this view is true of people of all kinds without exception, the superior excellence being only an addition to the function; for it is the function of a harpist to play the harp, and of a good harpist to

---

7. In other words life may be taken to mean either the mere possession of certain faculties or their active exercise.

play the harp well. This being so, if we define the function of Man as a kind of life, and this life as an activity of soul, or a course of action in conformity with reason, if the function of a good man is such activity or action of a good and noble kind, and if everything is successfully performed when it is performed in accordance with its proper excellence, it follows that the good of Man is an activity of soul in accordance with virtue or, if there are more virtues than one, in accordance with the best and most complete virtue. But it is necessary to add the words "in a complete life." For as one swallow or one day does not make a spring, so one day or a short time does not make a fortunate or happy man.

This may be taken as a sufficiently accurate sketch of the good; for it is right, I think, to draw the outlines first and afterwards to fill in the details. It would seem that anybody can carry on and complete what has been satisfactorily sketched in outline, and that time is a good inventor or cooperator in so doing. This is the way in which the arts have made their advances, as anybody can supply a deficiency.

* * *

SAINT AUGUSTINE

From On Free Choice of the Will, Book 3[†]

EVODIUS: It has been demonstrated to my satisfaction that free will **1.** is to be numbered among good things, and indeed not among the least of them, and therefore that it was given to us by God, who acted rightly in giving it. So now, if you think that this is a good time, I would like you to explain the source of the movement by which the will turns away from the common and unchangeable good toward its own good, or the good of others, or lower goods, all of which are changeable.

AUGUSTINE: Why do we need to know that?

EVODIUS: Because if the will was given to us in such a way that it had this movement naturally, then it turned to changeable goods by necessity, and there is no blame involved when nature and necessity determine an action.

AUGUSTINE: Does this movement please you or displease you?

EVODIUS: It displeases me.

AUGUSTINE: So you find fault with it.

[†] From *On Free Choice of the Will*, Book 3, trans. Thomas Williams (Cambridge, MA: Hackett Publishing Company, 1993). © 1993 by Hackett Publishing Company, Inc. Reprinted by permission of Hackett Publishing Company, Inc. All rights reserved. The footnotes are the translator's.

EVODIUS: Of course.

AUGUSTINE: Then you find fault with a blameless movement of the soul.

EVODIUS: No, it's just that I don't know whether there is any blame involved when the soul deserts the unchangeable good and turns toward changeable goods.

AUGUSTINE: Then you find fault with what you don't know.

EVODIUS: Don't quibble over words. In saying "I don't know whether there is any blame involved," I meant it to be understood that there undoubtedly *is* blame involved. The "I don't know" implied that it was ridiculous to have doubts about such an obvious fact.

AUGUSTINE: Then pay close attention to this most certain truth, which has caused you to forget so quickly what you just said. If that movement existed by nature or necessity, it could in no way be blameworthy. But you are so firmly convinced that this movement is indeed blameworthy that you think it would be ridiculous to entertain doubts about something so certain. Why then did you affirm, or at least tentatively assert, something that now seems to you clearly false? For this is what you said: "If the will was given to us in such a way that it had this movement naturally, then it turned to changeable goods by necessity, and there is no blame involved when nature and necessity determine an action." Since you are sure that this movement was blameworthy, you should have been quite sure that the will was not given to us in such a way.

EVODIUS: I said that this movement was blameworthy and that therefore it displeases me. And I am surely right to find fault with it. But I deny that a soul ought to be blamed when this movement pulls it away from the unchangeable good toward changeable goods, if this movement is so much a part of its nature that it is moved by necessity.

AUGUSTINE: You admit that this movement certainly deserves blame; but *whose* movement is it?

EVODIUS: I see that the movement is in the soul, but I don't know whose it is.

AUGUSTINE: Surely you don't deny that the soul is moved by this movement.

EVODIUS: No.

AUGUSTINE: Do you deny that a movement by which a stone is moved is a movement of the stone? I'm not talking about a movement that is caused by us or some other force, as when it is thrown into the air, but the movement that occurs when it falls to the earth by its own weight.

EVODIUS: I don't deny that this movement, by which the stone seeks the lowest place, is a movement of the stone. But it is a natural movement. If that's the sort of movement the soul has, then the soul's movement is also natural. And if it is moved naturally, it cannot justly be blamed; even if it is moved toward something evil, it is compelled by its own nature. But since we don't doubt that this movement is blameworthy, we must absolutely deny that it is natural, and so it is not similar to the natural movement of a stone.

AUGUSTINE: Did we accomplish anything in our first two discussions?

EVODIUS: Of course we did.

AUGUSTINE: I'm sure you recall that in Book One we agreed that nothing can make the mind a slave to inordinate desire except its own will. For the will cannot be forced into such iniquity by anything superior or equal to it, since that would be unjust; or by anything inferior to it, since that is impossible. Only one possibility remains: the movement by which the will turns from enjoying the Creator to enjoying his creatures belongs to the will itself. So if that movement deserves blame (and you said it was ridiculous to entertain doubts on that score), then it is not natural, but voluntary.

This movement of the will is similar to the downward movement of a stone in that it belongs to the will just as that downward movement belongs to the stone. But the two movements are dissimilar in this respect: the stone has no power to check its downward movement, but the soul is not moved to abandon higher things and love inferior things unless it wills to do so. And so the movement of the stone is natural, but the movement of the soul is voluntary. If someone were to say that a stone is sinning because its weight carries it downward, I would not merely say that he was more senseless than the stone itself; I would consider him completely insane. But we accuse a soul of sin when we are convinced that it has abandoned higher things and chosen to enjoy inferior things. Now we admit that this movement belongs to the will alone, and that it is voluntary and therefore blameworthy; and the only useful teaching on this topic is that which condemns and checks this movement and thus serves to rescue our wills from their fall into temporal goods and turn them toward the enjoyment of the eternal good. Therefore, what need is there to ask about the source of the movement by which the will turns away from the unchangeable good toward changeable good?

EVODIUS: I see that what you are saying is true, and in a way I understand it. There is nothing I feel so firmly and so intimately as that I have a will by which I am moved to enjoy something. If the will by which I choose or refuse things is not mine, then I don't know what I can call mine. So if I use my will to do something evil, whom can I hold responsible but myself? For a good God made me, and I can do nothing good except through my will; therefore, it is quite clear that the will was given to me by a good God so that I might do good. If the movement of the will by which it turns this way or that were not voluntary and under its own control, a person would not deserve praise for turning to higher things or blame for turning to lower things, as if swinging on the hinge of the will. Furthermore, there would be no point in admonishing people to forget about lower things and strive for what is eternal, so that they might refuse to live badly but instead will to live rightly. And anyone who does not think that we ought to admonish people in this way deserves to be banished from the human race.

2.   Since these things are true, I very much wonder how God can have foreknowledge of everything in the future, and yet we do not sin by necessity. It would be an irreligious and completely insane attack on God's foreknowledge to say that something could happen otherwise than as God foreknew. So suppose that God foreknew that the first human being was going to sin. Anyone who admits, as I do, that God foreknows everything in the future will have to grant me that. Now I won't say that God would not have made him—for God made him good, and no sin of his can harm God, who not only made him good but showed His own goodness by creating him, as He also shows His justice by punishing him and His mercy by redeeming him—but I will say this: since God foreknew that he was going to sin, his sin necessarily had to happen. How, then, is the will free when such inescapable necessity is found in it?

AUGUSTINE: You have knocked powerfully on the door of God's mercy; may it be present and open the door to those who knock. Nevertheless, I think the only reason that most people are tormented by this question is that they do not ask it piously; they are more eager to excuse than to confess their sins. Some people gladly believe that there is no divine providence in charge of human affairs. They put their bodies and their souls at the mercy of chance and give themselves up to be beaten and mangled by inordinate desires. They disbelieve divine judgments and evade human judgments, thinking that fortune will defend them from those who accuse them. They depict this "fortune" as blind, implying either that they are better than fortune, by which they think they are ruled, or that they themselves suffer from the same blindness. It is perfectly reasonable to admit that such people do everything by chance, since in whatever they do, they fall.[1] But we said enough in Book Two to combat this opinion, which is full of the most foolish and insane error.

Others, however, are not impertinent enough to deny that the providence of God rules over human life; but they prefer the wicked error of believing that it is weak, or unjust, or evil, rather than confessing their sins with humble supplication. If only they would let themselves be convinced that, when they think of what is best and

---

1. The Latin word for 'chance' ('casus') is derived from the verb 'to fall' ('cado').

most just and most powerful, the goodness and justice and power of God are far greater and far higher than anything they can conceive; if only they would consider themselves and understand that they would owe thanks to God even if he had willed to make them lower than they are. Then the very bone and marrow of their conscience would cry out, "I said, 'O Lord, have mercy upon me; heal my soul, for I have sinned against you'."[2] Thus they would be led in the secure paths of divine mercy along the road to wisdom, not becoming conceited when they made new discoveries or disheartened when they failed to do so. Their new knowledge would simply prepare them to see more, and their ignorance would make them more patient in seeking the truth. Of course I'm sure that you already believe this. But you will see how easily I can answer your difficult question once I have answered a few preliminary questions.

Surely this is the problem that is disturbing and puzzling you. **3.** How is it that these two propositions are not contradictory and inconsistent: (1) God has foreknowledge of everything in the future; and (2) We sin by the will, not by necessity? For, you say, if God foreknows that someone is going to sin, then it is necessary that he sin. But if it is necessary, the will has no choice about whether to sin; there is an inescapable and fixed necessity. And so you fear that this argument forces us into one of two positions: either we draw the heretical conclusion that God does not foreknow everything in the future; or, if we cannot accept this conclusion, we must admit that sin happens by necessity and not by will. Isn't that what is bothering you?

EVODIUS: That's it exactly.

AUGUSTINE: So you think that anything that God foreknows happens by necessity and not by will.

EVODIUS: Precisely.

AUGUSTINE: Now pay close attention. Look inside yourself for a little while, and tell me, if you can, what sort of will you are going to have tomorrow: a will to do right or a will to sin?

EVODIUS: I don't know.

AUGUSTINE: Do you think that God doesn't know either?

EVODIUS: Not at all—God certainly does know.

AUGUSTINE: Well then, if God knows what you are going to will tomorrow, and foresees the future wills of every human being, both those who exist now and those who will exist in the future, he surely foresees how he is going to treat the just and the irreligious.

EVODIUS: Clearly, if I say that God foreknows all of my actions, I can much more confidently say that he foreknows his own actions and foresees with absolute certainty what he is going to do.

2. Psalm 41:4

AUGUSTINE: Then aren't you worried that someone might object that God himself will act out of necessity rather than by his will in everything that he is going to do? After all, you said that whatever God foreknows happens by necessity, not by will.

EVODIUS: When I said that, I was thinking only of what happens in his creation and not of what happens within himself. For those things do not come into being; they are eternal.

AUGUSTINE: So God does nothing in his creation.

EVODIUS: He has already established, once for all, the ways in which the universe that he created is to be governed; he does not administer anything by a new act of will.

AUGUSTINE: Doesn't he make anyone happy?

EVODIUS: Of course he does.

AUGUSTINE: And he does this when that person is made happy.

EVODIUS: Right.

AUGUSTINE: Then suppose, for example, that you are going to be happy a year from now. That means that a year from now God is going to make you happy.

EVODIUS: That's right too.

AUGUSTINE: And God knows today what he is going to do a year from now.

EVODIUS: He has always foreknown this, so I admit that he foreknows it now, if indeed it is really going to happen.

AUGUSTINE: Then surely you are not God's creature, or else your happiness does not take place in you.

EVODIUS: But I am God's creature, and my happiness does take place in me.

AUGUSTINE: Then the happiness that God gives you takes place by necessity and not by will.

EVODIUS: His will *is* my necessity.

AUGUSTINE: And so you will be happy against your will.

EVODIUS: If I had the power to be happy I would be happy right now. Even now I will to be happy, but I'm not, since it is God who makes me happy. I cannot do it for myself.

AUGUSTINE: How clearly the truth speaks through you! You could not help thinking that the only thing that is within our power is that which we do when we will it. Therefore, nothing is so much within our power as the will itself, for it is near at hand the very moment that we will. So we can rightly say, "We grow old by necessity, not by will"; or "We become feeble by necessity, not by will"; or "We die by necessity, not by will," and other such things. But who would be crazy enough to say "We do not will by the will"? Therefore, although God foreknows what we are going to will in the future, it does not follow that we do not will by the will.

When you said that you cannot make yourself happy, you said it as if I had denied it. Not at all; I am merely saying that when you do become happy, it will be in accordance with your will, not against your will. Simply because God foreknows your future happiness—and nothing can happen except as God foreknows it, since otherwise it would not be foreknowledge—it does not follow that you will be happy against your will. That would be completely absurd and far from the truth. So God's foreknowledge, which is certain even today of your future happiness, does not take away your will for happiness once you have begun to be happy; and in the same way, your blame-worthy will (if indeed you are going to have such a will) does not cease to be a will simply because God foreknows that you are going to have it.

Just notice how imperceptive someone would have to be to argue thus: "If God has foreknown my future will, it is necessary that I will what he has foreknown, since nothing can happen otherwise than as he has foreknown it. But if it is necessary, then one must concede that I will it by necessity and not by will." What extraordinary fool-ishness! If God foreknew a future will that turned out not to be a will at all, things would indeed happen otherwise than as God foreknew them. And I will overlook this objector's equally monstrous state-ment that "it is necessary that I will," for by assuming necessity he tries to abolish will. For if his willing is necessary, how does he will, since there is no will?

Suppose he expressed it in another way and said that, since his willing is necessary, his will is not in his own power. This would run up against the same problem that you had when I asked whether you were going to be happy against your will. You replied that you would already be happy if you had the power; you said that you have the will but not the power. I answered that the truth had spoken through you. For we can deny that something is in our power only if it is not present even when we will it; but if we will, and yet the will remains absent, then we are not really willing at all. Now if it is impossible for us not to will when we are willing, then the will is present to those who will; and if something is present when we will it, then it is in our power. So our will would not be a will if it were not in our power. And since it is in our power, we are free with respect to it. But we are not free with respect to anything that we do not have in our power, and anything that we have cannot be nothing.

Thus, we believe both that God has foreknowledge of everything in the future and that nonetheless we will whatever we will. Since God foreknows our will, the very will that he foreknows will be what comes about. Therefore, it will be a will, since it is a will that he foreknows. And it could not be a will unless it were in our power.

Therefore, he also foreknows this power. It follows, then, that his foreknowledge does not take away my power; in fact, it is all the more certain that I will have that power, since he whose foreknowledge never errs foreknows that I will have it.

EVODIUS: I agree now that it is necessary that whatever God has foreknown will happen, and that he foreknows our sins in such a way that our wills remain free and are within our power.

4. AUGUSTINE: Then what is troubling you? Have you perhaps forgotten the results of our first discussion? Will you deny that nothing at all, whether superior, equal, or inferior, can coerce the will, and that we sin by our own wills?

EVODIUS: I certainly wouldn't dream of denying any of those things. But still, I must admit that I can't quite see how God's foreknowledge of our sins can be consistent with our free choice in sinning. For we must admit that God is just, and that he has foreknowledge. But I would like to know how it can be just to punish sins that happen necessarily, or how things that God foreknows do not happen necessarily, or how whatever happens necessarily in creation should not be attributed to the Creator.

AUGUSTINE: Why do you think that our free choice is inconsistent with God's foreknowledge? Because it's foreknowledge, or because it's God's foreknowledge?

EVODIUS: Because it's God's foreknowledge.

AUGUSTINE: If you knew that someone was going to sin, he wouldn't sin necessarily, would he?

EVODIUS: Indeed he would. Unless I foreknew something with certainty, it wouldn't be foreknowledge at all.

AUGUSTINE: Then it's not God's foreknowledge that makes his sin necessary but any foreknowledge, since if something is not foreknown with certainty, it is not foreknown at all.

EVODIUS: I agree. But where are you headed with this?

AUGUSTINE: Unless I am mistaken, you do not force someone to sin just because you foreknow that he is going to sin. Nor does your foreknowledge force him to sin, even if he is undoubtedly going to sin—since otherwise you would not have genuine foreknowledge. So if your foreknowledge is consistent with his freedom in sinning, so that you foreknow what someone else is going to do by his own will, then God forces no one to sin, even though he foresees those who are going to sin by their own will.

Why then can't our just God punish those things that his foreknowledge does not force to happen? Just as your memory does not force the past to have happened, God's foreknowledge does not force the future to happen. And just as you remember some things that you have done but did not do everything that you remember, God foreknows everything that he causes but does not cause everything that he foreknows. Of such things he is not the evil cause, but the just avenger. Therefore, you must understand that God justly punishes the sins that he foreknows but does not cause. If the fact that God foresees their sins means that he should not punish sinners, then he should also not reward those who act rightly, for he also foresees their righteous actions. Let us rather confess that nothing in the future is hidden from God's foreknowledge, and that no sin is left unpunished by his justice, for sin is committed by the will, not coerced by God's foreknowledge.

As for your third question, about how the Creator can escape **5.** blame for whatever happens necessarily in his creation, it will not easily overcome that rule of piety that we ought to bear in mind, namely, that we owe thanks to our Creator. His most abundant goodness would be most justly praised even if he had created us at a lower level of creation. For even though our souls are decayed with sin, they are better and more sublime than they would be if they were transformed into visible light. And you see that even souls that are addicted to the bodily senses give God great praise for the grandeur of light. Therefore, don't let the fact that sinful souls are condemned lead you to say in your heart that it would be better if they did not exist. For they are condemned only in comparison with what they would have been if they had refused to sin. Nonetheless, God their Creator deserves the most noble praise that human beings can offer him, not only because he places them in a just order when they sin, but also because he created them in such a way that even the filth of sin could in no way make them inferior to corporeal light, for which he is nonetheless praised.

So you should not say that it would be better if sinful souls had never existed. But I must also warn you not to say that they ought to have been created differently. Whatever might rightly occur to you as being better, you may be sure, that God, as the Creator of all good things, has made that too. When you think that something better should have been made, it is not right reason, but grudging weakness, to will that nothing lower had been made, as if you looked upon the heavens and wished that the earth had not been made. Such a wish is utterly unjust.

If you saw that the earth had been made but not the heavens, then you would have a legitimate complaint, for you could say that the earth ought to have been made like the heavens that you can imagine. But since you see that the pattern to which you wanted the earth to conform has indeed been made (but it is called 'the heavens' and not 'the earth'), I'm sure that you would not begrudge the fact that the inferior thing has also been made, and that the earth exists, since you are not deprived of the better thing. And there is so great a variety of parts in the earth that we cannot conceive of any earthly form that God has not created. By intermediate steps one passes gradually from the most fertile and pleasant land to the briniest and most barren, so that you would not dream of disparaging any of them except in comparison with a better. Thus you ascend through every degree of praise, so that even when you come to the very best land, you would not want it to exist without the others. And how great a distance there is between the whole earth and the heavens! For between the two is interposed the watery and airy nature. From these four elements come a variety of forms and species too numerous for us to count, although God has numbered them all.

Therefore, it is possible for something to exist in the universe that you do not conceive with your reason, but it is not possible for something that you conceive by right reason not to exist. For you cannot conceive anything better in creation that has slipped the mind of the Creator. Indeed, the human soul is naturally connected with the divine reasons on which it depends. When it says "It would be better to make this than that," if what it says is true, and it sees what it is saying, then it sees that truth in the reasons to which it is connected. If, therefore, it knows by right reason that God ought to have made something, let it believe that God has in fact done so, even if it does not see the thing among those that God has made.

For example, suppose we could not see the heavens. Nonetheless, if right reason showed that some such thing ought to have been made, it would be right for us to believe that it was made, even if we did not see it with our own eyes. For if we see by thought that something ought to have been made, we see it only in those reasons by which all things were made. But no truthful thinking can enable someone to see what is not in those reasons, for whatever is not there is not true.

Many people go astray when they have seen better things with their mind because in searching for it with their eyes they look in the wrong places. They are like someone who understands perfect roundness and is angry because he does not find it in a nut, if that is the only round object that he sees. In the same way, some people see by the truest reason that a creature is better if it is so firmly dedicated to God that it will never sin, even though it has free will. Then, when they look upon the sins of human beings, they do not use their sorrow over sin to stop people from sinning; they bemoan the fact that human beings were created in the first place. "He ought to have made us," they say, "so that we would always enjoy his unchangeable truth, so that we would never will to sin." Let them not moan and complain! God, who gave them the power to will, did not force them to sin; and there are angels who never have sinned and never will sin.

Therefore, if you take delight in a creature whose will is so perfectly steadfast that he does not sin, it is by right reason that you prefer this creature to one that sins. And just as you give it a higher rank in your thinking, the Creator gave it a higher rank in his ordering. So be sure that such a creature exists in the higher places and in the splendor of the heavens, since if the Creator manifested his goodness in creating something that he foresaw would sin, he certainly manifested his goodness in creating something that he foreknew would not sin.

That sublime creature has perpetual happiness in the perpetual enjoyment of its Creator, a happiness that it deserves because it perpetually wills to retain justice. Next, there is a proper place even for the sinful nature that by its sins has lost happiness but not thrown away the power to recover happiness. This nature is in turn higher than one that perpetually wills to sin. It occupies a sort of intermediate position between those that persist in willing justice and those that persist in willing to sin. It receives its greatness from the lowliness of repentance.

But God, in the bounty of his goodness, did not shrink from creating even that creature whom he foreknew would not merely sin, but would persist in willing to sin. For a runaway horse is better than a stone that stays in the right place only because it has no movement or perception of its own; and in the same way, a creature that sins by free will is more excellent than one that does not sin only because it has no free will. I would praise wine as a thing good of its kind, but condemn a person who got drunk on that wine. And yet I would prefer that person, condemned and drunk, to the wine that I praised, on which he got drunk. In the same way, the material creation is rightly praised on its own level, but those who turn away from the perception of the truth by immoderately using the material creation deserve condemnation. And yet even those perverse and drunken people who are ruined by this greed are to be preferred to the material creation, praiseworthy though it is in its own order, not because of the merit of their sins, but because of the dignity of their nature.

Therefore, any soul is better than any material object. Now no sinful soul, however far it may fall, is ever changed into a material object; it never ceases to be a soul. Therefore, no soul ceases to be better than a material object. Consequently, the lowest soul is still better than light, which is the foremost among material objects. It may be that the body in which a certain soul exists is inferior to some other body, but the soul itself can in no way be inferior to a body.

Why, then, should we not praise God with unspeakable praise, simply because when he made those souls who would persevere in the laws of justice, he made others who he foresaw would sin, even some who would persevere in sin? For even such souls are better than souls that cannot sin because they lack reason and the free choice of the will. And these souls are in turn better than the brilliance of any material object, however splendid, which some people mistakenly worship instead of the Most High God. In the order of material creation, from the heavenly choirs to the number of the hairs of our heads, the beauty of good things at every level is so perfectly harmonious that only the most ignorant could say, "What is this? Why is this?"—for all things were created in their proper order. How much more ignorant, then, to say this of a soul whose glory, however dimmed and tarnished it might become, far exceeds the dignity of any material object!

Reason judges in one way, custom in another. Reason judges by the light of truth, so that by right judgment it subjects lesser things to greater. Custom is often swayed by agreeable habits, so that it esteems as greater what truth reveals as lower. Reason accords the heavenly bodies far greater honor than earthly bodies. And yet who among carnal human beings would not much rather have many stars gone from the heavens than one sapling missing from his field or one cow from his pasture? Children would rather see a man die (unless it is someone they love) than their pet bird, especially if the man frightens them and the bird is beautiful and can sing; but adults utterly despise their judgments, or at least wait patiently until they can be corrected. In the same way, there are those who praise God for his lesser creatures, which are better suited to their carnal senses. But when it comes to his superior and better creatures, some of these people praise him less or not at all; some even try to find fault with them or change them; and some do not believe that God created them. But those who have advanced along the road to wisdom regard such people as ignorant judges of things. Until they can correct the ignorant, they learn to bear with them patiently; but if they cannot correct them, they utterly repudiate their judgments.

6. Since this is the case, it is quite wrong to think that the sins of the creature should be attributed to the Creator, even though it is necessary that whatever he foreknows will happen. So much so, that when you said you could find no way to avoid attributing to him everything in his creation that happens necessarily, I on the other hand could find no way—nor can any way be found, for I am convinced that there is no way—to attribute to him anything in his creation that happens necessarily by the will of sinners.

Someone might say, "I would rather not exist at all than be unhappy." I would reply, "You're lying. You're unhappy now, and the only reason you don't want to die is to go on existing. You don't want to be unhappy, but you do want to exist. Give thanks, therefore, for what you are willingly, so that what you are against your will might be taken away; for you willingly exist, but you are unhappy against your will. If you are ungrateful for what you will to be, you are justly compelled to be what you do not will. So I praise the goodness of your Creator, for even though you are ungrateful you have what you will; and I praise the justice of your Lawgiver, for because you are ungrateful you suffer what you do not will."

But then he might say, "It is not because I would rather be unhappy than not exist at all that I am unwilling to die; it's because I'm afraid that I might be even more unhappy after death." I would reply, "If it is unjust for you to be even more unhappy, you won't be so; but if it is just, let us praise him by whose laws you will be so."

Next he might ask, "Why should I assume that if it is unjust I won't be more unhappy?" I would reply, "If at that time you are in your own power, either you will not be unhappy, or you will be governing yourself unjustly, in which case you will deserve your unhappiness. But suppose instead that you wish to govern yourself justly but cannot. That means that you are not in your own power, so either someone else has power over you, or no one has. If no one has power over you, you will act either willingly or unwillingly. It cannot be unwillingly, because nothing happens to you unwillingly unless you are overcome by some force, and you cannot be overcome by any force if no one has power over you. And if it is willingly, you are in fact in your own power, and the earlier argument applies: either you deserve your unhappiness for governing yourself unjustly, or, since you have whatever you will, you have reason to give thanks for the goodness of your Creator.

"Therefore, if you are not in your own power, some other thing must have control over you. This thing is either stronger or weaker than you. If it is weaker than you, your servitude is your own fault and your unhappiness is just, since you could overpower this thing if you willed to do so. And if a stronger thing has control over you, its control is in accordance with proper order, and you cannot rightly think that so right an order is unjust. I was therefore quite correct to say, 'If it is unjust for you to be even more unhappy, you won't be so; but if it is just, let us praise him by whose laws you will be so'."

Then he might say, "The only reason that I will to be unhappy 7. rather than not to exist at all is that I already exist; if somehow I could have been consulted on this matter before I existed, I would have chosen not to exist rather than to be unhappy. The fact that I am now afraid not to exist, even though I am unhappy, is itself part of that very unhappiness because of which I do not will what I ought to will. For I ought to will not to exist rather than to be unhappy. And yet I admit that in fact I would rather be unhappy than be nothing. But the more unhappy I am, the more foolish I am to will this; and the more truly I see that I ought not will this, the more unhappy I am."

I would reply, "Be careful that you are not mistaken when you think you see the truth. For if you were happy, you would certainly prefer existence to nonexistence. Even as it is, although you are unhappy and do not will to be unhappy, you would rather exist and be unhappy than not exist at all. Consider, then, as well as you can, how great is the good of existence, which the happy and the unhappy alike will. If you consider it well, you will realize three things. First, you are unhappy to the extent that you are far from him who exists in the highest degree. Second, the more you think that it is better for someone not to exist than to be unhappy, the less you will see him who exists in the highest degree. Finally, you nonetheless will to exist because you are from him who exists in the highest degree."

So if you will to escape from unhappiness, cherish your will to exist. For if you will more and more to exist, you will approach him who exists in the highest degree. And give thanks that you exist now, for even though you are inferior to those who are happy, you are superior to things that do not have even the will to be happy—and many such things are praised even by those who are unhappy. Nonetheless, all things that exist deserve praise simply in virtue of the fact that they exist, for they are good simply in virtue of the fact that they exist.

The more you love existence, the more you will desire eternal life, and so the more you will long to be refashioned so that your affections are no longer temporal, branded upon you by the love of temporal things that are nothing before they exist, and then, once they do exist, flee from existence until they exist no more. And so when their existence is still to come, they do not yet exist; and when their existence is past, they exist no more. How can you expect such things to endure, when for them to begin to exist is to set out on the road to nonexistence?

Someone who loves existence approves of such things insofar as they exist and loves that which always exists. If once he used to waver in the love of temporal things, he now grows firm in the love of the eternal. Once he wallowed in the love of fleeting things, but he will stand steadfast in the love of what is permanent. Then he will obtain the very existence that he willed when he was afraid not to exist but could not stand upright because he was entangled in the love of fleeting things.

Therefore, do not grieve that you would rather exist and be unhappy than not exist and be nothing at all. Instead, rejoice greatly, for your will to exist is like a first step. If you go on from there to set your sights more and more on existence, you will rise to him who exists in the highest degree. Thus you will keep yourself from the kind of fall in which that which exists in the lowest degree ceases to exist and thereby devastates the one who loves it. Hence, someone who prefers not to exist rather than to be unhappy has no choice but to be unhappy, since he cannot fail to exist; but someone who loves existence more than he hates being unhappy can banish what he hates by cleaving more and more to what he loves. For someone who has come to enjoy an existence that is perfect for a thing of his kind cannot be unhappy.

Notice how absurd and illogical it would be to say "I would prefer **8.** not to exist rather than to be unhappy." For someone who says "I would prefer this rather than that" is choosing something. But not to exist is not something, but nothing. Therefore, you can't properly choose it, since what you are choosing does not exist.

Perhaps you will say that you do in fact will to exist, even though you are unhappy, but that you *shouldn't* will to exist. Then what should you will? "Not to exist," you say. Well, if that is what you ought to will, it must be better; but that which does not exist cannot be better. Therefore, you should not will not to exist, and the frame of mind that keeps you from willing it is closer to the truth than your belief that you ought to will it.

Furthermore, if someone is right in choosing to pursue something, it must be the case that he becomes better when he attains it. But whoever does not exist cannot be better, and so no one can be right in choosing not to exist. We should not be swayed by the judgment of those whose unhappiness has driven them to suicide. Either they thought that they would be better off after death, in which case they were doing nothing contrary to our argument (whether they were right in thinking so or not); or else they thought that they would be nothing after death, in which case there is even less reason for us to bother with them, since they falsely chose nothing. For how am I supposed to concur in the choice of someone who, if I asked him what he was choosing, would say "Nothing"? And someone who chooses not to exist is clearly choosing nothing, even if he won't admit it.

To tell you quite frankly what I think about this whole issue, it seems to me that someone who kills himself or in some way wants to die has the feeling that he will not exist after death, whatever his conscious opinion may be. Opinion, whether true or false, has to do with reason or faith; but feeling derives its power from either habit or nature. It can happen that opinion leads in one direction and feeling in another. This is easy to see in cases where we believe that we ought to do one thing but enjoy doing just the opposite. And sometimes feeling is closer to the truth than opinion is, as when the opinion is in error and the feeling is from nature. For example, a sick man will often enjoy drinking cold water, which is good for him, even if he believes that it will kill him. But sometimes opinion is closer to the truth than feeling is, as when someone's knowledge of medicine tells him that cold water would be harmful when in fact it *would* be harmful, even though it would be pleasant to drink. Sometimes both are right, as when one rightly believes that something is beneficial and also finds it pleasing. Sometimes both are wrong, as when one believes that something is beneficial when it is actually harmful and one is also happy not to give it up.

It often happens that right opinion corrects perverted habits and that perverted opinion distorts an upright nature, so great is the power of the dominion and rule of reason. Therefore, someone who believes that after death he will not exist is driven by his unbearable troubles to desire death with all his heart; he chooses death and takes hold of it. His opinion is completely false, but his feeling is simply a natural desire for peace. And something that has peace is not nothing; indeed, it is greater than something that is restless. For restlessness generates one conflicting passion after another, whereas peace has the constancy that is the most conspicuous characteristic of Being.

So the will's desire for death is not a desire for nonexistence but a desire for peace. When someone wrongly believes that he will not exist, he desires by nature to be at peace; that is, he desires to exist in a higher degree. Therefore, just as no one can desire not to exist, no one ought to be ungrateful to the goodness of the Creator for the fact that he exists.

* * *

CRITICISM

HENRY CHADWICK

Introduction to *Boethius: His Life, Thought, and Influence*[†]

By writing the *Consolation of Philosophy* Boethius provided all educated people of the Middle Ages and the Renaissance with one of their principal classics, a work of both intellectual profundity and literary delight to be read not only in Latin by clerks in their study but also by laymen at leisure, and therefore often in the vernacular. The author, it is true, wrote some pages on Christian theology which are of the greatest consequence. But he did not write them as a theologian in the ordinary sense of the word; he is addressing himself only indirectly to a pastoral or 'political' situation in the Church, as a logician who thought there was some tidying up to be done in the ecclesiastical garden. He writes as a layman and has been loved by laymen. In its philosophical content the *Consolation* attracted commentaries from several medieval authors, not as momentous as the commentaries called forth by his theological tractates, but a significant sign of the seriousness with which men took his philosophical reflections on the dealings of providence with a world beset by so much evil. But the common experience of apparently purposeless evil has attracted all thoughtful readers to Boethius' pages. His stylistic grace and above all his radical analysis of the true sources of human happiness contribute to making the book one that still retains its place among the masterpieces and jewels of western literature. Boethius' English translators alone include King Alfred, Geoffrey Chaucer and Queen Elizabeth I, which is not a weak list of admirers.

Nevertheless, there is a certain isolation about Boethius. This isolation has perhaps become akin to neglect since the Renaissance.

His world is the old world of antiquity with an intellectual framework dominated by Ptolemaic ideas about the world, by Aristotle's doctrines of substance and accidents, by a Platonic metaphysic setting asunder mind and matter, by Pythagorean ideas of mathematics and of musical proportion as the key to the structure of the cosmos. A sense of isolation is felt even during his lifetime. He had his intimate circle of friends: his father-in-law Symmachus to whom he felt himself to owe a profound intellectual debt; a Roman advocate

---

[†] From *Boethius: His Life, Thought, and Influence*, ed. Margaret Gibson (Oxford: Basil Blackwell, 1981), 1–12. Reprinted by permission.

named Patricius for whom he composed, late in his career, a commentary on Cicero's *Topics*; a learned deacon of the Roman church named John (probably, not quite certainly, to be identified with Pope John I, 523–6), who shared his enthusiasm for questions of logic; a Roman senator in the bureaucracy at Ravenna named Renatus, like Boethius fluent in Greek, who seems first to have collected a corpus of Boethius' dialectical treatises a year or two after his death. But it is a small circle, and the treatises on logic did not make him new friends. They contain a large number of unhappy references to contemporary critics who were altogether failing to see any value in his labours on Aristotle and suspected him of writing for ostentation rather than for use. These critics are evidently not barbarian Goths, but fellow senators. His writing was caviare to the general and pleased not the million.

Boethius was by temperament a man who liked to strike out on his own. In all the fields that he touched he had some Latin predecessors. Apuleius anticipated him in writing a short guide to Aristotle's difficult treatise on *Interpretation*. It is likely that Boethius knew Apuleius' work, but he never mentions it by name. Apuleius also anticipated him in making an adaptation of the *Arithmetic* of Nicomachus of Gerasa, but Boethius sets about his own version of Nicomachus as if he had no predecessor. Marius Victorinus, the African rhetor of the mid-fourth century whose conversion to Christianity astonished high Roman society about 355, directly covered some of the ground that Boethius was to claim as his own. He made a translation of Porphyry's *Isagoge* or introduction (Porphyry did not explain what he was introducing, but in the sixth century it was assumed to be an introduction to Aristotle's *Categories*); a version, with eight books of commentary, of Aristotle's *Categories*; a version of Aristotle on *Interpretation*; a tract on the hypothetical syllogism; and a commentary on Cicero's *Topics*. Boethius acknowledges that Victorinus was the most eminent orator of his time, but loses no opportunity of drawing attention to Victorinus' blunders either in logic or in translation from the Greek. Nevertheless, it can hardly be accidental that the portion of Boethius' dialectical work which became most widely known covers much the same area as that laid down as the standard curriculum by Victorinus in the fourth century. Although Boethius succeeded in making careful translations, which were then given a further meticulous revision, of both *Analytics, Topics*, and *Sophistic Refutations*, the transmission of these last treatises is a thin line. Until the twelfth century they were little known or not at all.

Neither in his dialectical studies nor in his works on mathematics did Boethius claim to be original. For arithmetic he closely follows his Greek model in the Pythagorean Nicomachus of Gerasa. This study is intended as a preparation for the introduction to music, a much longer work dependent on Nicomachus and on Ptolemy. The

Institutio Musica is transmitted incomplete in the manuscript tradition, which breaks off in the middle of a sentence halfway through the fifth book. Originally the work must have run to six or seven books. The matter preserved follows the Platonic/Pythagorean tradition in preferring theory to practice and in discounting the potent criticisms of the Pythagorean tradition from Aristoxenus of Tarentum in the fourth century B.C. Aristoxenus insisted on the primacy of the ear over abstract mathematical theory. Boethius has to concede to Aristoxenus that the judgement of the ear has some claim to consideration. In making these concessions he follows Ptolemy's extant *Harmonics*. Ptolemy's book is likely to have been the model for his discussion (in the lost books at the end) of cosmic and human music; that is of the way in which harmonic ratios and exact proportionality are exemplified in the structure of the cosmos (e.g. the distance of the planets from the earth) and in the fitting together of the human soul and body. Boethius' introduction to music is not intended to assist in the practice of the art, and has been held to have done disservice to music by instilling into generations of readers the doctrine that the true 'musicus' is master exclusively of the theory, and that practical skills can be left to the inferior orders of society. That prejudice, however, is virtually universal among ancient writers on the subject. We need not put all the blame on Boethius. In the *Consolation* he tells us that listening to music meant much to him. He felt that music should not merely be used to express one's feelings when one is either sad or glad, and attributed to it the dignity of being a clue to the providential ordering of things.

In his logical treatises there stands one monograph which had special interest for him, namely, that on the hypothetical syllogism of the conditional form: 'if A, then B; but A, therefore B', or 'if A, then B; but not B, therefore not A.' The school of Aristotle had begun the investigation of the logic of conditional statements of this kind. The Stoics had taken the matter considerably further, treating the variables AB as symbols not (as in Aristotle) for terms but for entire propositions. Cicero took some notice of this Stoic logic, so that it was not bringing out matter of which the Latin world knew nothing. But Boethius' monograph is the most careful and detailed study in logic to come from his pen, and without it our knowledge of ancient propositional logic would be thin. To medieval logicians this treatise was not perhaps of the greatest interest. John of Salisbury regarded it without enthusiasm, but conceded that it was at least clearer than anything that Aristotle would have written on the subject, had he done so. In recent times modern logicians have shown a more benevolent interest in Boethius' work in this complex field.

John of Salisbury felt that some of Boethius' logical studies were too abstract to be of any use. There is no doubt that his expositions of Aristotle are academic and detached, but written with the conviction that they train the mind to detect fallacies. In his second commentary on Porphyry's *Isagoge* he utters the warning: 'Those who reject logic are bound to make mistakes. Unless reason shows the right path, the incorrupt truth of reality cannot be found'.

In the commentary on Aristotle's *Categories* he writes in pain of the threat to the survival of culture in his own time, and speaks of the imminent collapse of liberal studies unless drastic action is taken to preserve the values of the classical past. Knowledge is not only gained in the process of historical change; it is even more easily lost. Human culture can suffer impoverishment more readily than it can achieve enrichment. Hence Boethius' sweat and toil in his study to make available to the Latin world those works which the best philosophers of his age regarded as the proper ladder of true education. They were Neoplatonists and set action far below contemplation. Their educational ideal was relatively little concerned with politics or economics or even ethics (though Boethius' contemporary Simplicius wrote a commentary on the *Enchiridion* of Epictetus which must be reckoned a treatise on the moral life), but was directed towards what they called 'theoria', rendered by Boethius 'speculatio'. Under the heading of speculative philosophy they wrote of physics, i.e. the scientific study of the natural order; or of mathematics; or of metaphysics and 'theology'.

The late Platonists are schoolmen in the sense that they approach Plato and Aristotle not simply as acute thinkers whose arguments could and should provoke continued independent thinking on the part of their readers; but as authoritative figures, masters of philosophical truth, whose metaphysical beliefs deserve to be received with respect and awe by their pigmy successors. It followed that distress would be caused if these authorities seemed at important points to be speaking with divergent or even contradictory voices. Plotinus' biographer Porphyry accepted Plotinus' view that in Peripatetic logic there is much of the highest value, but it concerns truth in this world of time and space. The ten categories, according to Plotinus, have a limited applicability to the realm of the Ideas in the intelligible world beyond time and space. So Porphyry set out to prove Plato and Aristotle to be concordant on fundamental questions and to be in disagreement only in secondary matters. This scheme was facilitated by treating Plato as the master guide to the mathematical and metaphysical world of unchanging truth, and Aristotle as the master scientist, moralist and political theorist who best understood terrestrial matters. It followed that Aristotle's *Metaphysics* needed a certain amount of careful exegesis to bring the doctrines of the book into a Platonic line. On one major point of confrontation, namely the kind of reality to be ascribed to universals such as genera and species, Porphyry was able to keep his authorities from discord simply by not making up his mind. In his second commentary on Porphyry Boethius follows a decisively Peripatetic line, in agreement with the Aristotelian master of A.D. 200, Alexander of Aphrodisias, viz. that universals can have a reality only in so far as there actually exist concrete particulars, independent of our minds, for which universal terms such as genera and species serve as a convenient classification system. Admittedly Boethius juxtaposes this with a much more Platonising statement, that the reality of universals can be discovered not by collecting and putting together a large number of instances, but rather by a negative way of abstraction from matter.

An analogous procedure appears in the treatment of the problem of 'future contingents', in Boethius' commentary on the ninth chapter of Aristotle's *De Interpretatione* and then in the last book of the *Consolation of Philosophy*. The commentary deals with divine foreknowledge of events that might or might not occur in a wholly Peripatetic framework. Foreknowledge makes nothing to happen, even if it is God's. If the cosmos has in its structure a certain indeterminacy, then God knows indeterminate things as indeterminate. If he believed them to be certainly predictable, he would hold false beliefs (which is incompatible with the concept of God). God's knowledge of future contingents is therefore a true knowledge that the possibilities are open, and that while a great deal in the world may take place by necessary causation, this is not true of everything. So the commentary. But in the *Consolation* the profound influence on Boethius of Proclus of Athens is directly felt, and the answer to the same questions is now found in a Platonic framework: what is an open and uncertain future to us is certain to God who foreknows all things and in whose world an element of indeterminacy would appear to a Neoplatonist to be some kind of defect in the order of things. Therefore Boethius has to embark on his argument that in God there is no before and after, but everything is known in the simultaneity of eternity: 'interminabilis uitae tota simul et perfecta possessio' (V pr. vi. 4).

Both the mathematical treatises and the studies in Aristotelian logic are concerned with knowledge for its own sake, not because it may lead to some enlargement of the wealth of Italy. No doubt Boethius was not displeased when Theoderic invited him to design for the Burgundian king a sundial and a waterclock, or invited him to express a view about the proper exchange rate between the gold solidus and the absurdly devalued copper denarius, out of compliment to his mathematical distinction. His *Institutio Musica* won him an invitation to select a harpist to be sent to Clovis, in the simple hope that music might tame his dangerous aggressiveness on Theoderic's borders. No special public service was expected of consuls in the sixth century, and his service as sole consul for the year 510 (for which office he must have been appointed by the Eastern emperor Anastasius on the nomination of Theoderic) did not lay heavy governmental burdens on his shoulders. Consuls had to be rich and dispense vast munificence in donatives and in the provision of public spectacles. Even so, Boethius used the dignity of his office to oppose the prefect Faustus when, at a time of famine and high food prices, he proposed compulsory purchase of food from farmers in Campania at prices that would have left them destitute. Otherwise his consulship did not much bring him out of his study; he tells us that the duties of the office have done something to delay his commentary on the *Categories*, a work which he sees as a civic duty.

Paradoxically it seems to have been an interest in theology and in the logic of the ecclesiastical *usus loquendi*, or 'tradition of talking', which did more than anything else to bring him out of his library.

Until the last three years of his long reign, Theoderic's regime in Italy was distinguished for its rare liberality. His toleration was extraordinary. It did not extend to sorcerers, Manichees, and those who offered pagan sacrifices. His dealings with the Jewish communities in Italy were marked by justice rather than by acts of positive encouragement. As a Goth he was an Arian king presiding over a self-consciously separate race whom he wished to keep apart from the Romans especially by enforcing a religious apartheid of Arian and Catholic. He cordially disliked conversions from Catholic to Arian or vice versa. The Catholic churches of Italy he treated with liberality and fairmindedness. When in 500 he visited Rome, he came to St Peter's 'as if he were a Catholic'. It was easy for the churches in Italy to look to him for protection, though an Arian, because from 484 until 519 there was a breach of communion between Rome and the Greek patriarchates, the Acacian schism, caused by Rome's indignation when the patriarch Acacius of Constantinople established communion with the patriarch of Alexandria on a basis other than that of the Council of Chalcedon (451) and without reference to Rome. The new basis for communion was the emperor Zeno's Henoticon, or 'reunion formula' which, without expressly censuring the Council of Chalcedon referred to it in very cool terms. After Zeno his successor Anastasius (491–518) upheld the Henoticon as the standard of orthodoxy in his dominions, and sought to remain 'above parties'. His toleration of the Monophysite critics of Chalcedon seemed unendurable to Rome, and various endeavours from either side to reestablish understanding and communion ended in abrasive exchanges, especially with Pope Symmachus (498–514) who had a schism on his hands at Rome and was very uncertain of himself. Symmachus' successor Hormisdas (513–23) reopened negotiations with Theoderic's consent, but no progress was made until suddenly in 518 Anastasius died and was succeeded by Justin I.

Assisted by his nephew Justinian, Justin's policy was to reestablish unity with the West on any terms the Pope cared to specify, the ultimate objective being to encourage the church in Italy to look to Constantinople rather than to the Gothic king at Ravenna, and so to make possible the ultimate overthrow of the Gothic kingdom.

Theology, however, lay at the heart of the ecclesiastical controversy, the terms of which were bewildering to the Latin West. When about 513 a Greek bishop wrote to Pope Symmachus begging him to adopt a less anti-Greek attitude and to take initiatives to heal the schism, the Roman clergy and senators were filled with alarm to learn that this professedly Chalcedonian and pro-Roman bishop wished to affirm as orthodox not only the Chalcedonian formula that Christ, God and man, is known as one person *in* two natures, but also that he is *of* two natures. Boethius was present at the resulting tumult and felt that a logician had something to contribute to the clarification of the issue. After some long pondering (which may have lasted five years rather than five weeks), Boethius wrote the earliest of his theological tractates, the fifth, 'against Eutyches and Nestorius', the most original work on any subject that came from his pen. Its content manifests affinity with the positions advocated both at Constantinople and at Rome by a group of Gothic ('Scythian', because they came from the Dobrudja) monks led by Maxentius and Leontius. Maxentius was firm for the Chalcedonian 'in two natures', but wished to meet its critics by adding that there is 'one nature of the divine Word incarnate', that Christ is both *of* and *in* two natures, and that the incarnate, crucified Lord is 'one of the Trinity'. He explained that this last formula implies neither that God can suffer nor that there is plurality in the divine being. However, at Rome Pope Hormisdas was alarmed by such doctrines, perhaps especially for any hint of an implication that Chalcedon needed supplementation or qualification. The Pope's advisers were suspicious of any concession to Byzantine compromise. Boethius' fifth tractate shows that he thought otherwise. In essentials he supports Maxentius, whose formulae were also congenial to Justinian, though he would not be so imprudent as to say so before he had won the Pope's approval.

Boethius' classic definition of person as 'the individual substance of rational nature' is formulated with the eastern Christological controversy in mind. It had its sixth century critics as well as adverse comment from Richard of St Victor (*De Trinitate* iv. 21f.). Boethius was aware that the term 'persona' may be obscure, but is easier to use of human kind than of God, in which context its meaning becomes unclear.

The first tractate, *De Trinitate*, written for his father-in-law Symmachus, displays an Augustinian reserve towards the word 'persona' in the exposition of the doctrine of the Trinity. Father, Son and Spirit are one God, not three. Yet these three biblical terms are not describing accidental qualities of the one divine substance, since it is axiomatic that what God is, he has; there are no accidents in God. But Neoplatonic logic can help with its analysis of the relationship of identity and difference. When we say that x and y are 'the same', some distinction between them is necessary if the assertion is to be of interest. The language of Father and Son is that of relation, a word which implies otherness. But within the Christian Trinity, relation is that between equals and identicals, a kind of relation not to be found among perishable, finite things. The second tractate, for John the deacon, pursues the question further. The term 'Trinitas' is not a term of substance, but of relation. For John Boethius also composed his third tractate, in which there is no discussion of any point of Christian dogma, but exclusively of a problem in Platonic metaphysics: Plato teaches that the good transcends being. All that exists derives from the good, and its existence as such is a good. If an existent entity is good, is it good in the same way as the supreme Good is good, or is goodness something it has rather than something it is? Boethius follows Proclus in proceeding on a mathematical analogy. First establish the axioms and definitions, and then, like Euclid, ask what must necessarily follow.

Boethius' role as a 'boffin' in the discussions at Rome will not have passed unnoticed at Constantinople. In the year 522 Boethius' two young sons were nominated as consuls for the year, which can hardly have happened unless Boethius' name was being spoken of at Constantinople as a personage carrying weight in the pro-Byzantine interest at Rome. From 1 September, probably of 522, Boethius took up a major administrative post at Ravenna as Master of the Offices. He used his position to protect his friends and to frustrate the corruption of court officials. In short, he made many enemies. The storm broke when he was accused of suppressing damning evidence that the senator Albinus had engaged in treasonable correspondence with Constantinople to the danger of Theoderic's kingdom. For the harsh realities of political life Boethius was too much of an academic to survive.

But his long imprisonment at Pavia gave him the opportunity to write his greatest book, *The Consolation of Philosophy*. From an apologia protesting his innocence of the charge he goes on to an analysis of human misery and happiness. In serious trouble one quickly discovers by pain and disillusionment who are one's real friends (I pr. viii.6). How bitter is the sadness of remembering one's past happiness (II pr. iv. 1); perhaps an echo of Augustine's 'tristis gaudium pristinum recolo' in the *Confessions* (X xxi. 30). But Boethius reproaches himself, through the lady Philosophy who represents his better self, for his self-pity. Nothing is miserable unless thinking makes it so (II pr. iv. 18). Those who trust to the deceitful lady Fortuna have no right to complain when her proverbial wheel

turns (II pr. viii). But from the middle of the third book, with its literary climax in the poem 'O qui perpetua', the vindication of providence moves into a Platonic key, and owes much to the writings of
Proclus. In the first book Proclus' authority is recognised in passing
in the quotation, taken from his commentary on the *Parmenides*
(1056 Cousin): 'If there is a God, whence comes evil? But whence
comes good, if there is not?' (I pr. iv. 30). Boethius tells his readers
that for some time past he has been studying the arguments about
providence and evil, and the many parallels with Proclus' three
opuscula on this subject illustrate his reading there.

At the beginning of his monograph on the hypothetical syllogism
he remarks that the study of philosophy has been the solamen of his
life. Now in prison, perhaps with a few books brought by Symmachus or his wife Rusticiana, he must compose his confession of
philosophical faith. It is a profoundly religious view of the nature
and destiny of man, but it is notoriously not a Christian book. There
is nothing of the remission of sins or eternal life or redemption.
There are a number of tantalising, near-echoes of biblical texts; it is
characteristic of the style of the book that they can be otherwise
interpreted, except one, the citation of a phrase from the Wisdom of
Solomon 8:1 in III pr. xii. 22–23 to the effect that God 'rules everything firmly and gently disposes them', where Boethius expresses
delight not only at the content of the lady Philosophy's statement
but also at the very words she uses ('haec ipsa verba'). It is, however,
to be emphasised that the truth conveyed by this biblical citation is a
matter of natural theology, not of revealed.

The *Consolation* does not read like crypto-paganism; that is to
say, like a manifesto of the inner pagan religion of a man who now
has nothing to lose and has torn the Christian façade aside. But nor
does it read like crypto-Christianity; that is to say, expressing
thoughts that are inwardly Christian but, by way of literary conceit,
adopt the outward dress of a Platonic metaphysic. The essential
shape of the *Consolation* is a Neoplatonic thesis that the imperfec-
tions of this world are allowed to facilitate the return of the soul to
its origin in God. But it is not very easy to specify themes admitted
by Boethius which are frankly inconceivable within a Christian
scheme of thought. There is one emphatic assertion of agreement
with the Platonic doctrine of the pre-existence of the soul: 'Platoni
vehementer assentior' (III pr. xii. 1; cf. m. xi) in the context of
Boethius' forgetfulness of his true destiny. But the transmigration of
souls merely becomes an innocuous description of the different
beasts that various types of wicked men come to resemble (IV pr. iii.
16–21, where the final clause 'uertatur in beluam' is quoted from
Cicero, *De Officiis* iii. 20, 82). Porphyry would have said the same.
But the point is that in this form a Christian vigilante would have

found nothing to object to. There are no Platonisms in the *Consolation* that one cannot also find somewhere in Augustine, notably in the Cassiciacum dialogues written between his conversion and his baptism where Augustine experiments with a juxtaposition of Christianity and Neoplatonism. It is possible to draw up a considerable list of anticipations in Augustine's writings, though none where one can establish a verbal echo or the probability of a literary dependence. Perhaps the closest analogies occur in Augustine's *Soliloquies* which, like Boethius, speak of the wings of the soul; of the need to know your own self to be immortal, simple and uncompounded; above all, of the embodied soul's need to recover gradually its sense of true identity by a process of 'remembering' (*Solil.* i. 14, 24; ii. 1, 1; 20, 34f.).

This is not to say that Augustine is a source for Boethius' Platonism, but rather that the early dialogues may have offered him a model that he was glad to accept.

Nineteenth-century scholars used to contrast the Christian author of the *Opuscula* with the pagan author of the *Consolation,* and wove fantastic hypotheses that they were two different authors. Obsessions blinded them to the paradox of Boethius' most serious works: there is even more Neoplatonism in the *Opuscula* (except for the very different fourth, *De Fide Catholica,* whose diction is nevertheless wholly Boethian) than in the *Consolation.* And the *Consolation,* though it contains nothing either specifically pagan or specifically Christian, is composed by a man who is throughout aware of Christianity, and is therefore adopting no philosophical positions that he has good reason to think incompatible with an Augustinian version of the faith.

Boethius' mind is retrospective, so far as its content is concerned, soaked in Plato and Aristotle and in their Neoplatonic exegetes of his own time. Yet the opuscula and dialectical treatises injected an essential ingredient into the formation of scholastic theology and philosophy, and the music and arithmetic long remained to educate medieval men in matters of which they would otherwise have been remarkably ignorant. If tragedy had never overtaken him and if he had never written the *Consolation of Philosophy*, charged from start to finish with intellectual and moral passion, no doubt his influence on posterity would have been greatly reduced, but it would still have been far from negligible. He set the feet of western men on the ladder that ascends from practical philosophy (morality, politics, economics) to contemplative questions of pure and abstract truth, transcending objects of sense-perception. He taught the Latin West to judge the validity of an inference, to be aware of the foundations of mathematics, and to envisage reason and revelation as related but very distinct ways of apprehending the mystery of God.

NELSON PIKE

The Predicate "Timeless"[†]

In *The Christian Faith*, Friedrich Schleiermacher says that God is eternal in the sense of 'timeless' ('*zeitlos*').[1] He says, too, that God is 'spaceless'.[2] Further, Schleiermacher says that timelessness and spacelessness are directly parallel concepts.[3] What one says about God *vis-à-vis* time when one says that He is timeless, is precisely what one says about God *vis-à-vis* space when one says that He is spaceless. I think it will be easier to grasp the details of the notion of timelessness if we look briefly at what Schleiermacher says in his text about the corresponding notion of spacelessness.

On Schleiermacher's account, the claim that God is spaceless involves two closely related ideas. First, God is not, as he says, 'space-filling'. This is to say that God has no spatial extension. He is not, e.g., three feet tall. Secondly, Schleiermacher says that there are no 'spatial contrasts' between God and other things. The point seems to be that God bears no special relation to other things. God is not, e.g., three feet to the left of Jones or four miles above the clouds.[4]

It is important to see that we have two distinct (though related) ideas working here. To say that God does not bear spatial contrasts with other things is not the same as to say that God is not 'space-filling'. A Euclidean point has spatial location but no spatial extension. If we could allow the possibility of there being a spatially extensionless thing (e.g., a mind or an idea), we might still insist that this thing has spatial location. (John Locke said that minds and ideas have location in space.) Thus, to say that a given thing lacks spatial extension does not not commit one to the view that that thing also lacks spatial location. A thing might have spatial location without having spatial extension. However, I think that these two ideas are logically connected in the other direction. With the possible exception of the universe considered as a single unit (which requires very special treatment) if something lacks spatial location, it also lacks spatial extension. Crudely speaking, to have spatial extension is to occupy more than one spatial position at a time. Thus, we might summarize the claim that God is spaceless in the statement: 'God lacks spatial location'. This formula would probably entail that God also lacks

---

† From *God and Timelessness* (Eugene, OR: Wipf and Stock, 2002) 6–16. Reprinted by permission.

1. *The Christian Faith*, numbered para. 52, sec. 1. English translation of the second edition, ed. by H. R. Mackintosh and J. S. Stewart, Edinburgh, Clark, 1956; pp. 203–5.

2. *Ibid.*, numbered para. 53, sec. 1, pp. 206–8.

3. *Ibid.*

4. *Ibid.*, numbered para. 53, sec. 2, p. 209.

spatial extension. For present purposes, however, I shall keep these two conceptual elements distinct. It will be to our advantage if we work with the expanded (though less elegant) version of the claim that God is spaceless.

What now of time? Following Schleiermacher's idea that space-lessness and timelessness are directly parallel concepts, we must divide the notion of timelessness into two closely related ideas. First, if God is timeless, He has no duration, i.e., He lacks temporal exten-sion. Schleiermacher introduces this thesis by contrasting the life of God with the life of the Universe of natural objects.[5] Let it be true that the universe has a history that is indefinitely extended both for-ward and backward in time. The history of the universe has no tem-poral limits. Still the world has a history. It is, as it were, 'spread out in time'. This is what is denied of God when it is said that His life lacks duration. It is not just that the life of God lacks temporal lim-its: the point is that it has no temporal spread at all. Secondly, if God is timeless, God also lacks temporal location. God did not exist *before* Columbus discovered America nor will He exist *after* the turn of the century. Schleiermacher says that with respect to God, there is no 'temporal opposition of before and after'.[6] This looks to be the temporal counterpart of the idea that the life of God lacks 'spatial contrasts'. As a general comment, Schleiermacher insists that God is 'utterly timeless'[7]—completely 'outside all contact with time'.[8] The point seems to be that God is not to be qualified by temporal predi-cates of any kind—neither time-extension predicates (such as, e.g., 'six years old') nor time-location predicates (such as, e.g., 'before Columbus').

Again, it is important to see that we have two distinct (though closely related) ideas operating here. Let us call the temporal coun-terpart of the Euclidean point a 'moment'. A moment has temporal location, but no temporal extension. Two p.m., 16 March 1822 might count as a moment. Now suppose that it makes sense to speak of a thing having momentary existence. Such a thing would have temporal location but no duration. Given this much, if we knew that a given thing lacked temporal extension, we could not conclude that it also lacked temporal location. Something might have location in time without having duration. However, as I suggested when work-ing with the elements of the notion of spacelessness, I think that the elements of timelessness are logically related in the other direction. With the possible exception of the universe considered as a whole, if something has temporal extension, it also has temporal position. In

5. *Ibid.*, numbered para. 52, secs. 1 and 2, pp. 204–5.
6. *Ibid.*
7. *Ibid.*
8. *Ibid.*, numbered para. 41, sec. 1, p. 154.

a manner of speaking, to have duration is, simply, to occupy a number of consecutive temporal positions. Thus, the claim that God is timeless might be compressed into the single statement: 'God lacks temporal location'. But for present purposes I shall keep these two ideas distinct. We shall get a better look into the interior of timelessness if we keep its ingredients as isolated as possible.

The claim that God is timeless in the sense just outlined is rich with tradition. Keeping its two conceptual elements distinct in our minds, let us look briefly at some of its more important medieval sources.

Concerning the thesis that the life of God lacks duration (or temporal extension), consider the following somewhat vague remark from Bk. XI, Ch. 13 of St. Augustine's *Confessions*.[9]

> Thy years do not come and go; while these years of ours do come and go, in order that they all may come. All Thy years stand together [and in one non-extended instant], for they stand still, nor are those going away cut off by those coming, for they do not pass away, but these years of ours shall all be when they are all no more. Thy years are but one day, and Thy day is not a daily recurrent, but today. Thy present day does not give place to tomorrow, nor, indeed, does it take the place of yesterday. Thy present day is eternity.

This same theme is developed in considerably more detail and with much greater clarity in Bk. V, sec. 6 of Boethius's *Consolation*. It is taken over from Boethius by St. Thomas in Pt. I, Q. X of the *Summa Theologica*. Boethius (anticipating Schleiermacher) introduced this thesis by contrasting the life of God with the life of the Universe. Grant that the Universe has limitless temporal spread. The life of God is to be distinguished from the life of the Universe in that the former involves no temporal extension at all.

Focus now on the idea that the life of God lacks temporal location as well as temporal extension. Perhaps the clearest and most emphatic expression of this thesis is to be found in the writings of St. Anselm. In Ch. XIX of the *Proslogium*, Anselm writes:[1]

> Thou wast not, then, yesterday, nor wilt thou be tomorrow; but yesterday and today and tomorrow thou art; or, rather, neither yesterday, nor today nor tomorrow thou art; but simply, thou art, outside all time. For yesterday and today and tomorrow have no existence, except in time; but thou, although nothing

---

9. This passage translated by V. J. Bourke, New York (*Fathers of the Church*), The Catholic University of America Press, 1953, pp. 342–3. The phrase in brackets is added by Bourke in an explanatory footnote.
1. This passage translated by Sidney Deane, *St. Anselm*, La Salle, Court, 1958, p. 25.

exists without thee, nevertheless dost not exist in space or time, but all things exist in thee.

Again, in Ch. XXII of the *Monologium* this same point is repeated:[2]

In no place or time, then, is this being properly said to exist, since it is contained by no other at all . . . [The Supreme Being has no place or time because] it has not taken to itself distinctions of place or time, neither here, nor there, nor anywhere, nor then, nor now, nor at any time; nor does it exist in terms of the fleeting present in which we live, nor has it existed, nor will it exist in terms of the past or future, since these are restricted to things finite and mutable, which it is not.

In both these passages Anselm insists that time-location predicates (as well as space-location predicates) are not to be used when characterizing God. God did not exist *before* the outbreak of civil war in America, nor will He exist after the coming election. It is never true to say that God exist*ed*, or that He *will* exist. But, further, Anselm also makes clear that God cannot be said to exist *now*. A being existing at the present moment, would be, as he says, 'contained' in time.[3]

Following Boethius, St. Thomas defines the term 'eternity' in the odd formula: 'The simultaneously-whole and perfect possession of indeterminable life.'[4] St. Thomas unfolds the implications of this definition in the following remark from the Pt. I, Q. X of the *Summa Theologica*:[5]

Two things are to be considered in time; time itself which is successive, and the *now* of time which is imperfect. Hence, the expression *simultaneously-whole* is used to remove the idea of time, and the word *perfect* is used to exclude the *now* of time.

Thomas here seems to be making the distinction made above between the notion of temporal extension (which involves the idea of succession) and the notion of temporal location, i.e., the idea of existing at a given moment—a given 'now of time'. The latter as well as the former is denied application to God in the claim that God is eternal. St. Thomas seems to be committed to the view that with respect to any given location in time (before Columbus discovered America, after the turn of the century, right now, i.e., at the present moment) God cannot be said to exist at that time.

---

2. *Ibid.*, p. 81. (In the first section of Ch. 7, I cite and discuss those portions of this passage that I have here omitted.)

3. *Monologium*, Ch. XXIII, Deane, p. 83.

4. See *Consolation*, Bk. V, sec. 6, 11. 9–11. *Boethius*, translated by H. F. Stewart and E. K. Rand, Cambridge, Harvard University Press, 1962, p. 401. Anselm also used this formula. See *Monologium*, Ch. XXIV, Deane, p. 83.

5. Article 1, reply to objection 5. This passage taken from *The Basic Writings of St. Thomas*, ed. A. C. Pegis, New York, Random House, 1945, p. 75.

As regards Boethius's position on the question of God's location in time, the matter is a little less clear than it is in the case of Anselm and St. Thomas. Boethius clearly says that God cannot be located either *before* or *after* a given time or event, but there is some obscurity in his text as to whether God can be located in the temporal *present*. I should like to conclude *** with a brief examination of the sources of this obscurity. I think there is something important to be learned from a study of Boethius's remarks on this topic.

In Pt. V of the *Consolation*, Boethius formulates two quite different theses using two Latin locutions, both of which are generally translated into English with the help of the single term 'present'. First, Boethius says that temporal objects and events are *present* to God in the sense that he 'sees'[6] or 'beholds'[7] them, i.e., in the sense that He is directly aware of them. He says that the Supreme Being has ' . . . an infinity of movable time present (*praesentam*) to it'.[8] I doubt that Boethius would regard this claim as relevant to the topic we are now discussing. I think he intended that it carry no implications as regards God's temporal qualities or lack thereof. Let y be a temporal object, circumstance or event and let x be some (knowing) individual who is aware of y. x might exist before y or after y (allowing the logical possibility of directly observing past or future events as in a crystal ball) and, of course, x and y might exist simultaneously. Given only that x is aware of y, one would not conclude that x exists before y, one would not conclude that x exists after y; and one would not conclude that x and y exist simultaneously. But further (and this is the point of real importance), given only that x is aware of y, one might be able to hold that x and y bear no temporal relation to one another at all. We here need a distinction between the *awareness of time* (let this phrase cover the awareness of temporal objects and events as well as the awareness of the passage of time) and the *time of awareness* (i.e., the temporal position of the awareness itself or the individual who is aware). Boethius says that God is directly aware of time and its contents, i.e., that time and its contents are present to God. But I don't think he means for us to conclude that God's awareness (or God Himself) has location in time. I think Boethius is here counting on us to make the distinction between the awareness of time and the time of awareness. (Kant made use of this distinction in the *First Critique* when discussing the relation between the Transcendental Ego and spatio-temporal phenomena.) ***

Secondly, there are places in Boethius's texts in which he says that God 'has always an eternal and present (*praesentarius*) state'.[9] God

---

6. *Consolation*, II. 140–60. Stewart and Rand translation, p. 409.
7. *Ibid.*, 1. 176, p. 411.
8. *Ibid.*, Bk. V. sec. 6, II. 32–4, p. 401.
9. *Ibid.*, II. 61–2, p. 403.

exists in the 'eternal-present'. Augustine called this 'ever-present eternity' and the 'everlasting present'.[1] This does not seem to be a claim about God's *awareness* of temporal objects. It seems to be a comment about God's metaphysical (as opposed to epistemological) relation to time and the objects it contains. Further, this thesis is very difficult to grasp. I think that there are at least two ways in which it might be understood.

It might be that what Boethius had in mind when he said that God exists in the 'eternal-present' is that given a position at any one moment in time, one could correctly assert that God exists *now* (i.e., at this moment). This would be to deny St. Thomas's claim that God does not exist in the 'now of time'. However, if we were to accept this reading of the passages in question I think they would then conflict openly with the idea that the life of God lacks duration. If at each moment between three o'clock and four o'clock one could say, truly, that God exists *now* (i.e., at this moment), it would then follow that God exists at each moment between three o'clock and four o'clock. This would entail that the life of God *has* duration; for what is it to have duration if it is not to exist at each moment in a temporally extended interval?

On the other hand, it might be that what Boethius meant to be affirming in the passages in which he said that God exists in the 'eternal-present' is not that God exists at each moment in time, but rather that God exists in a special sense of 'exists' (or that God possesses a special mode of existence) that is unique to individuals having no location in time. Let me explain this second possibility a little further.[2]

We say that there exists a prime number between 5 and 9. Some contemporary philosophers have suggested the following account of the term 'exists' as it occurs in this statement. Suppose that at three o'clock I said: 'There exists a prime number between 5 and 9.' What I said was true. But it does not follow that at four o'clock the statement: 'There exist*ed* a prime number between 5 and 9' could have been uttered truly; nor does it follow that at two o'clock the statement: 'There *will* exist a prime number between 5 and 9' could have been uttered truly. There is no use for the locutions 'exist*ed*' or '*will* exist' when talking about numbers. It follows (on this account) that had I said at three o'clock that there exists a prime number between 5 and 9 *now* (meaning *at this moment*), my remark would have been incorrect. Had the prime existed at three o'clock (as would have been

---

1. *Confessions*, Tr. V. J. Bourke, Bk. XI, Ch. 13 (fifth paragraph) and Ch. 11 (second paragraph).
2. For what follows in the next three paragraphs, I am indebted to suggestions made by William Kneale in his article 'Time and Eternity in Theology', *Proceedings of the Aristotelian Society*, 1961, especially sec. III; and to G. E. L. Owen in his article, 'Plato and Parmenides on the 'Timeless Present', *Monist*, 1966.

affirmed had I said at that time that it exists *now*), it would follow by the ordinary meaning of tensed phrases, that at two o'clock the future tense existential claim could have been made correctly and at four o'clock the past tense existential claim could have been made correctly. The conclusion is that there is a sense of 'exists' (present tense) that does not bear the usual logical relations to 'existed' (past tense) and 'will exist' (future tense). To affirm of something that it exists in this special sense of 'exists' is not to affirm that the thing in question exists in the temporal present.

Now let's suppose that Boethius was thinking of God as existing in this a-temporal sense of 'exists' (or in this a-temporal mode of existence). He might well have used terms usually reserved for marking the temporal present as ways of underscoring the idea that the sense of 'exists' involved in 'God exists' is a sense of this term that does not bear the usual logical relations to sentences utilizing past and future tenses of this term. The prime number between 5 and 9 might be characterized as 'eternally present' or as existing in an 'eternal now' meaning that whenever uttered, the claim that it *exists* (present tense) is correct, but that whenever uttered, the claim that it exist*ed* (past tense) or *will* exist (future tense) is incorrect. The phrase 'simultaneously-whole' seems to allow this sort of interpretation too. If taken literally, 'God is simultaneously-whole' would appear to mean that the life of God has temporal compactness—it occurs *all at once*. (Boethius actually says this in some places.) It would then tend to suggest that God has a single location—that He is a momentary being. But I don't think that we must read the text in this way. Boethius may have employed the phrase 'simultaneously-whole' as a way of emphasizing the idea that God exists in a sense of 'exists' that is incompatible with the concept of temporal spread. The prime number between 5 and 9 might be said to be 'simultaneously-whole' in the sense that it has no history—there are no earlier or later *parts* of its existence. Of course, if the temporal terms used by Boethius to characterize God can be interpreted as having this sort of import, then the passages in which Boethius says that God exists in the 'eternal-present', that God is 'simultaneously-whole', etc., need not be understood as assigning God location in the 'now of time'. To be sure, these passages contain locutions that suggest that God has temporal location, but on the interpretation we are now considering these locutions are being used as figurative ways of underscoring certain aspects of the idea that God exists in an a-temporal sense of the word 'exists'.

I shall not claim categorically that the second of the interpretations just suggested is the right way of understanding the passages in which Boethius says that God exists in the 'eternal-present'. I think, however, that there are at least two reasons for thinking that this is so. In the first place, it seems unlikely that a theologian of the stature of Boethius would have failed to detect the rather obvious logical conflict that would have resulted had he claimed both that the life of God lacks duration and that God is temporally present at each moment in time. The first interpretation of these passages thus seems initially implausible. It would require that we accuse Boethius of what would appear to be a relatively simple logical error regarding the conceptual connection between existing at a number of consecutive temporal locations and having duration. Secondly, Boethius explicitly says that the concept of eternity he is employing in his text is one that he borrowed from Plato.[3] Now, to be sure, Plato's remarks on the topic of eternity are not paradigms of precision and clarity, but I think that it is worth noting that in the *Timaeus* (at least), Plato says that if something is eternal, one cannot say that it *was* or that it *will be*, but only that it *is*. He writes:[4]

> . . . 'was' and 'will be' are created species of time which we in our carelessness mistakenly apply to eternal being. For we say that it was, is, and will be; but, in truth, 'is' applies to it, while 'was' and 'will be' are properly said of becoming in time. They are motions, but that which is immovably the same for ever cannot become older or younger in time.

As was suggested above, if something *is*, but is such that it is never correct to say that it *was*, or that it *will be*, it *is* in a sense of '*is*' that does not mean 'is now'. If something *is now*, then it *is* in a sense of '*is*' for which there will be times when it is correct to say that it *was* and that it *will be*. The object in question must exist in an a-temporal sense of 'exists'.

Schleiermacher said that God is eternal in the sense of timeless, i.e., that the life of God lacks temporal position and temporal extension. St. Thomas also held this view and I think that a sympathetic interpretation of the passages referred to above from Boethius's *Consolation* would attribute this position to him as well. In the *Confessions*, St. Augustine said that God lacks temporal extension and that He exists in 'ever-present eternity'. I am inclined to interpret these remarks as I interpreted similar remarks of Boethius above. Lastly, Anselm emphasized that God lacks temporal location. Considerations of consistency would commit him to the idea that God also lacks temporal extension. That God is timeless in the sense outlined in the fourth paragraph of this chapter would thus appear to be a doctrine that has been endorsed by a number of important figures in the history of Christian theology.

---

3. *Consolation*, I. 36, Stewart and Rand translation, p. 401. I am indebted to Mrs. Marilyn McCord Adams for pointing out the importance of this reference to Plato.
4. *Timaeus*, 37E6–38A6. This passage translated by William Kneale, 'Time and Eternity in Theology', pp. 92–3.

WILLIAM BARK

Theodoric vs. Boethius: Vindication and Apology[†]

The background of the tragedy which cut short the brilliant career of Anicius Manlius Severinus Boethius has always remained obscure and puzzling. This talented scion of one of the noblest of Roman families rose to positions of the greatest eminence under Theodoric the Ostrogoth. In 522 his two young sons shared the consulship and Boethius pronounced the panegyric in praise of the king. Later in the year he was signally honored by appointment as Master of the Offices. Then disaster struck. Albinus the consular was accused of treason; Boethius defended him, only to be himself accused, arrested, and, in 524 or 525, executed.[1] The obvious sources of information concerning the background of the case are meager. The best one, Boethius' tantalizing defense written in prison, hints vaguely but tells little.[2] He was charged with treason along with Albinus and also with sacrilege, whereas in reality, he maintains, he was defending the whole senate against the accusation of treason.[3] Although his brief statement, that he was censured for obstructing evidence concerning the senate's guilt, has led to much speculation, the vitally important theological evidence has received insufficient attention.[4] It now seems possible that this heretofore neglected source of information may clear up the mystery of Boethius' downfall, as it is the purpose of this paper to show.

[†] From *The American Historical Review* 49.3 (April 1944): 410–26. Reprinted by permission of the American Historical Association.

1. For an eloquent account of the whole case stated at some length see Thomas Hodgkin, *Italy and Her Invaders* (2d ed., Oxford, 1896), III, 481–98. In the matter of dating, Charles H. Coster, *The Indicium Quinquevirale* (Cambridge, 1935), passed over Hermann Usener's *Anecdoton Holderi* and consequently went astray. See M. L. W. Laistner's review, *Am. Hist. Rev.*, XIII, 284–85.

2. *Philosophiae Consolatio*, I. iv. 142–58, in the edition of Edward K. Rand and Hugh F. Stewart in the Loeb series (New York, 1918). All references to the works of Boethius are to this edition. The evidence of Agnellus' *Liber Pontificalis Ecclesiae Ravennatis*, the *Liber Pontificalis*, the *Anonymus Valesianus*, Procopius, and Cassiodorus has been recently reexamined by Coster, particularly pp. 43–63 and notes. Boethius's own account of what took place, to which he refers in his defense (*Phil. Consol.*, I. iv. 86–88), regrettably has never come to light.

3. *Ibid.*, I. iv. 48–154.

4. Contributions to the subject are indeed assuming mountainous proportions. It is not my intention in this brief article to review the older writers, who were altogether or largely unaware of the true importance of the theological side of the affair. Coster has gone over the arguments of such writers as Cessi, Sundwall, Hartmann, and Bury exhaustively. For other views see Viktor Schurr, *Die Trinitätslehre des Boethius im Lichte der "skythischen Kontroversen"* (Paderborn, 1935). Note also E. K. Rand's chapter on Boethius in *Founders of the Middle Ages* (Cambridge, 1928) and his briefer references in *The Building of Eternal Rome* (Cambridge, 1943), especially pp. 237–39. See also his review of Schurr's book, *Speculum*, XI (1936), 153–56. The work of H. F. Stewart, *Boethius, an Essay* (Edinburgh and London, 1891), has now been superseded in many respects by later contributions.

It has always been recognized that the history of the Patristic Age cannot be understood apart from the theological controversies which raged continuously for centuries and eventually lead to a separation of the churches of East and West.[5] In the fourth, fifth, and sixth centuries of the Christian era doctrinal disputes were matters of the greatest interest and importance not merely to theologians but even to the man in the street. And the fate of many a ruler was sharply influenced by his theological views. In the Greek East, where the passion for subtle distinctions of dogma was particularly strong, the most violent battles were waged over the abstruse but highly significant subjects of the Trinity and the person and nature of Christ.

In the fifth century there arose two Christological heresies which threw the whole Orient into turmoil, eventually drew in even the bishop of Rome, and in the next century threatened Justinian's entire imperial policy. The heresiarch Nestorius, archbishop of Constantinople, agreed with the orthodox dogma in confessing two natures in Jesus Christ but taught that he also had two persons. Monophysitism, which was introduced in the Eastern capital by the archimandrite Eutyches, taught correctly that Christ had just one person but then heretically insisted that he had only one nature. The Monophysites were especially strong in Alexandria, whence Eutyches' chief support had come, but they won adherents everywhere and finally threatened to disrupt dangerously the unity of the East, calling all who opposed them Nestorians and rejecting with special violence the oecumenical Council of Chalcedon, which they regarded as too sympathetic to the Nestorians. In a well-meant effort to restore internal peace, the Emperor Zeno along with Acacius, the Patriarch of Constantinople, in 482 gave his support to a compromise known as the Henoticon, which it was hoped would reconcile the dissident factions.

The Henoticon miscarried. Not only did it fail to establish unity in the East, but, by passing over the decrees of Chalcedon in silence, it also gave affront to the papacy. As a consequence Felix III excommunicated Acacius, thus precipitating the Acacian schism (484–519). This meant that when the successors of Zeno, Anastasius I (491–518), Justin I (518–27), and the famous nephew of the latter, Justinian (527–65), attempted to bring the West back into their

---

5. For a full and scholarly treatment of the events quickly sketched in the following paragraphs the reader is referred to these standard works: Hefele-Leclercq, *Histoire des conciles*, II (Paris, 1908); Erich Caspar, *Geschichte des Papsttums von den Anfängen bis zur Höhe der Weltherrschaft* (2 vols., Tübingen, 1930–33); Louis Duchesne, *L'histoire ancienne de l'église*, III (Paris, 1911), and *L'église au VIe siècle* (Paris, 1925); Adolf von Harnack, *Lehrbuch der Dogmengeschichte*, II–III (Freiburg i.B., 1888, 1890).

orbit, they had first to come to an agreement with Rome. No less important of course was the restoration of ecclesiastical harmony in the Orient. The diplomacy of Justinian, who directed the Byzantine foreign policy long before he became emperor, is particularly important for the present study. Justinian at last found in the theological formula of a group of Latin-speaking monks residing in Scythia Minor what he considered a solution to his problem. These Scythian monks, who defended their position with violence and objurgation, instigated the Theopaschite controversy (thus named because the Scythian formula maintained that "one of the Trinity suffered in the flesh"), and with this dispute and the accompanying imperial diplomacy Boethius was closely connected, as will appear.

The way to an understanding of Boethius' position in respect of Byzantine policy and the reasons for his fall from Theodoric's grace was prepared by the discovery that he was an accomplished theologian as well as a philosopher, scientist, and statesman.[6] The acceptance of the theological tractates as authentic made certain very significant conclusions inevitable. Before the Cassiodorus fragment came to light, it had been easy to believe that a pagan Boethius could look on unmoved while orthodox emperors tried to wrest Italy from the Arian Theodoric. But that discovery showed the Boethius who served Theodoric as Master of Offices also serving the cause of orthodoxy in Rome, which altered the situation considerably.

In the sixth century political affairs were often inseparably bound up with matters of religion, and it has been recognized for some time that the arraignment of Boethius, the Catholic theologian, had theological as well as political aspects.[7] But precisely how Boethius was linked with the confused Roman-Byzantine negotiations has not been clear. Now, however, Father Schurr, by means of his intensive study of Boethius' Trinitarian doctrine, has demonstrated that Boethius took an active interest in doctrinal disputes of the greatest political importance. Apparently Boethius started out innocently

---

6. Recognition of this exceedingly important fact began in 1877 with Hermann Usener's publication of the *Anecdoton Holderi*, a fragment of Cassiodorus discovered by Alfred Holder, which stated that Boethius wrote a treatise on the Trinity, some doctrinal tractates, and a treatise against Nestorius. Coster's neglect of this work led him to state, in note 214, "It is quite possible that Boethius was not in fact the author of many of the theological works which have been attributed to him." This view is no longer tenable. Professor E. K. Rand has long upheld the authenticity of the theological works, even the disputed fourth tractate, which he once questioned. In Rand's acceptance of all five treatises H. F. Stewart concurs; see their discussion in the introduction of their edition, pp. xi and 52. See also Rand, *Founders*, pp. 149–57, 315, n. 28, and Rand, *Building of Eternal Rome*, p. 239, n. 104. Father Schurr accepts four of the tractates as unquestionably genuine but still rejects Tr. IV (Schurr, pp. 6–9). *Cf.* Rand's comment, *Speculum*, XI, 153–54. In any case the status of Tr. IV does not alter the fact that Boethius was a distinguished theologian.

7. Rand, *Founders*, pp. 322–23, n. 75.

enough in 512, intervening in a matter which at the time appeared to have no vast significance. In that year certain bishops of the Eastern European provinces of the Byzantine Empire appealed to Pope Symmachus. Caught between Eutychians and Nestorians, they asked for the pope's advice and presented their Christological formula, *et ex et in duabus naturis*, as a safe guide to orthodoxy.[8] The pope gave the bishops only the theologically sound but unsympathetic advice that they should renounce communion with the successors of the heretical Acacius of Constantinople, even if it meant martyrdom.[9] Boethius treated the Easterners more kindly; after careful study of their theology, he concluded that they pointed the way to a clear understanding of the Christological problem at issue.[1] In his *Liber contra Eutychen et Nestorium*, one of the first notable contributions to scholastic studies, he brilliantly defended their position, thus for the first time engaging in a dispute in which the Scythian monks figured.[2]

Before Boethius was to return to the subject of theology, certain important developments, including and following the settlement of the Acacian schism, were to take place. Guided by his astute nephew Justinian, Justin I succeeded in healing the breach where this predecessor, Anastasius I, had failed. Late in March, 519, the delegates of Pope Hormisdas, come to settle the long dispute, were led into Constantinople by Justinian and Vitalian, the Master of Soldiers.[3] The presence of Justinian is noteworthy, for from the first he devoted himself to the ecclesiastical problems facing the empire he was to rule, even engaging actively in doctrinal controversy. His chief purpose was to put an end to the dangerous theological dissension which rent the empire, since there could be no thought of political unification until the Eastern church had made its peace with Rome.[4] And at the same

8. Schurr, pp. 108, 124–27. The bishops' letter is no. 12 in Thiel, and Symmachus' answer is no. 13. The Eastern provinces included Scythia, where the famous Scythian monks must already have become active. Boethius' course at this time could not have been thought dangerous by Theodoric, if indeed the king was aware of it at all.

9. For the background see Schurr, pp. 108–36, and Peter Charanis, *Church and State in the Later Roman Empire: The Religious Policy of Anastasius the First, 491–518* (Madison, 1939), pp. 13–50.

1. As he indicates in the preface of Tr. V.

2. Note that this tractate, No. V, was chronologically the earliest, Schurr, p. 127. For Boethius as the first of the scholastics, see Rand, *Founders*, pp. 150, 152, 155–56.

3. *Collectio Avellana*, no. 167, in *Corpus Scriptorum Ecclesiasticorum Latinorum* 35, edited by Otto Günther; hereafter cited as *Col. Avel.* See also Henricus de Noris, *Dissertatio I. In Historiam Controversiae de Uno ex Trinitate Passo*, in *Opera Omnia* (Verona, 1729), III, 790–91; hereafter cited as de Noris, *Dis. I.* Vitalian had tried in vain to force Anastasius I to come to an understanding with the pope (Schurr, pp. 127–36, and Charanis, pp. 51–71). Vitalian, who was a Goth, came from Scythia and was related to Leontius, one of the Scythian monks (*Col. Avel.*, p. 216).

4. See Pierre Batiffol, "L'empereur Justinien et le siège apostolique," *Recherches de Science Religieuse*, XXVI (Paris, 1916), 193–264, and also Friedrich Loofs, *Leontius von Byzanz und die gleichnamigen Schriftsteller der griechischen Kirche. Erstes Buch: Das Leben und die polemischen Werke des Leontius von Byzanz.* In *Texte und Untersuchungen zur Geschichte der altchristlichen Literatur.* Band III, Hefte I und 2 (Leipzig, 1887), pp. 304, 315–16.

time some compromise satisfactory to the dissident religious groups in the Orient, particularly the large body friendly to Monophysitism, had to be found. In March, 519, then, Justinian looked hopefully forward to the solution of some of these problems in the conclusion of the Acacian schism and the winning of papal approval.

It is at this point that the Scythian monks, led by John Maxentius, a disputant as ardent as he was skillful, appear upon the scene. Our best source, though a prejudiced one, is the deacon Dioscorus, a member of the papal delegation and an intimate and influential friend of Pope Hormisdas.[5] Of Maxentius and the other monks Dioscorus had nothing good to say; he claimed indeed that they made trouble for all concerned—the papal representatives, the emperor, the patriarch, their patron Vitalian, and Justinian—and held up the work of peacemaking. They particularly desired that their Theopaschite formula, *unus ex trinitate passus carne*, be accepted, and when rebuffed, they fled to Rome, hoping to win the approval of the pope himself for their views.[6]

The attitude of Justinian during the negotiations which began in March is especially interesting. As late as the end of June, 519, he agreed with the papal legates in regarding the monks as an obstacle to the settlement of the Acacian schism.[7] But his sentiments had changed only a few days later and he then and thereafter adopted a very friendly tone in referring to the monks. In a letter to Hormisdas, Justinian explained his new position in language carefully veiled but quite intelligible.[8] A great dispute had arisen in the East and apparently Justinian had now become convinced that the peace of the church could best be salvaged through the Scythian formula.[9] Hence he urged Hormisdas to give the monks the approval which had been denied them by the papal delegates in the East. What had happened there is clear enough. Constantinople was willing to make peace at the expense of Acacius and the adherents of the Henoticon, but the party of Monophysite sympathies proved too strong. Rome insisted upon the recognition of Chalcedon, but the Monophysite party was willing to accept the decrees of that council only if they were properly interpreted, *i.e.*, against Nestorianism. Since the Scythians offered a solution which would make Chalcedon acceptable to the

---

5. For his private reports see the *Col. Avel.*

6. *Ibid.*, no. 216, dated June 29, 519. See also nos. 217, 224, and de Noris, *Dis. I*, pp. 798–99. The legates refused even to receive the *Libellus fidei*, which Maxentius wrote in behalf of his brothers. Hormisdas accepted it, however, and it was also presented to the bishops, church, and Senate in Rome.

7. As he shows in a severely critical letter to Hormisdas, which Günther dates June 29, 519, *Col. Avel.*, no. 187.

8. *Ibid.*, no. 191. See Schurr's comments, pp. 157–58, n. 184.

9. And that is of course the policy he adopted and put into effect at the fifth oecumenical council in 553. See also Loofs, pp. 315–16, and Schurr, pp. 152–54.

East, their formula was exactly what Justinian needed. No wonder he urged the pope to treat the monks well.[1]

The pope remained aloof, however, and the monks unsatisfied, though not silent. They actually—and this, too, is significant—presented their case both to the people and to the senate in Rome, much to the pope's annoyance.[2] Moreover, while still waiting for papal approval they wrote to the African bishops exiled in Sardinia and were well received by them.[3] With their departure from Rome the Scythian monks as a group disappear from history, but their position was staunchly upheld by the work both of their leader, John Maxentius, and of their famous countryman, Dionysius Exiguus, who at the time of the controversy had long lived in Rome.

The Scythian Theopaschite formula has a direct bearing upon the affairs of Boethius, for Father Schurr has proved that the Patrician's first and second theological tractates were called forth by the controversy over that formula. These treatises were written in 523, the year before Boethius was imprisoned.[4] Does this mean that he actively entered into the most important dispute of the time? Not at all, according to Father Schurr. Boethius' interest was purely scientific and speculative. That is, his philosophical curiosity was aroused when the Theopaschite question became an issue in Rome, and he at that time occupied himself with the Trinitarian problem which it presented.[5] In Father Schurr's opinion, then, Boethius was stirred to write Tr. I and II by the Theopaschite formula, but he wrote only for his own satisfaction. If this view is correct, Boethius can by no

---

1. See the very revealing letters of Dioscorus and Justinian, *Col. Avel.*, nos. 224 and 196. For the efficacy of the Scythian formula against the Nestorian sympathies of Chalcedon, see de Noris, *Dis. I*, pp. 791–810; Harnack, *Dogmengeschichte*, II, 382; G. Krüger, "Theopaschiten," *Realencyklopädie für protestantische Theologie und Kirche*, XIX, 659. The formula had been approved not only by such orthodox leaders as Proclus and Cyril of Alexandria but also, in a heretical sense, by Peter the Fuller, a Monophysite theologian, and it had been included in the Henoticon. Justinian, whose aim was utilitarian, soon saw that he could make good use of the formula. Catholics, like the Scythians, could accept the proposition as orthodox, Monophysites could interpret it as Peter the Fuller had, and moderates could remember its inclusion in Zeno's Henoticon. Justinian regarded it only as a means to an end.

2. *Col. Avel.*, no. 231, and John Maxentius, *Responsio adversus Hormisdae epistulam*, *Acta Conciliorum Oecumenicorum*, Tome IV, vol. 2, pp. 54–55; the *Acta* are hereafter cited as ACO. Schurr, pp. 159–01, is of the opinion that the monks remained in Rome until September, 520.

3. *Ep.* 16 and 17, PL, LXV, 442–93. See also H. de Noris, *Historia Pelagiana et dissertatio de synodo V oecumenico* (Padua, 1673), p. 306.

4. Schurr, pp. 136–225. For a summary, see pp. 224–25. It is also shown (pp. 97–104) that Tr. II preceded Tr. I.

5. Schurr, pp. 217–21. Note particularly on p. 221: "Wir sagen also: Nicht eigentlich aus Parteitheologie schrieb Boethius seine trinitarischen Werkchen, sondern als diese in die kirchenpolitisch interessierten Senatorenkreise hineingetragen ward, wurde sie ihm zur *Anregung* mehr aus wissenschaftlichem Selbstzweck auf spekulative und disziplinierte Art über die Trinität zu forschen." He adds that we cannot infer that Boethius was friendly to the Scythians, but concludes, "immerhin legt unser Ergebnis nahe, dass er ähnlich wie Vitalian und Justinian zur theopaschitischen Formel stand."

means be regarded as an active disputant or even as a friendly partisan of the Scythian position.[6]

For a number of reasons Father Schurr's view may be regarded as excessively cautious. Justinian's plan for, first, theological and then political unification had many ramifications, and there is evidence that Boethius had something to do with certain aspects of this plan. At this point, however, the background must be described a little more fully. It was suggested above that Justinian adopted the Scythian Theopaschite formula because it purged Chalcedon of Nestorianism and thus pacified the influential group of anti-Nestorian and pro-Monophysite Easterners. If only the West could be persuaded to accept the Scythian position also, ecclesiastical harmony was assured. The leading opponent of Nestorianism in the fifth century had been Cyril of Alexandria, a bishop whose relations with Rome had been cordial and whose name in the sixth century still evoked the greatest reverence. It is not surprising then that the Scythians requested Dionysius Exiguus, their countryman, to translate several of the respectable Cyril's anti-Nestorian works into Latin, hoping thus to win sympathy and prestige for their cause.[7] It was for the same practical purpose that an anonymous Scythian scholar made the great anti-Pelagian, anti-Nestorian, and pro-Cyrillan compilation known as the *Collectio Palatina*.[8]

The evidence of the Palatine Collection has importance for the case of Boethius. Eduard Schwartz pointed out twenty years ago that the compilation was prepared for use in the disputes of Justinian's time and that the anonymous collector was closely associated with a certain John, bishop of Tomi in Scythia. Schwartz conjectured that John of Tomi was John Maxentius.[9] Additional evidence in the form of a brief *instructio* by John of Tomi makes it all but a certainty that John Maxentius and John of Tomi were the same man.[1] There can be

---

6. All Father Schurr believed he could say definitely was that Boethius' position in respect of the Theopaschite formula was similar to that of Vitalian and Justinian (p. 221). I imagine that he meant that Boethius regarded the formula as a means of achieving church unity, though I find the remark rather baffling. If Boethius wrote merely out of philosophical interest, as Schurr says, on what ground is an attitude similar to that of Vitalian and Justinian to be attributed to him?

7. Schurr, p. 152.

8. Edited by Eduard Schwartz, *ACO* I, 5, pars prior (Berlin and Leipzig, 1924–25). The anti-Pelagian portion was prepared by Marius Mercator, a disciple of St. Augustine. The rest of the collection, about two thirds of the whole, consists of translations from Greek to Latin.

9. For Schwartz's discussion see *ACO* I, 5, first preface and his article, "Die sogenannten Gegenanathematismen des Nestorius," *Sitzung. d. Bay. Akad. zu München,* hist.-phil. Klasse, (1922).

1. The *instructio* was discovered and published by Dom Morin, "Le témoignage perdu de Jean évêque de Tomi sur les hérésies de Nestorius et d'Eutychès," *Journal of Theological Studies,* VII (1906), 74–77. In my article "John Maxentius and the Collectio Palatina," *Harvard Theological Review,* XXXVI (1943), 93–107, I present the case for the identity of John Maxentius and John of Tomi.

no question that the purpose of the Palatine Collection was to win Roman support for the Scythian theology. By including the anti-Pelagian works of St. Augustine's disciple, Marius Mercator, the compiler probably hoped to make his own orthodoxy all the clearer to Western readers. At the end of the extant portion of the original collection the Scythian scholar provides the interesting information that both Nestorians and Eutychians by their wiles were deceiving the ignorant. He himself feared that because of his anti-Nestorianism he would be called a Eutychian by the Nestorians. He appealed, therefore, to Maxentius' *instructio* which simply and clearly defined both Nestorianism and Eutychianism.[2]

That John Maxentius and Boethius were interested in the same theological problems Father Schurr has amply proved, but no one hitherto has established any closer contact between the two.[3] The *instructio* found under the name of John of Tomi strongly suggests, however, that Maxentius relied on the arguments of Boethius as presented in Tr. V.[4] The most striking similarities are indicated below.

The chief purpose of the formula *unus ex trinitate passus carne*, first offered by the Scythians in 519, was to protect Christ's divinity by allowing for his suffering as a human, *i.e.*, in his passible nature. In his *Liber contra Eutychen et Nestorium*, written in 512, Boethius gave strong dialectical support to the orthodox Scythian position in defense of the divine nature, showing that what is immutable and impassible, *i.e.*, the Godhead, cannot be subjected to suffering and death.[5] Then in 520 or a little later John Maxentius pointed out that the Eutychians were guilty of precisely this error.[6]

The impressive similarity of the two theologians' language and argument may be made still clearer by comparing their remarks on

2. ACO I, 5, pp. 180–81. There is a gap in the collection at this point and the *instructio* is missing. Schwartz was not aware that Dom Morin had found it.

3. Maxentius was concerned not only with the later Scythian controversy but also the first, as shown by Schurr (pp. 142–43). Note also Maxentius' and Boethius' common interest in the problem of numbers in the Godhead (Schurr, pp. 211–14).

4. It will be remembered that the earlier and later controversies were closely related. It was because Christ subsists not only *ex* but also *in duabus naturis* that the Scythians insisted upon the later formula *unus ex trinitate passus carne*.

5. Note Boethius' discussion at the beginning of the sixth book of Tr. V, particularly II. 5–15. In II. 8–15 he says: "Sed si diuinitas in humanitatem translata est, factum est, quod credi nefas est, ut humanitate inmutabili substantia permanente diuinitas uerteretur et quod passibile atque mutabile naturaliter exsisteret, id inmutabile permaneret, quod uero inmutabile atque inpassibile naturaliter creditur, id in rem mutabilem uerteretur. Hoc igitur fieri nulla ratione contingit."

6. In making these comparisons differences of expression must be allowed for. Boethius wrote a philosophical treatise, while Maxentius provided in simple language for the needs of the layman. For Maxentius' indictment of the Eutychians see Morin, p. 76, 11. 24–30: "dum enim timet ne si duas in xpo confitetur naturas quartam introducat in trinitate personam, inpia confusione ipsum dei filium a deitatis suae natura pronuntiat demutatum ita ut inconuertibilem dicat & passionibus subdat immortalemque morti subiciat & eum qui non cecidit (nec enim fas erat deum in sua diuinitate posse occidi) resurrexisse contendat." Boethius disposed of the Eutychian fear that a fourth person might be added to the Trinity in Tr. V. vii. 46–56.

the Eutychian view of Christ's nature. Maxentius in his definition explains that there are two groups of the heretics.[7] Some believe Christ assumed his nature whence he wished, not from the flesh of the Virgin Mary (of our nature, that is), but yet passible, while others think he had a nature coeternal with heavenly and spiritual beings and hold that he passed through the womb of Mary as water through a reed, assuming no flesh from her. Nevertheless, all the Eutychians assert that the word and the flesh are of one nature by a wicked mixture and confusion.[8] Boethius, in considering all conceivable Eutychian views as to the source of Christ's body, includes these two, which he shows to be untenable.[9] Boethius demonstrated why it was foolish to say Christ did not take his body from Mary. In effect he declared that if Eutyches believed this, that, or the other, he was in error. John briefly noted that some Eutychians actually did believe this, while others believed that, which was enough for a definition designed for plain people.

One more point in Tr. V requires attention. Toward the close of the seventh chapter Boethius gives a masterful summary of the orthodox position on the Christological and Trinitarian question.[1] In the course of this penetrating analysis he resolves succinctly and definitely the problem that had been so confused by both Nestorians and Monophysites, explaining that Christ, who is one of the Trinity, perfect man and God, suffered in the manhood.[2] This is nothing less than the Scythian contention that one member of the Trinity suffered in the flesh! Boethius does not actually say, *unus ex trinitate passus carne*. It is nevertheless highly significant that he should have stated so cogently the Scythian view in a passage written in 512 in defense of the first formula. It was only a few years later, in 519, that the monks appeared in Constantinople, brandishing their Theopaschite formula like a sword before the startled eyes of the papal delegation.

The significance of this evidence now begins to appear. Boethius was an enthusiastic advocate of orthodoxy, following closely the theological developments of his day. In 512 he attended the assembly at

7. It was only later that Monophysitism split up into many sects.
8. Morin, p. 76, II, 30–37: "Alii autem eiusdem perfidiae sectatores dicunt. quod filius dei non de Mariae uirginis carne hoc est nostrae naturae sed passibilem unde uoluit sibi adsumpsit, ali de caelestibus eum & spiritalibus coaeternam habuisse existimant. ac per uterum Mariae uirginis ueluti aquam per fistualam nihil ex ea carnis adsumens transisse contendunt omnes tamen hi uerbum & carnem unius esse naturae impia permixtione confusioneque confirmant."
9. Tr. V. v. 24–35. Note especially (27–32): "Sed si tempore generationis [adunatio] facta est, uidetur putare et ante generationem fuisse humanam carnem non a Maria sumptam sed aliquo modo alio praeparatam, Mariam uero uirginem appositam ex qua caro nasceretur quae ab ea sumpta non esset." And below, II, 97–101: "Traxisse autem hanc sententiam uidetur, si tamen huius erroris fuit ut crederet non fuisse corpus Christi uere ex homine sed extra atque adeo in caelo formatum, quoniam cum eo in caelum creditur ascendisse."
1. *Ibid.*, V. vii. 46–79.
2. Note particularly II. 46–56.

which the Eastern bishops' plea for help was read.[3] Seeing at once the importance of the issue raised by the bishops, he effectively lent them his aid by means of Tr. V.[4] A comparison of Tr. V and John Maxentius' *instructio*, written in 520 or later, seems to indicate that the Scythian leader borrowed directly from the work of the Roman writer.[5] In 519 the monks appear, upholding the same views as Boethius and even offering a formula suggested, though not in so many words, in Boethius' earliest treatise. And then in 523 Boethius was stimulated by the Theopaschite controversy to write two more tractates. Are we to believe that he wrote only for a friend or two, as he says in the introductory remarks of Tr. I and V? It seems wiser to attribute his rather pretentious lack of interest in the public to rhetorical exaggeration or perhaps to caution, for the tractates obviously had considerable currency and influence. To conclude that Boethius meant his carefully worked-out clarification of the question only for his friends is to assume that he solved an important, troublesome, and potentially dangerous problem out of intellectual curiosity alone. This assumption hardly seems borne out by the evidence, since in the years after 512 the theology he expounded in Tr. V was adopted by some of those whose plight had impelled him to write in the first place. And this theology became the nucleus around which the imperial plans revolved.

It must be admitted, however, that Boethius' profound interest in theological matters and the probable use of his writings by the Scythians do not prove that the Roman Patrician was a partner in Justinian's policy of ecclesiastical and political unification. At the same time it is only fair to say that if Boethius' purpose in supporting the Scythian theology was the same as Justinian's, both men would have made every effort to conceal the fact. We know that in the years immediately preceding Boethius' arrest prolonged negotiations were carried on between the Byzantine court and the leaders of the Roman church and senate.[6] But always Boethius remained in the background, and one wonders why so prominent a man kept himself so ostentatiously aloof from a matter in which he was unquestionably interested. In a puzzle such as this many of the questions that we should like to ask cannot be answered, even though strong probabilities may be established. In the matter of the dealings between Rome and Constantinople, however, there is some rather impressive

---

3. Tr. V, preface.
4. Note the parallel passages from the episcopal letter and Tr. V, cited by Schurr, pp. 108–109.
5. The explanation may be that Maxentius hoped, through his reliance upon Boethius, to win Western support more easily. His *instructio*, like the Palatine Collection, must have been prepared primarily for use in Rome.
6. Duchesne, *L'église au VIe siècle*, pp. 130–31.

information which serves to implicate Boethius. This, together with the evidence of his theological activities, makes his co-operation with Justinian seem more than likely.

It is well established that the Roman senate had actively engaged in the ecclesiastical struggle from the time of Felix III (483–92). One prominent senator after another had visited the Eastern capital, hoping to bring the long conflict to an end. Theodoric, who had great respect for the position of the emperor, had acquiesced in these efforts; in fact he had given his definite approval when consulted by the cautious Hormisdas.[7] Clearly it was to the king's advantage to live at peace with the great power in the East, and for a long time, it is plain, he suspected nothing of Justinian's political scheme. Then suddenly Theodoric's attitude changed. He ordered the arrest of three prominent aristocrats, Albinus, Boethius, and Symmachus, and according to Boethius, questioned the loyalty of the whole senate.[8] It seems evident that the negotiations with Constantinople were responsible.[9] But what did Boethius have to do with them? The question is answered by an examination of the activities of Albinus and Symmachus.

Albinus' keen interest in the theological conflict is indicated in a letter addressed by Hormisdas to Dioscorus, asking about the status of those who rejected the Council of Chalcedon.[1] Albinus had raised the question, whether those who condemned the council in speech were to be regarded in the same way as those who had condemned it in writing, and the pope wanted Dioscorus' opinion. The allusion to those who opposed Chalcedon in speech is illuminating. Who could they have been but the Scythian monks who were at that very moment in Rome? Although the monks had not attacked the council in writing, Dioscorus had done his best to turn the pope against them, insisting that they were hostile to Chalcedon.[2] It would appear that Albinus intervened in behalf of the monks. Even if that was not the purpose of his inquiry, there can be no doubt that this prominent senator carefully followed the negotiations by means of which Justinian's highly prized *ecclesiarum concordia* was to be won.

Symmachus' connection with the unification movement is revealed, rather circuitously, through one of Maxentius' pamphlets and a

---

7. *Ibid.*, pp. 128–31; Schurr, pp. 111–12, 198–207; and Coster, p. 41.
8. *Phil. Consol.*, I. iv. 112–17.
9. Duchesne, *L'église au VIe siècle*, pp. 130–31.
1. *Col. Avel.*, no. 173, but it is significant that this letter was not sent. A different version, from which the incriminating references to Albinus and Chalcedon were omitted, was dispatched on December 3, 519. On the same date Hormisdas wrote to the other delegates dealing with the Scythian monks in no admiring terms.
2. *Ibid.*, nos. 216, 224. In no. 224 Dioscorus charged that the monks clamored for the addition of their Theopaschite formula, because Chalcedon alone did not suffice to counteract Nestorianism.

papal letter. Maxentius' *Responsio adversus Hormisdae Epistulam*, composed after the monks' departure from Rome, was a reply to an attack directed against the monks by the pope.[3] In a remarkable passage in this defense the Scythian leader proudly proclaimed that Hormisdas had unequivocally approved of the Scythian position. He pointed out that the pope well knew the Scythian view on *unus ex trinitate*, and if he had considered this teaching heretical the pontiff obviously would not have admitted the monks to his communion in the period of almost fourteen months during which he kept them at Rome. Moreover, in the presence of many distinguished men, Hormisdas had asked the Byzantine *magister militum*, Romanus, to tell the emperor that if Dioscorus, who was still in the Eastern capital, would not accept the Scythian formula, he should be cast into the sea.[4]

In spite of the rather strong language used of Dioscorus, there is, so far as I can see, no conceivable reason for doubting the reliability of this statement. It is true, as Maxentius says, that Hormisdas forcibly detained the monks in Rome, even while Justinian was asking for their safe return.[5] And Maxentius would hardly have dared to manufacture the pope's remark to Romanus, made in the presence of many witnesses. Then how is the pope's later attack on the monks to be explained? Maxentius himself suggests the most likely answer: perhaps Dioscorus persuaded Hormisdas to repudiate his decision in favor of the monks.[6]

Whatever the explanation of Hormisdas' reversal of policy, the importance of Maxentius' evidence can hardly be exaggerated. The message entrusted to Romanus, supporting the formula adopted by Justinian in July, 519, shows that the pope kept the closest watch over all aspects of the Eastern situation.[7] The consultations with Romanus also indicate that the affairs of the Byzantine court, the pope, and the Scythian monks were bound up together.

That the pope actually was in touch with Romanus is revealed by none other than Hormisdas himself, and so we have a further witness to the reliability of John Maxentius. Hormisdas' reference to

3. *ACO* IV, 2, 46–62. The attack of Hormisdas, dated August 13, 520, is to be found in *ibid.*, IV, 2, 44–46, and *Col. Avel.*, no. 231. Maxentius pretended that the letter was a forgery, thus leaving himself quite free to answer the pope's attack.
4. *ACO* IV, 2, 51.
5. *Col. Avel.*, no. 227.
6. *ACO* IV, 2, 51. Another possibility is that fear of Theodoric led the pope to change his position. It is not always easy to understand Hormisdas' policy but one should remember that he was a cautious as well as a clever diplomat, and that his position was perilous: his successor, John I, who had incurred the wrath of Theodoric, died in prison.
7. Romanus must be the Byzantine military leader who fought the Arabs and Persians and helped lead a raid on the Apulian coast in 508 (Hodgkin, III, 399; and Pauly-Wissowa, Romanus 13). In any case he was a high official of the Eastern court and therefore without doubt close to Justinian.

Romanus is contained in an anxious letter addressed to the legates in Constantinople, urgently requesting news.[8] The pope announced in his letter that both Romanus and the *uir magnificus patricius Symmachus* had promised the embassy's return without delay. It seems very likely that the Symmachus thus mentioned was Boethius' father-in-law. Had there been another Symmachus considered worthy of dealing with both pope and emperor in so vital a matter, some other record of him would almost surely survive.[9] If my surmise as to the identity of Symmachus is correct, the appearance of his name together with that of a high Byzantine official is very enlightening. The Roman Symmachus was probably among the many distinguished men present, according to Maxentius, when Hormisdas gave his message to Romanus. Whether Symmachus went to Constantinople at the same time as Romanus we cannot tell. Both dignitaries were active in the ecclesiastical dispute, however, and the participation of so notable a member of the Roman aristocracy would again show how close was the relationship between powerful Eastern and Western groups interested in unification. We cannot doubt that Boethius was keenly aware of all that transpired. His theological activity alone is sufficient guarantee of that. If the Symmachus mentioned by Hormisdas is Boethius' intimate friend and beloved patron, Boethius' knowledge of the conspiracy is put beyond question.[1]

Now, in a brief summation, the case against Boethius amounts to this:

I. It is certain that Boethius, one of the ablest philosopher-theologians of his time, was directly stimulated by the Scythian controversies to write three of his theological tractates.

II. It appears likely that John Maxentius, the Scythian leader, drew upon Boethius' Tr. V, the *Liber contra Eutychen et Nestorium,*

---

8. *Col. Avel.*, no. 229, dated July 15, 520. Apparently Hormisdas was as conservative as ever, for on July 9 Justinian wrote asking him to be more lenient with the Easterners and again urging acceptance of the Scythian formula (*ibid.*, no. 196).

9. Yet the Symmachus referred to in Hormisdas' correspondence is described in Pauly-Wissowa, Symmachus 36, only as "*Patricius und Magister officiorum am Hofe von Konstantinopel.*" I suppose he is thus designated because a certain *magistrianus* of Symmachus is mentioned in another of Hormisdas' letters (*ibid.*, no. 221). *Magistriani* were officials connected with the post under the *magister officiorum*, but I am not convinced that the papal letter meant to indicate such service. Yet, even if it be granted that this Symmachus was Master of the Offices, why should it be assumed that he was an Eastern, rather than a Western, official? The Roman Patrician had already been honored by positions of trust; perhaps in 519 and 520 he held the office which we know was given to his son-in-law in 522. This would help explain Theodoric's rage against both men. One other point is worth mentioning. Symmachus is not described as *magister officiorum* in the *Anecdoton Holderi*, but then neither is Boethius, and it is certain that he held the position.

1. Boethius' respect for his father-in-law was profound, as shown by the prefaces of Tr. I and Tr. V. Tr. I, inspired by the Scythian Theopaschite controversy and written in 523, just before Boethius' fall, was dedicated to Symmachus. One may feel unusually sure that if Symmachus was involved in Justinian's larger plan, Boethius was also.

in preparing for Roman perusal his brief definitions of Eutychianism and Nestorianism.

III. It is certain that Albinus, one of the pro-Byzantine party in the Roman senate, took a lively interest in the Theopaschite dispute. When Albinus was charged with treason, Boethius was his ardent defender.

IV. It is probable that Symmachus, the friend and father-in-law of Boethius, also engaged actively in the negotiations with the Eastern court, and it is known that Boethius dedicated Tr. I to Symmachus.

V. These two important members of the Roman aristocracy were arrested for treason along with Boethius. All three were in one way or another connected either with the theological issue or with the negotiations by which Justinian hoped to pacify Eastern Christendom and then to unite both East and West.

Even if we did not know that Boethius was arraigned for treason, we might suspect him of the crime on the basis of this evidence. For it cannot be denied that he appears deeply enmeshed, both through his theological writings and through his personal ties, in the imperial plan aiming at unification.

In defense of Boethius two points may be made. First, there is the fact that he did not consider himself guilty of any crime and that he impugned the reliability of his accusers.[2] While proclaiming his innocence, however, Boethius confessed with pride that he tried to hold back information by which the senate would have been proved guilty of treason.[3] There is an apparent contradiction here: he denies guilt but admits tampering with evidence. The explanation, it seems to me, is simply that a man of Boethius' views would not regard either support of ecclesiastical union or the protection of the senate as treasonable. His savage references to the greed and rapacity of upstart Gothic officials, against whom he stood in defense of the Romans, show that he resented the treatment of his countrymen.[4] In the *Consolation of Philosophy* Boethius declares his loyalty, not to the king, to whom he does not even refer by name, but to the Roman senate. In short, what was commendable to Boethius was treason to Theodoric. As for Boethius' vituperative condemnation of his three accusers, two of the three are highly praised by Cassiodorus.[5] Consequently the

2. *Phil. Consol.*, I, iv. 57–75, 120–23.
3. *Ibid.*, I. iv. 71–81, 111–17.
4. *Ibid.*, I. iv. 34–51.
5. Hodgkin, III, 491–93. Nothing more is definitely known of the third accuser. See also Coster, pp. 51, 63. I am not convinced by Coster's argument (p. 63) for believing Boethius rather than Cassiodorus, chiefly because I think the latter was in a better position to speak the truth and also because we cannot be sure that Boethius had given up hope of pardon.

zealous defender of Boethius must damn Cassiodorus, in the circumstances a harsh alternative, since Cassiodorus was fully as well informed as Boethius and less likely to be swayed by passion. It would be safer to attribute Boethius' denunciation to a natural hatred of those who testified against him.

The second point in favor of Boethius' innocence is that in 522 Theodoric gave proof of his confidence in the Patrician by making him *magister officiorum*. Father Schurr relies quite heavily on this seeming indication of Boethius' blamelessness.[6] That Boethius maintained treasonable relations with Constantinople he considers untenable.[7] But is it not more likely that Boethius enjoyed the king's favor in 522 because Theodoric was still ignorant of the Patrician's relations with the East? It appears that Theodoric did not guess the exact nature of Justinian's plan until 523, the year in which the diplomatic Pope Hormisdas died. Then the efforts of Boethius in behalf of unity may have taken on an entirely different aspect. When the king at last became aware of Justinian's political design, masked by the apparently harmless negotiations between the Eastern and Western churches, his rage must have been boundless. He had been betrayed by men whom he trusted. His surprise must have been all the greater since the Emperor Justin had seemed well disposed and Boethius devoted.[8] Yet when Albinus was charged with dealing treasonably with Justin, Boethius rushed to his defense.[9] What was more natural at this point than that Theodoric should investigate the activities of the man who sought to defend a traitor and to whom the great powers of *magister officiorum* had been entrusted? Then the *Liber contra Eutychen et Nestorium*, which ten years before would have seemed unobjectionable, must have begun to appear dangerous. For in it, as well as in two other treatises, Boethius supported the

6. Schurr considers it improbable (p. 201, n. 316) that Boethius' and Albinus' interest or participation in the settlement of the Acacian schism afterward worked against them. But Albinus and Boethius kept on working for Justinian's larger plan of unification *after* that preliminary union was achieved in 519. It was surely to carry out this larger plan aiming at political unification that Justinian in July, 519, adopted the Scythian Theopaschite formula which in 523 induced Boethius to write Tr. I and II.

7. Schurr (p. 201, n. 316) appeals for support to the article of Giovanni B. Picotti, "Il senato romano e il processo di Boezio," *Archivio storico italiano*, Ser. VII, Vol. XV (Firenze, 1931), pp. 205–28. I am surprised that Father Schurr should regard Picotti's article as *eine gediegene Zurückweisung* of the charge of treason, since Picotti throughout neglects the theological aspect of the affair, going so far indeed as to say (p. 208) that it can be doubted whether Boethius was a Christian. Picotti makes much of Boethius' silence, in his defense, in respect of the religious question, but that is what one would expect of a guilty man.

8. Justin had agreed to the appointment of Theodoric's son-in-law to the consulship in 519 (Coster, p. 41).

9. The referendarius, Cyprian, who brought the charges against both Albinus and Boethius, had got wind of suspicious negotiations carried on between Roman senators and Eastern officials. See Stewart, *Boethius*, p. 43. It is no wonder Cyprian became alarmed, since such influential men as Justinian, Symmachus, Albinus, Romanus, and Vitalian were involved, as indicated by the *Collectio Avellana*.

position maintained by the Scythian monks. And it was the position of these monks, who had been so active among the people and senate of Rome, that Justinian had seized upon in 519 in his search for a theology which might unify all the East and also appeal to the West. That Albinus and Symmachus had likewise been much interested in the supposedly ecclesiastical negotiations helped to bind them closely to what must have seemed to the king clearly a revolutionary movement. Theodoric faced the failure of his regime and the destruction of his power. All who had been connected with the affair became suspect, and among these was Boethius.[1]

We must conclude that Boethius, the Roman noble, was proud of the Roman tradition and loyal to it. He was also an orthodox Christian who could not approve of his country's subservience to Theodoric's Arian barbarians. We know for a certainty that he took up the theological position of the Scythian monks, by means of which Justinian's plan of empire was to be furthered. Thus he had both a motive and a method for combating the tyranny of the Goths. Finally we know that he fell under the king's suspicion and, charged with treason and sacrilege, was arrested. It is easy, out of a desire to defend Boethius, to overlook Theodoric's side of the case. Are we to believe that the king, a man of balance and unusual tolerance, who had greatly honored Boethius, suddenly turned on him without good cause? Are we to assume that Theodoric accepted weak evidence? Everything is against it. Coming after all the trust which the king had reposed in Boethius, the disclosure of his treachery must have been exceedingly painful to Theodoric. It was a discovery no man would like to make and one for which he would insist upon incontrovertible proof. There is then all the more reason to believe that there was strong indication of treason.[2] What could it have been but Boethius' unmistakable sympathy with Justinian's imperial policy, a sympathy made plain both by his support of the Scythian theology

1. Note that, though Stewart, *Boethius*, pp. 156–57, realized that the question dealt with in Tr. V was "fraught with an interest quite as much political as religious," the "political" interest which Stewart had in mind was not the same as that put forward here. Stewart believed that Boethius meant to support the see of Rome as against the see of Constantinople and thereby to add luster to Theodoric's own position as ruler of the West. On pp. 158–59 Stewart offers a rather ingenious explanation of Boethius' strange failure to mention Christianity in the *Consolation of Philosophy*. To suggest another, the tone of Boethius' defense of himself leads me to suspect that he still hoped to regain his freedom. If so, might he not have thought it wise to leave the subject of religion alone?

2. For the charge of divination see Coster, p. 63. For another view see R. Bonnaud, "L'éducation scientifique de Boèce," *Speculum*, IV (1929), 198–206, especially pp. 200–201. The temptation to exculpate the "last of the Romans" at the expense of a "barbarian" must be guarded against. Stewart, *Boethius*, p. 51, accuses Theodoric of "an act of blind cruelty, such as the condemnation of Boethius and Symmachus undoubtedly was." Why "undoubtedly"? Theodoric's character is no more open to censure than Boethius' own. Though Stewart admits that Boethius had faults, he defends him rather vigorously against Dr. Hodgkin's strictures. I cannot avoid the conclusion that Boethius could be harsh, selfish, and arrogant, and that he well knew how to consult his own interest.

and by his close contact with those who strove for an ecclesiastical harmony which they hoped would be followed by political unification based on the destruction of Theodoric's power.

Boethius did not suffer "martyrdom." It was not because of his theological activities that he fell from Theodoric's favor but because the theological activities were part of a program aiming at political unity. There is no evidence that Arianism was involved.[3] In itself Boethius' orthodox theology was no more dangerous to the Gothic regime in 523 than it had been in 512. So it was the combination of theology and politics that brought about Boethius' fall. The political aspect accounts for the condemnation, but the political aspect cannot be explained apart from the theological. Boethius' part in this affair will hardly improve his reputation. He lacked the steadfastness of Cassiodorus, being apparently unaware of the inconsistency of accepting gifts of power and prestige from Theodoric while working for the king's overthrow. At the end at least he was loyal to what he believed in and risked everything for it. And in prison he turned again, happily, to philosophy. It was unfortunate, for the cause of learning as well as for Boethius, that he ever abandoned her. Theodoric's fame is enhanced. There is little reason now to cling to the belief that this king, renowned for his extraordinary wisdom and justice, reversed his policy at the end of his life and wantonly murdered Boethius.

* * *

EDMUND REISS

The Fall of Boethius and the Fiction of the *Consolatio Philosophiae*[†]

Although it is something of an exaggeration to claim that the fall of Boethius has been "almost as much discussed as the fall of Adam," for all the ink that has been spilled we know remarkably little about what actually happened in the early 520's to King Theodoric's Master of the Offices.[1] When in Book I of the *Consolatio Philosophiae* Boethius the narrator tells Lady Philosophy of his fall, he says, "you

---

3. Schurr, pp. 222–23; Picotti, pp. 206–207; Rand, *Speculum*, XI, 155, and *Building of Eternal Rome*, p. 239.

† From *The Classical Journal* 77.1 (Oct.–Nov. 1981): 37–47. © 1981 by Classical Association of the Middle West and South. Reprinted by permission of Classical Association of the Middle West and South via Copyright Clearance Center.

1. This is the point of C. H. Coster, "The Fall of Boethius: His Character," *Annuaire de l'Institut de Philologie et d'Histoire Orientales et Slaves*, 12(1952) *Méanges Henri Grégoire*, 4 (Brussels 1953) 45.

remember how at Verona a charge of treason was made against Albinus and how in his eagerness to see the total destruction of the Senate the king tried to extend the charge to them all in spite of their universal innocence; and you remember how I defended them with complete indifference to any danger, and you know that I am telling the truth."[2] He says that he took public office so as to put into practice his philosophical principles. He worked for what was right, and even when it meant opposing those who wielded greater power than he, he protected the poor and helpless from the oppressions of the mighty. In particular, he writes, he saved ex-Consul Paulinus from "the very mouth of the gaping courtiers, who like ravenous curs had already . . . devoured his riches." And in order to save ex-Consul Albinus from being punished wholly on the basis of presumed guilt, he risked incurring the enmity of Cyprian, Albinus' accuser. The resentment provoked by these noble actions led to his being struck down by false informers:

> Yet who were the informers who struck me down? One was Basilius. He had previously been dismissed from the royal service and was forced into impeaching me by his debts. Two others were Opilio and Gaudentius. A royal decree had sentenced them to banishment because of their countless frauds, and to avoid complying they had protected themselves by seeking sanctuary. When the news reached the king, he made a proclamation that unless they had left the city of Ravenna by the appointed day they would be driven out with their foreheads branded. There could scarcely be greater severity than that. Yet the very same day they laid information against me and the denunciation was accepted. Surely my actions didn't deserve that? And surely the fact that my conviction was prejudged didn't make just men of my accusers? Fortune should have blushed at the sight of innocence accused, or at least at the depravity of my accusers.

Boethius' overt concern in this impassioned defence is less with clarifying the charges against him or with recording the events leading to these charges than with protesting his innocence and with lamenting the injustice done to him. What he offers is obviously neither an impartial nor a complete account of what actually happened. This he says he has offered elsewhere: "That posterity may not be ignorant of the course and truth of the matter I have put it down in writing." But since no such account has come down to us, we can only won-

---

2. *De consolatione Philosophiae*, I, prose 4; tr. V. E. Watts (Baltimore 1969) 44. For Boethius' original see *Anicii Menlii Severini Boethii Philosophiae consolatio*, ed. Ludovicus Bieler, *Boethius, Opera I*, Corpus Christianorum, Series Latina, 94 (Turnholt 1957).

der how much of what Boethius includes of his fall in the *Consolatio* can be taken at face value.

The few extant historical sources do not help much. The official letters written by Boethius' contemporary Cassiodorus, when he was Theodoric's quaestor, and collected by him in his *Variae*, though otherwise providing valuable details about Theodoric's reign, say nothing about the fall of Boethius. The *History of the Gothic War*, written later in the century by Procopius of Caesarea, says only that when "men of worthless character" laid false information against Boethius and his father-in-law Symmachus, the king believed they were guilty and after confiscating their property had them put to death on the charge of treason.[3] Procopius is more concerned with the subsequent marvels that supposedly showed Theodoric his error than with the facts of Boethius' fall. The marvellous also permeates the fragmentary mid-sixth century chronicle known as the *Anonymous Valesii*. Reporting the wonders that occurred after the devil found a way to subvert Theodoric, it notes that a woman gave birth to four dragons, a comet fell for two weeks, and earthquakes were commonplace. Such is the setting of Boethius' fall: Cyprian the referendarius—the official who made an impartial statement of law cases that came before the King's Court—being "driven by greed," accused Albinus the Patrician of sending letters to the Emperor Julian in Constantinople that were hostile to Theodoric. When Albinus, summoned before the court, denied the accusation, Boethius said in the king's presence, "False is the information of Cyprian, but if Albinus did it, both I and the whole Senate did it with one accord. It is false, my lord, Oh King." Cyprian then brought forward false witnesses against both Albinus and Boethius, and Boethius was arrested. Without even a hearing he received sentence, and soon afterwards he was executed: "He was tortured for a very long time by a cord that was twisted round his forehead so that his eyes started from his head. Then at last amidst his torments he was killed with a club."[4]

In both Procopius' *History* and the *Anonymous Valesii*, because of the mixture of history and legend, it is difficult to ascertain what is valid. Even if we assume to be factual only those details that are in accord with the account of Boethius' fall included in the *Consolatio*, we are faced with a further problem, for we do not know that the accounts in these chronicles are independent of that in the *Consolatio*. Moreover, even the scant evidence we have is not without ambiguity. Notwithstanding his identification in the *Anonymous Valesii*, it is

---

3. Procopius, *History of the Gothic Wars*, V.1; *Procopius*, ed. and tr. H. B. Dewing, Loeb Classical Library (London 1919) 12–15.
4. *Anonymous Valesii*, sect. 83–87; ed. Roberto Cessi, *Fragmenta historica ab Henrico et Hadriano Valesio*, Rerum Italicarum Scriptores, 24.4 (Città di Castello 1913) 19–20.

not clear that Cyprian would have been referendarius at the time of
Albinus' accusation. Furthermore, the historicity of the main actors in
the drama of Boethius' fall is not at all certain. Cassiodorus' collection
contains letters to a Cyprian on the occasion of his being appointed
finance minister and again when he is named Patrician, and to an
Opilio, brother to this Cyprian, when he succeeds him as finance minister. Also one of the letters praising this Opilio cites the noble family
of Basilius, with whom Opilio has allied himself in marriage.[5] The
striking differences between these figures celebrated by Cassiodorus
and those reviled by Boethius have been explained by saying, on the
one hand, that Cassiodorus, who was serving as Theodoric's mouth-
piece, was not offering his private opinion, and, on the other hand,
that Boethius' assessment was hardly impartial. As John Moorhead
has recently argued, Boethius' opinions of the Romans who served the
Goths clearly differed from the opinions they held of themselves.[6]

A further possibility, which should at least be considered, is that the
eminent citizens of Cassiodorus' letters and the false accusers of
Boethius' Consolatio only coincidentally have the same names. Not
uncommon at the time, these names may not refer to the same people
at all. This is what is customarily said about the name Basilius, which
in Cassiodorus is both that of a member of a noble family and that of a
senator charged with practicing magical arts. Perhaps Cyprian, Opilio,
and Basilius should be joined to Gaudentius, about whom, all scholars
agree, nothing is known outside Boethius' account.[7]

While the identities of the rogues cited in the Consolatio may be
understandably unclear, we might expect more positive identification of the two noble ex-Consuls whom Boethius says he aided.
Unfortunately, the situation is no better. Though an Albinus is
addressed in several letters of Cassiodorus, none of these records
any accusation against him. In fact, aside from what is said of the
accusation and arrest in the Consolatio and the Anonymous Valesii—
which may be based on the Consolatio—no record exists of his fate.
Paulinus, the other ex-Consul whom Boethius says he helped, may
seem to be the Paulinus who, according to Cassiodorus, was Consul
in 493 and later prosecuted by certain Senators—perhaps explaining Boethius' reference to the "ravenous curs" who had already
devoured Paulinus' wealth. But since Boethius' father-in-law,

5. Cassiodorus, Variae, 40, 41; VIII. 16, 17, 21, 22; IV. 22, 23; ed. Theodorus Monumenta
   Germaniae Historica, Auctorum Antiquissimorum, 12 (Berlin 1894). See also Coster,
   65–67.
6. See Moorhead, "Boethius and Romans in Ostrogothic Service," Historia 27 (1978) esp.
   609 ff.
7. See The Letters of Cassiodorus, ed. Thomas Hodgkin (London 1886) p. 246 n.: also Watts,
   p. 180. While acknowledging that "no surviving evidence" for identifying Gaudentius
   exists, Moorhead feels that the name of one "Fl[avius] Gaudentius,v[ir] c[larissimus]" in
   a multilated piece of papyrus "probably refers to him" (pp. 609–10 and n. 34).

Symmachus, was one of the Senators involved in prosecuting this Paulinus, it is hardly likely that Boethius would have celebrated Paulinus or criticized Symmachus in this manner.[8]

Rather than take at face value Boethius' account of his fall, we should realize that it is part of the fictional account of a conversation between the victim Boethius and Lady Philosophy who has come to console him and, indeed, to teach him a proper understanding of happiness. While several of the specific details of the *Consolatio* may very well be factual, these are included mainly as part of the picture, created by the author at the beginning of his work, of man, here the narrator, grieving over undeserved misfortune. And, as Wolfgang Schmid first demonstrated, the initial physical condition of the narrator, that of man overcome by lethargy, or sloth, is an expression of a familiar tradition and would have indicated to Boethius' audience the inadequate spiritual condition of the narrator.[9] Regardless of whether or not this sickness represents the actual condition of Boethius after his fall, it functions in the *Consolatio* to show the narrator's lack of proper understanding. It is hardly accidental that after the narrator finishes his long lament, Philosophy responds by saying unsympathetically that she had not realized how sick he was or how far he had been led astray by his grief (I, pr. 5).

As the point of the *Consolatio* is to take the narrator beyond the sorrowful and the emotional to the rational, so it is to go beyond the personal to an understanding of man's place in God's creation. Inasmuch as Boethius the philosopher proceeds by "ruthlessly exposing Boethius the natural man," the work should be understood less as a personal autobiography than as a manifestation of the didactic literature common in the sixth century in such forms as the *consolatio* and the *confessio*.[1] As Salvian, for instance, could use personal experience in his *De gubernatione Dei* to reassure Christians who could

8. See also the reference to "the excellent Patrician Paulinus" in Cassiodorus, *Variae*, II. 3; Hodgkin, *Letters*, 173. See the analysis of evidence in Helen M. Barrett, *Boethius. Some Aspects of His Times and Work* (Cambridge: University Press, 1940; repr. New York 1965) 67–69.

9. Schmid, "Philosophisches und Medizinisches in der *Consolatio Philosophiae* des Boethius," *Festschrift Bruno Snell* (Munich 1956) 113–44; repr. *Römische Philosophie*, Wege der Forschung, 193 (Darmstadt 1976) 341–84; also Schmid, "Boethius and the Claims of Philosophy," *Studia Patristica*, II.2; Texte und Untersuchungen, 64 (Berlin 1957) 368–75. See also the later refinement by Christine Wolf, "Untersuchungen zum Krankheitsbild in dem ersten Buch der *Consolatio Philosophiae* des Boethius," *Rivista di Cultura Classica e Medievale* 6 (1964) 213–23. On the symbolic use of lethargy in Augustine's sermons and *Confessiones*, see Schmid, *Studia Patristica*, 371 ff. Also see the recent correlation of philosophy and therapy, in which healing is seen to come with insight, by Donald F. Duclow, "Perspective and Therapy in Boethius' *Consolation of Philosphy*," *Journal of Medicine and Philosophy* 4 (1979) 334–43.

1. See C. S. Lewis, *The Discarded Image. An Introduction to Medieval and Renaissance Literature* (Cambridge 1964) 80; Peter von Moos, *Consolatio. Studien zur mittellateinischen Trostliteratur über den Tod und zum Problem der christlichen Trauer*, Münstersche Mittelalter-Schriften, 3 (Munich 1971–72) I, 59 ff.; and Georg Misch, *A History of Autobiography in Antiquity*, tr. E. W. Dickes (Cambridge 1951) II, 670 ff.

not understand how God could permit the faithful to suffer at the hands of unbelievers, so Boethius could use the personal as a way to demonstrate the workings of Providence. And as Augustine in his *Confessiones* could use the personal to make meaningful the journey of the mind to God and, finally, to emphasize the hidden workings of the divine in human thought and effort, so the *Consolatio* could use personal autobiography—particularly what purports to be an account of the author's misfortunes—as a springboard for moral and meta-physical instruction. While for the narrator his undeserved misfor-tune is initially of paramount importance, as he begins to understand Philosophy's teachings, he moves beyond his concern with self to issues that are not immediately pertinent to him. To say this is not to deny that the *Consolatio* has as its starting point the situation of the fallen virtuous man Boethius. Rather it is to insist that the personal details be taken less as historical facts than as details chosen by Boethius the author—not the character who changes in the course of the narrative—for their thematic significance. Their point is finally not to assert the innocence of Boethius but to justify the ways of God to man.

Symbolic details are the norm in Book I of the *Consolatio*, and the personal details about Boethius should be understood as having no more literal significance than those describing Lady Philosophy. Notwithstanding the abundance of specific details in her description, we have no doubt that those showing her to be both old and ageless, both of average height and higher than the very heavens (I, pr. 1), are to be taken metaphorically as revealing the nature, scope, and purpose of philosophy itself. Similarly metaphoric are the personal details found in the opening song where the narrator—whose depic-tion may derive from that of the gray-haired narrator at the beginning of Martianus Capella's *De nuptiis Philologiae et Mercurii*—speaks of being old, with white hair and loose skin quaking on his bones (I, m.1). It is unlikely that Boethius, probably in his early forties at the time of writing, is giving a realistic picture of himself. Compara-ble to these details may be those of Boethius' fall including refer-ences to figures who would seem to be historical personages. Whatever the historicity of the victimized ex-Consuls and the false accusers, Boethius may be using them symbolically. Names like Cyprian and Albinus may have been chosen more for their typicality and their symbolic potential than for their historical accuracy. Even if Albinus was indeed the actual name of the ex-Consul whom Boethius protected, it was especially appropriate in its connotations, seen in its Latin root, of whiteness and, by extension, of innocence.

Looking at the names of Boethius' false accusers in terms of their symbolic significations, we find that the Latin roots of the names Basilius, Opilio, and Gaudentius suggest respectively Power, Wealth,

and Pleasure. The allegorical sense of the names Basilius and Gaudentius is especially apparent, for these names are synonymous with
the Latin words for power and pleasure. But Opilio presents some
difficulties. As a variant form of *ovilio* or *upilio*, both terms meaning
"shepherd," the name Opilio would suggest the opposite of wealth. A
name like Opulentius would have been more suggestive of riches,
but it would have functioned only to create an allegorical personification. Boethius seems to have been concerned with choosing for
his accusers names that were actual Roman names, as Basilius and
Gaudentius were. Opilio, containing the root *op-* and suggesting a
reference to the Roman goddess Ops, associated with wealth and
money, may have been selected as an actual Roman name that could
function to suggest wealth.

Viewed symbolically instead of historically, Basilius, Opilio, and
Gaudentius take on quite different significances. Basilius, who is
described as having been dismissed from royal service, returns to
accuse falsely; and Opilio and Gaudentius, having been banished
because of "their countless frauds," return also to work against the
truth. It seems more than coincidental that Power, Wealth, and
Pleasure, here figures of corruption and fraud, are precisely those
false gifts of Fortune later singled out by Lady Philosophy in Books
II and III of the *Consolatio*. While appearing to give man happiness,
they are actually deceptive, for they bring only misery.

In focusing here on Power, Wealth, and Pleasure—whereas later
in the *Consolatio* these false bringers of happiness are joined by
High Office and Fame as well—Boethius would seem to be following a Hellenistic tradition of three false goods or false states of
being, related perhaps to the commonly understood three parts of
the soul. Included in this tradition are Aristotle's discussion in the
Nicomachean Ethics of the three kinds of life—honor, money-making, and pleasure—which one could mistakenly think good; Plato's
criticism in the *Republic* of the three concerns—with honors,
wealth, and indulgence of appetite—that cause the decline of the
State; and the Christian idea of the three temptations of man, as
listed in 1 John—pride of life, lust of the eyes, and lust of the flesh—
which were the subject of notable exegesis by the Church Fathers,
including Augustine's Commentary on the Epistle of John and also
his *Confessiones*.[2] Boethius' point in the *Consolatio* is not necessarily
to identify his three false accusers with any one set of these false

2. See Aristotle, *Nicomachean Ethics*, I.5 (1095b–1096a); and Plato, *Republic*, VIII.
544–56. For the temptations of 1 John 2:15–16—also related to the temptations of Adam
and Eve (Genesis 3) and of Christ (Matthew 4:1–11, Luke 4:1–13)—see, e.g., Augustine,
Confessiones, X. 30–40. On Hellenistic and early Christian versions of the temptations
and their possible relationship to the tripartite soul, see Donald R. Howard, *The Three
Temptations: Medieval Man in Search of the World* (Princeton 1966) 45 ff.

concerns or temptations but, rather, to relate them to a familiar tradition that would have made clear the significance of their adversary relationship.

Precedent for Boethius' using details that though apparently autobiographical are actually symbolic may be found in his writings as early as his first commentary on Porphyry's *Isagoge*. There, as a basis for the philosophical discussion, he establishes a fictional dialogue between himself and a friend who supposedly meet one winter's night in the mountains of Aurelia outside Rome, and while the wind blows violently discuss the usefulness of commentaries. This leads to a discussion of Porphyry and Aristotle. The wild setting provides a contrast with the placid discourse on the mind, and significantly at the conclusion of the instruction, when the friend arrives at understanding, the darkness, turbulence, and wilderness are replaced by dawn, calm, and civilization.[3] It may be that in the *Consolatio Philosophiae* Boethius created a comparable symbolic setting.

Further precedent for Boethius' using such symbolic details may be found in both Neoplatonic and Christian tradition. And statements like Augustine's in the *Confessiones* and *De doctrina Christiana* about the need to get beyond the name to the thing reflect a general awareness of the symbolic significance of names throughout the centuries immediately preceding Isidore of Seville's *Etymologiae*. Even names found in the New Testament were taken symbolically. Origen and Ambrose, for instance, in their commentaries on the Gospel according to Luke matter-of-factly explain the significance of Luke's addressing his work to someone named Theophilus, a name meaning lover of God. As they make clear, this is what one must truly be if one is to understand Luke's message. Another basis for Boethius' symbolic use of names may be found in a passage in his second commentary on Aristotle's *Peri Hermeneias* (*On Interpretation*), where, in what has been described as the first explicit recognition in Western writing that proper nouns express essences, Boethius speaks of fabricating names "so that the form of what is proposed would become clearer."[4]

To refer to Boethius' false accusers as symbols of Power, Wealth, and Pleasure is not to negate the reality of his fall, but rather to insist that as Boethius presents his predicament, it is to be understood as

3. See *In Isagogen Porphyrii commenta, editio prima*, I.1; in *Anicii Manlii Severini Boetii in Isagogen Porphyii commenta*, ed. Georg Schepss, rev. Samuel Brandt, Corpus Scriptorum Ecclesiasticorum Latinorum, 48 (Leipzig 1906) 3–4.
4. See *In Aristotelis de interpresatione, editio secunda*, II.7; in *Anicii Manlii Severini Boetli commentarii in librum Aristotelis Peri hermeneias*, ed. Carolus Meiser, pars posterior (Leipzig 1880); 137; and Alvin Plantinga, "The Boethian Compromise," *American Philosophical Quarterly* 15 (1978) 132.

more than something personal or individual. In the fiction that Boethius has created, his downfall functions as an object lesson of how a good man may be destroyed by relying on the impermanent and illusory goods of this world. We should realize that Boethius did not write the *Consolatio* "to help him to bear overwhelming sorrow."[5] The woebegone prisoner depicted in Book I is not in the same state as the author of the work, who already possesses the understanding attained by the narrator only at the end. Had Boethius not already been consoled, he could not have offered the consolation he does. Far from being the spontaneous overflow of the powerful emotions of one who viewed himself as unfairly persecuted, the *Consolatio* is a planned, contrived, and artful creation whose every detail of literary structure and philosophical content seems to have been carefully considered.

We should therefore not find it surprising that the controlling structural principle of Book I, pr. 4, the so-called autobiographical section, where the narrator delivers what amounts to an apologia for his life, is the traditional five-part division of oration that Boethius would have known from Quintilian. Using the *exordium* (or *proemium*), where the speaker traditionally prepares the audience to be well-disposed to his argument, Boethius has his narrator make the point that his misfortune is undeserved; in the *narratio*, or recounting of the facts, he shows how he has always opposed injustice and worked for the common good; in the *probatio*, or proof, he states how he has been falsely accused; in the *refutatio* he rebukes his accusers and reaffirms his innocence; and in the *peroratio*, using eloquence and emotion, he relates his particular case to what he takes to be the state of the world: the innocent being overcome by the wicked. In terms of the rhetoric, the so-called personal details in this section of the *Consolation*—including the mentions of Basilius, Opilio, and Gaudentius—function as *topoi* to develop the oration at hand.[6]

Recognizing the contrived and artful nature of the *Consolatio*, we should address two questions still bothering many readers of the work. First, if Boethius was actually in the exile or prison—the narrator bitterly asks Philosophy if she thinks the place he is in looks like the library of his house in Rome (I, pr. 4)—we are faced with the difficulty of explaining how he could have brought together such a wealth of material from Stoic, Aristotelian, and Neoplatonic sources and how he could have alluded to and quoted from so many pieces

---

5. Cf. Barrett, 73.
6. See Kurt Reichenberger, *Untersuchungen zur literarischen Stellung der Consolatio Philosophiae*, Romanistische Arbeiten 3 (Cologne 1954) 35–76; also Quintilian, *Institutio oratoria*, III.ix; and cf. Cicero, *De inventione*, I.xiv.19; and *Rhetorica ad Herennium*, I.iii.4.

of poetry—by Homer, Sophocles, Euripides, and Menander among the Greeks; and by Catullus, Claudian, Juvenal, Lucan, Ovid, Seneca, Statius, and Virgil among the Romans. Furthermore, we might wonder how Boethius had the leisure and peace of mind to create a prose style which is the nearest thing to the Ciceronian ideal that had been written in Latin for five hundred years, and how he could have penned thirty-nine poems that employ not only virtually every meter known in the sixth century but two or three apparently invented by Boethius himself.[7]

Unless we wish to say that the *Consolatio* is only a pastiche of some now-lost Greek works which Boethius merely translated and put within a personal frame, we are forced to appeal to the faculty of remembering, which Boethius would have had to possess to a degree now lost to most of us, or to recognize that the story of Boethius' fall is essentially a literary device designed to provide a setting for the philosophy.[8] Moreover, if we view the thought of the *Consolatio* not as the result of Boethius' fall but as the product of his life's work, the book does not seem at all surprising or strange. Nothing in it is antithetical to Boethius' thoughts elsewhere, and indeed its combination of Aristotelian and Neoplatonic elements is wholly in accord with the principle of harmonizing the two philosophies which he affirmed in his second commentary on the *Peri Hermeneias* to be the ultimate aim of his writings.[9]

Even though we may recognize this, we are faced with a second question: Why in his last work would Boethius, a practicing Christian, not have turned to the consolation offered by his religion? To rephrase this question, how could he, awaiting torture and death, have written a work that, while full of Aristotle and Plato, of elegant poetry and references to classical literature, never once mentions Christ and, for that matter, never presents teachings and conceptions that are unequivocally Christian? To assert, as C. S. Lewis does, that Boethius was writing a consolation of philosophy, not one of religion, and that he purposely "wrote philosophically, not religiously," is unfortunately to beg the question, for it does not address the issue of why, on what has been taken to be the threshold of death, Boethius was concerned with matters of reason instead of faith, with thoughts of the providential order instead of the eschatological ultimates.[1] And to point out, as Christine Mohrmann does, that expressions of piety

7. See, e.g., Barrett, 166–67; and E. K. Rand, "Boethius, the First of the Scholastics," *Founders of the Middle Ages* (Cambridge 1928; repr. New York 1957) 162.
8. See Hermann Usener, *Anecdoton Holderi. Ein Beitrag zur Geschichte Roms in ostgothischer Zeit* (Bonn, 1877; repr. Hildenheim 1969), esp. 51–52; and Rand, 164.
9. *In Aristotelis de interpretatione, editio secunda*, II.3; ed. Meiser, pars posterior, 79–80.
1. See Lewis, 78; and, e.g., Hans von Camperhausen, *The Fathers of the Latin Church*, tr. M. Hoffmann (London 1964) 308.

having their source in the liturgy show through the philosophical dialogue, does not explain why Boethius intended to focus on philosophy in the first place.[2] The answers offered over the centuries are, first, that Boethius chose a purely rational form so that his *consolatio* could be understood by all; second, that the work is unfinished and would ultimately have included Christian doctrine; and, third, that though nominally a Christian, Boethius at the end of his life found consolation in the study of philosophy, which in his *De syllogismis hypotheticis* he had called the "chief solace in life.'[3]

The premises of these explanations—not only that the *Consolatio* reflects Boethius' actual state of mind after his fall but that it was written while he was awaiting death—are suspect. Although death is mentioned in the poem that opens the work, it is there a desideratum: the unhappy narrator laments that "happy death" is deaf to his cries (I, m.1). And although the narrator says later in Book I that without a trial or conviction he has been "condemned to death and proscription," the reference is more likely to exile—a symbolic death—than to execution; for, as he says in the same passage, he has been "conveyed five hundred miles" from his home (I, pr.4). In like manner, the narrator asks Philosophy why she has come down from heaven to his "place of solitary banishment" (I, pr.3); and Philosophy later remarks that "this very place, which you call banishment" is home to others (II, pr.4). Notwithstanding Philosophy's sense that the narrator fears he will be killed (II, pr.5), the general tone of the *Consolatio* is, as Lewis notes, "not that of a prisoner awaiting death but that of a noble and a statesman lamenting his fall—exiled, financially damaged, parted from his beautiful library, stripped of his official dignities, his name scandalously traduced." Not only is the language not that of "the condemned cell," the consolation sought is apparently "not for death but for ruin."[4]

The literature of imprisonment and banishment enjoyed in Boethius' time a long tradition dating back to Plato's *Apology* and *Crito*, dialogues whose setting was the prison where Socrates awaited death, and in Roman times to, notably, Ovid's sorrowful *Tristia* and *Epistulae ex Ponto*, written while he was in exile. In

2. Mohrmann, "Some Remarks on the Language of Boethius, *Consolatio Philosophiae*," *Latin Script and Letters, A.D. 400–900. Festschrift Presented to Ludwig Bieler* (Leiden 1976) 61.

3. The first view was stated by Conrad of Hirsau in the twelfth century; the second by Petrus Bertius in the seventeenth century; and the third, though old, was recently restated by Philip Merian, "Ammonius Hermiae, Zacharias Scholasticus and Boethius," *Greek, Roman and Byzantine Studies*, 9(1968) 202–03. See also C. J. de Vogel, "The Problem of Philosophy and Christian Faith in Boethius' *Consolatio*," *Romanitas et Christianitas. Studia Iano Henrico Waszink* (Amsterdam 1973), 359–60; and *De syllogismis hypotheticis*, I, 1.3; in A. M. *Severino Boezio, De hypotheticis syllogismis*, ed. and tr. Luca Obertello (Brescia 1969).

4. Lewis, 77.

Christian times this literature also took the form of theodicies, or affirmations of divine justice, such as Dracontius' *De laudibus Dei*, written at the end of the fifth century after the author, who was imprisoned by the Vandals, was able to see beyond his personal misfortune. At the same time, imprisonment and exile were common metaphors in both Neoplatonic and early Christian writings for the condition of man in this world, in that the soul imprisoned in the body and man trapped in the world of matter were both exiles from their proper spiritual homeland.[5] Whatever the actual condition of Boethius after his fall from power, we might wonder whether as author of the *Consolatio* he was not using the facts of his fall as a basis for developing the metaphysical condition of imprisonment and exile.

In any case, there is absolutely no indication that Boethius himself viewed the *Consolatio* as his final piece of writing. Regardless of whether or not it is finished as it stands—and I would argue that it is—Boethius may well have intended to write other works after it. The philosophical contents of the *Consolatio* seem out of place only when readers insist that the work should represent a religious consolation. And the lack of overt Christian elements becomes significant only when readers insist on regarding the work as Boethius' farewell address to the world.

Boethius' earlier writings may be meaningfully viewed as forming an educational program that moved from the analysis of number to language—mainly logic but also rhetoric—to theology. From his works on arithmetic and music to his commentaries on Porphyry, Aristotle, and Cicero, and his original philosophical treatises, as well as his investigations of Trinitarian and Christological issues, Boethius was continually concerned with synthesizing and harmonizing—Greek and Latin thought, Aristotle and Plato, philosophy and theology, logic and rhetoric, the secular and the religious. The *Consolatio Philosophiae*, a blend of verse and prose, of the personal and the philosophical, as well as an amalgamation of classical thought, may also be considered an important part of Boethius' educational program in its investigation of such basic moral and metaphysical issues as the role of Fortune in the world, man's true and false happiness, evil, the relationship between Providence and Fate, and between God's foreknowledge and man's free will.

---

5. See Rand, 160, 201–02; also Pierre Courcelle, "Tradition platonicienne et traditions chrétiennes du corps-prison," *Revue des Etudes Latines* 43 (1965) 406–42; "L'âme en cage," *Parusia. Studien zur Philosophie Platons und zur Problemgeschichte des Platonismus. Festgabe für Johannes Hirschberger* (Frankfurt 1965) 103–16; and "Le corps-tombeau," *Revue des Etudes Anciennes* 68 (1966) 101–22.

If, as is likely, Boethius had already been thinking about these issues, his own personal fall from power, loss of wealth, and general unhappiness would have provided an apt context for making the issues particularly meaningful. Regardless of whether, by using the fiction of consoling the good man who had fallen, Boethius hoped to regain what he had lost, this fiction provided him with the opportunity to record his investigations of issues that were at the heart of philosophy and that he clearly felt must be considered by one seeking truth. From this point of view his fall should be related to the fall of Socrates which provided Plato with a basis for his analysis of whether, even to preserve his life, the good man should return evil for evil. That Boethius apparently died before writing anything after the five books comprising the *Consolatio* does not mean that he wrote the work in the shadow of execution. But we can hardly ignore the fact that the account of the execution—stemming from that in the *Anonymous Valesii*—has given the work a special poignancy and point.

The story of Boethius' being tortured by a cord twisted around his head so that his eyes popped out of their sockets, and then clubbed to death led to various apocryphal *vitae* and to the common view that he was a Christian martyr and saint—in one medieval version which shows him decapitated, he holds his severed head in his hands as he receives the Eucharist.[6] As Saint Severinus, Anicius Manlius Severinus Boethius becomes the subject of legends that show the influence of various saints' lives. In particular, he seems to have been linked to the famous Saint Severinus, who died about the time Boethius was born and whose life—in which, interestingly, Theodoric figures briefly—was written by Boethius' Roman contemporary, Eugippius.[7] But regardless of the various confusions that have existed, it seems clear that the story of Boethius' life and death developed in the popular mind and became, with little justification, the basis for interpreting Boethius' last work, the *Consolatio*.

While we may legitimately lament that fascination with Boethius the martyr has prevented proper interpretation of his work, we must also recognize that the identification of Boethius as martyr surely

---

6. For the *vitae*, see the edition of the *Consolation* by Rudolf Peiper (Leipzig 1871) xxxv. See also William Bark, "The Legend of Boethius' Martyrdom," *Speculum* 21 (1946) 312–17; Howard R. Patch, "The Beginnings of the Legend of Boethius," *Speculum* 22 (1947) 443–45; and C. H. Coster, "Procopius and Boethius," *Speculum* 23 (1948) 284–87; also Patch, *The Tradition of Boethius. A Study of His Importance in Medieval Culture* (New York 1935) 15; and Arturo Graf, "Severino Boezio," *Roma nella memoria e nelle immaginazioni del Medio Evo*, rev. ed. (Turin 1923) 624–49.

7. See E. M. Young, "Boethius," *A Dictionary of Christian Biography* (London 1877) I, 320–23; and Eugippius, *Vita S. Severini*, VII, XXXII, XLIV. On the possibility that Boethius was named after Saint Severinus, see Luca Obertello, *Severino Boezio* Genoa: Accademia Ligure di Scienze e Lettere, 1974) I, 17.

attracted readers to the work. Without the legend, the *Consolatio* would certainly not have fascinated men throughout the centuries as it did, and would not have exerted the influence it did on medieval thought, literature, and art. Admitting this, we should recognize that it is now time to study the *Consolatio* apart from the fall of Boethius and see just how it merits its reputation as one of the greatest books ever written.

JOHN MARENBON

Anicius Manlius Severinus Boethius[†]

1. Life and Works

Anicius Severinus Manlius Boethius was born into the Roman aristocracy c. 475–7 C.E.—about the same time as the last Roman Emperor, Romulus Augustulus was deposed (August 476). Boethius lived most of his life under the rule of Theoderic, an Ostrogoth educated at Constantinople, who was happy to let the old families keep up their traditions in Rome, while he wielded power in Ravenna. Boethius's privileged social position ensured that he was taught Greek thoroughly and, though it is unlikely that he travelled to Athens or Alexandria, the sites of the two remaining (Platonic) philosophical schools, he was certainly acquainted with a good deal of the work which had been going on there. He was able to spend most of his life in learned leisure, pursuing his vast project of translating and commenting philosophical texts. The Roman aristocracy was, by his day, thoroughly Christianized, and Boethius also became involved in some of the ecclesiastical disputes of his time, centring mainly around a schism between the Latin and the Greek Churches which was resolved shortly before his death.

Boethius's final years are well known to anyone who has read his most popular work, the *Consolation of Philosophy*. He agreed to become Theoderic's 'Master of Offices', one of the most senior officials, but he quickly fell out with many others at court, probably because he attacked their corruption. Accused of treason and of engaging in magic, he was imprisoned and (probably in 526) executed, but not before he had the chance to write his literary masterpiece.

[†] From *The Stanford Encyclopedia of Philosophy* <http://plato.stanford.edu/entries/boethius/>. Reprinted by permission of the author.

The *Consolation of Philosophy*, a prosimetrum (a prose work with verse interludes) which recounts, in polished literary language, an imagined dialogue between the prisoner Boethius and a lady who personifies Philosophy, contrasts with the rest of Boethius's *oeuvre*. Besides writing text-books on arithmetic and geometry, closely based on Greek models, Boethius devoted himself to translating Aristotle's logic and commenting on it; he produced a commentary on the *Categories* and two each on *On Interpretation* and on the *Isagoge* ('Introduction') by Porphyry, which had become a standard part of the logical curriculum. He also composed logical text-books on division, categorical syllogisms, and on two branches of logic: hypothetical syllogisms and topical reasoning (along with a commentary on Cicero's *Topics*). In three of his four *Theological Treatises* (often known as the *Opuscula sacra*), I, II and V, Boethius uses his logical equipment to tackle problems of Christian doctrine; IV, however, is a straightforward statement of Christian doctrine, a sort of confession of faith; whilst III is a brief, not specifically Christian philosophical treatise.

* * *

2. *The Theological Treatises*

The three *opuscula sacra* written to analyse points of Christian doctrine seem to have been occasioned by events of the time. Treatise V, against Eutyches and Nestorius, was apparently inspired by a letter (c. 513) from a group of Greek bishops, proposing a Christological formula which, they hoped, would unite the Western and Eastern Churches. The two treatises on the Trinity (II is a partial sketch for I) are related to the intervention in 519 by a group of Scythian monks, also designed to heal the schism. The works have, however, an interest far beyond their contributions to the immediate doctrinal debate. They pioneer a method of using logical analysis in a theological context which Augustine had anticipated but not developed. Both heretical positions (for example, the views about Christ and human nature held by Eutyches and Nestorius) and orthodox Christian doctrine are subjected to rigorous scrutiny, using the techniques of Aristotelian logic and, where necessary, ideas from Aristotelian physics. The heretical ideas are shown to contain logical contradictions. As for the orthodox understanding of God, it does not fit within the classifications of Aristotelian logic and natural science, but Boethius tries to chart exactly how far these distinctions, which are accommodated to the created world, also apply to the deity, and at what point they break down and provide us merely with an analogy.

This way of thinking about God is made especially clear in the longer treatise on the Trinity (I). When God is said to have an attribute, how is this predication to be understood? For created things, on the Aristotelian scheme, a predication is either substantial (when the genus, species or *differentia* is predicated of something: 'Socrates is an animal/man/rational') or accidental, when the predicate is any accident in any of the nine Aristotelian categories of accident. Augustine had already acknowledged that nothing is predicated of God accidentally. Predications about him may be relative, as when he is called 'Father' or 'Son', or substantial. Even when a quality or quantity is attributed to him, the predication is substantial. When we say of a created thing that it is great or good, we are affirming that it participates in greatness or goodness: it is one thing for the thing to exist, another for it to be great or good. But God is greatness itself and goodness itself, and so, when we say, 'God is good' or 'God is great', we are not affirming any attribute of him beyond what he is as a substance. This Augustinian view is faithfully set out in the brief Treatise II.

In Treatise I, Boethius develops this scheme. In especial, he distinguishes between predications in the categories of Substance, Quantity and Quality, which are proper and intrinsic, and those in the other six categories, excluding Relation, which he calls improper and extrinsic. The intuitive idea behind the distinction seems to be that predications in these other categories concern only how the subject relates to other things; only substantial, quantitative and qualitative attributes mark out the particular, given thing. Boethius goes on to say that, whereas all proper, intrinsic predications about God are substantial, extrinsic, improper predications about him are not: they do not concern what either God or his creatures *are*, but are rather about exterior things.

The discussion of Relation shows particularly clearly how Boethius applies logic to analysing God as far as he can, and then shows where and how the logic fails. He needs to explain how it can be true that the same, one God is both the Father and the Son. He does so by claiming that a predication of Relation, such as 'is the Father', does not concern the substance of the things related: that *a* is related to *b* in no way changes *a* or *b*. Moreover, there are some relationships which a thing can have to itself—for example, that of equality. Being-a-father and being-a-son are not, among created things, such relations: no one can be his own father or his own son. But it is here, says Boethius, that creaturely logic breaks down when it tries to comprehend the Trinity: we have in some way to try to grasp the idea of a relation of fatherhood or filiation which is reflexive.

Treatise III is also concerned with predication and God. But it differs sharply from the other treatises, in that it contains nothing specifically Christian. The question it addresses is how all substances are good in that they are, and yet are not substantial goods. Boethius takes it as a fundamental truth that all things tend to the good, and also that things are by nature like what they desire. Everything, therefore, is by nature good. But if so, then things must be good either by participation, or substantially (or 'essentially' as a modern philosopher would say). If they were merely good by participation, they would be good by accident, not by nature. But if they are good substantially, then their substance is goodness itself, and so nothing can be distinguished from the first good, God. In giving his answer, Boethius makes use of a set of axioms he states at the beginning of the piece, and undertakes a thought-experiment in which it is supposed *per impossibile* that God does not exist. The key to his solution lies in finding a principled way to distinguish between a thing *a* being *F* in that it exists, and a thing *a* being substantially *F*. For *a* to be substantially *F* means, Boethius's discussion implies, that '*a* is not-*F*' is inconceivable (we might say 'logically impossible'). For *a* to be *F* in that it exists means just that '*a* is not-*F*' is impossible (we might say 'impossible given the way the world is set up'). Whereas it is inconceivable that God is not good, it is merely impossible that everything is not good.

3. *The* Consolation of Philosophy: *The Argument of Books I–V.2*

The *Consolation of Philosophy* presents interpretative difficulties of a different order from the logical works or the theological treatises. Unlike them, it is written in an elaborately literary form: it consists of a dialogue between Boethius, sitting in his prison-cell awaiting execution, and a lady who personifies Philosophy, and its often highly rhetorical prose is interspersed with verse passages. Moreover, although it is true that elsewhere Boethius does not write in a way which identifies him as a Christian except in the Theological Treatises I, II, IV and V, the absence of any explicit reference to Christianity in the *Consolation* poses a special problem, when it is recalled that it is the work of a man about to face death and so very literally composing his philosophical and literary testament. These questions will appear in sharper focus when the argument of the *Consolation* has been examined.

Boethius's real predicament sets the scene for the argument of the *Consolation*. He represents himself as utterly confused and dejected by his sudden change of fortune. Philosophy's first job—true to the generic aim of a *consolatio*—is to console, not by offering sympathy, but by showing that Boethius has no good reason to complain: true happiness, she wishes to argue, is not damaged even by the sort of disaster he has experienced. She also identifies in Book I a wider objective: to show that it is not the case, as Boethius the character claims, that the wicked prosper and the good are oppressed.

Philosophy seems to have two different lines of argument to show Boethius that his predicament does not exclude him from true happiness. The first train of argument rests on a *complex* view of the highest good. The first (which is put forward in Book II and the first part of Book III) distinguishes between the ornamental goods of fortune, which are of very limited value—riches, status, power and sensual pleasure—and the true goods: the virtues and also sufficiency, which is what those who seek riches, status and power really desire. It also recognizes some non-ornamental goods of fortune, such as a person's friends and family, as having considerable genuine value. On the basis of these distinctions, Philosophy can argue that Boethius has not lost any true goods, and that he still even retains those goods of fortune—his family—which carry much real worth. She does not maintain that, in his fall from being powerful, rich and respected to the status of a condemned prisoner, Boethius has lost nothing of any worth at all. But his loss need not cut him off from true happiness, which is attained primarily by an austere life based on sufficiency, virtue and wisdom.

Philosophy's second line of argument is based on a *simple* view of the highest good. She begins to put it forward in III.10, a turning-point in the discussion, which is preceded by the most solemn poem of the whole work (III m. 9), an invocation to God in terms borrowed from Plato's *Timaeus*. Through a number of arguments which draw out the consequences of the Neoplatonic assumptions which Boethius accepts, Philosophy shows that the perfect good and perfect happiness are not merely in God: they *are* God. Perfect happiness is therefore completely untouched by changes in earthly fortune, however drastic. But what this second approach fails to explain is how the individual human, such as Boethius, is supposed to relate to the perfect happiness which is God. Philosophy seems to speak as if, merely by *knowing* that God is perfect happiness, Boethius himself will be rendered happy, although in the next section it seems that it is by acting well that a person can attain the good.

Philosophy now goes on (III.11–12) to explain how God rules the universe. He does so by acting as a final cause. He is the good which all things desire, and so he functions as 'a helm and rudder, by which the fabric of the world is kept stable and without decay.' Philosophy thus pictures an entirely non-interventionist God, presiding over a universe which is well-ordered simply because he exists. But how does this account fit with the apparent oppression of the good and triumph of the wicked, about which Boethius had begun by complaining? In Book IV.1–4, Philosophy shows, drawing on Plato's *Gorgias*, that the evil do not really prosper and they are in fact powerless. Her central argument is that what everyone wants is happiness, and happiness is identical with the good. The good have therefore gained happiness, whereas the wicked have not; and since people have power in so far as they can gain or bring about what they want, the wicked are powerless. She also argues that the good gain their reward automatically, since by being good, they attain the good, which is happiness. By contrast, since evil is not a thing but a privation of existence, by being wicked people punish themselves, because they cease even to exist—that is to say, they stop being the sort of things they were, humans, and become other, lower animals. Philosophy is therefore able to put forward emphatically two of the most counter-intuitive claims of the *Gorgias*: that the wicked are happier when they are prevented from their evil and punished for it, than when they carry it out with impunity, and that those who do injustice are unhappier than those who suffer it.

At the beginning of IV.5, however, there is another change of direction. Boethius the character is allowed to put forward the obvious, common-sense objections to the position Philosophy has been taking: 'which wise man', he asks, 'would prefer to be a penniless, disgraced exile rather than stay in his own city and lead there a flourishing life, mighty in wealth, revered in honour and strong in power?' Philosophy answers by abandoning completely the explanation developed from III.11 onwards, which presented God as a non-intervening final cause, and offers instead a view of God as the efficient cause of all things. Divine providence is the unified view in God's mind of the course of events which, unfolded in time, is called 'fate', and everything which takes place on earth is part of God's providence. Philosophy's change of direction might seem at first to make Boethius's common-sense objection even harder to answer, but in fact it is easy enough for her to explain that apparently unjust rewards and punishments on earth always serve a good, though to us hidden, purpose: for instance, exercising good people to increase their virtue, helping the wicked to repent or, alternatively, letting them bring themselves to ruin. A less tractable problem raised by Philosophy's new approach is that it seems to imply that the human will is causally determined. Unlike many modern philosophers, Boethius did not believe that the will can remain free, in the sense needed for attribution of moral responsibility, if it is determined causally. Moreover, Philosophy insists that the causal chain of providence, as worked out in fate, embraces all that happens. In V.1, when Boethius asks about chance, Philosophy explains that events are said to happen by chance when they are the result of a chain of causes which is unintended or unexpected, as when someone is digging in a field for vegetables and finds a buried treasure. Philosophy's solution is to argue (V.2) that rational acts of volition, unlike all external events, do not themselves belong to the causal chain of fate. This freedom, however, is enjoyed only by 'the divine and supernal substances' and by human beings engaged in the contemplation of God. It is reduced and lost as humans give their attentions to worldly things and allow themselves to be swayed by the passions.

4. Divine Prescience, Contingency and Eternity

In V.3, however, the character Boethius puts forward an argument, based on God's foreknowledge of future events, which threatens to show that even mental acts of willing are determined and so (as Boethius the author believed) unfree. He proposes the argument in two formulations:

7. If God sees all things and can in no way be mistaken, then there necessarily happens what he by providence will have foreseen will be.
8. If things are capable of turning out differently from how they have been foreseen, then there will no longer be firm foreknowledge of the future, but rather uncertain opinion.

Since it is accepted that God is omniscient, and that this implies that he *knows* what every future event—including mental events such as volitions—will be, (7) and (8) each seem to rule out any sort of freedom of the will requisite for attributing moral responsibility: a consequence the disastrous implications of which Boethius the character vividly describes.

Philosophy's answer to this difficulty is the most philosophically intricate and interesting section of the *Consolation*. It is one part of Boethius's work (perhaps the only one) which remains of interest in contemporary philosophy (of religion) and, for that reason, it has often been interpreted according to a framework provided by more recent thinking about the problem of divine prescience. The following is, rather, an attempt to present the discussion as it actually proceeds in the *Consolation*.

The first point which needs to be settled is what, precisely, is the problem which Boethius the character proposes? The reasoning behind (7) seems to be of the following form:

9. God knows every event, including all future ones.
10. When someone *knows* that an event will happen, then the event will happen.

11. (10) is true as a matter of necessity, because it is impossible to know that which is not the case.

12. If someone knows an event will happen, it will happen necessarily. (10, 11)

13. Every event, including future ones, happens necessarily. (9, 12)

The pattern behind (8) will be similar, but in reverse: from a negation of (13), the negation of (9) will be seen to follow. But, as it is easy to observe, (9–13) is a fallacious argument: (10) and (11) imply, not (12), but

14. Necessarily, if someone knows an event will happen, it will happen.

The fallacy, therefore, concerns the scope of the necessity operator. Boethius has mistakenly inferred the (narrow-scope) necessity of the consequent ('the event will happen'), when he is entitled only to infer the (wide-scope) necessity of the whole conditional ('if someone knows an event will happen, it will happen'). Boethius the character is clearly taken in by this fallacious argument, and there is no good reason to think that Boethius the author ever became aware of the fallacy (despite a passage later on which some modern commentators have interpreted in this sense). None the less, the discussion which follows does not, as the danger seems to be, address itself to a non-problem. Intuitively, Boethius sees that the threat which divine prescience poses to the contingency of future events arises not just from the claim that God's beliefs about the future constitute *knowledge*, but also from the fact that they are beliefs about the *future*. There is a real problem here, because if God knows now what I shall do tomorrow, then it seems that either what I shall do is already determined, or else that I shall have the power tomorrow to convert God's knowledge today into a false belief. Although his logical formulation does not capture this problem, the solution Boethius gives to Philosophy is clearly designed to tackle it.

Philosophy identifies (V.4) the character Boethius's central difficulty as lying in the apparent incompatibility between an event's not having a necessary outcome and yet its being foreknown. To foresee something 'as if it were certain' when it is uncertain how it will turn out is 'foreign to the integrity of knowledge', since it involves 'judging a thing as being other than it is.' Philosophy counters these doubts with the principle that 'everything that is known is grasped, not according to its own power, but rather according to the capacity of those who know it.' Her view, as she develops it (in V.5 and V.6), is based on what might be called the Principle of Modes of

Cognition: the idea that knowledge is always relativized to different levels of knowers, who have different sorts of objects of knowledge. Although she initially develops this scheme in a complex way, in relation to the different levels of the soul (intelligence, reason, imagination and the senses) and their different objects (pure Form, abstract universals, images, particular bodily things), for most of her discussion Philosophy concentrates on a rather simpler aspect of it. God's way of being and knowing, she argues, is eternal, and divine eternity, she says, is not the same as just lacking a beginning and end, but it is rather (V.6) 'the whole, simultaneous and perfect possession of unbounded life.'

A being who is eternal in this way, Philosophy argues, knows all things—past, present and future—in the same way as we, who live in time and not eternity, know what is present. She then goes on to show why, so long as God knows future events by their being present to him, this knowledge is compatible with the events' not being determined. There are, she explains, two sorts of necessity: simple and conditional. Simple necessities are what would now be called physical or nomic necessities: that the sun rises, or that a man will sometime die. By contrast, it is conditionally necessary that, for instance, I am walking, *when* I am walking (or when someone sees that I am walking); but from this conditional necessity it does not follow that it is simply necessary that I am walking. Although a number of modern commentators interpret this passage as Philosophy's way of noticing the scope-distinction fallacy in the original way Boethius the character presents the problem, she really seems to be making a rather different point. On an Aristotelian understanding of modality, which Boethius the author accepted, the present is necessary: 'what is, necessarily is, when it is' (*On Interpretation* 19a23). Philosophy is arguing that, since God knows all things as if they were present, future events are necessary, in relation to their being known by God, in just the way that anything which is presently the case is necessary. And this necessity of the present is an unconstraining necessity—those who accepted Aristotelian modalities did not think that because, when I am sitting, I am sitting necessarily, my freedom to stand has been at all curtailed. Indeed, as Philosophy stresses, in themselves the future events remain completely free. Philosophy is thus able to explain how, as known by God, future contingent events have the certainty which make them proper objects of knowledge, rather than opinion, whilst nevertheless retaining their indeterminacy.

It is important to add, however, that most contemporary interpreters do not read the argument of V.3–6 in quite this way. They hold that Philosophy is arguing that God is atemporal, so eliminating the problems about determinism, which arise when God's knowing future contingents is seen as an event in the past, and therefore, fixed.

However it is interpreted, Philosophy's argument takes a surprising turn at the very end of the book. When he gave his initial statement of the problem, Boethius the character had distinguished the problem at issue—that of divine prescience—from that of divine predetermination. He had explained (V.3) that, for the purposes of their discussion, he was assuming that God does not cause the events he foreknows: he knows them because they happen, rather than their happening because he foreknows them. He added, though, in passing, that he did not really accept this view: it is 'back to front' to think that 'the outcome of things in time should be the cause of eternal prescience.' Philosophy now returns to this point, conceding that God's act of knowing 'sets the measure for all things and owes nothing to things which follow on from it.' Although Philosophy considers that she has successfully resolved the character Boethius's problems, the reader is left asking whether this final concession, which makes God the determiner of all events, does not ruin the elaborate defence of the contingency of human volitions she has just been mounting.

5. Interpreting the Consolation

One, perfectly plausible way of reading the *Consolation* is to take it, as most philosophical works are taken, at face value. On this reading, Philosophy is recognized as a clearly authoritative figure, whose teaching should not be doubted and whose success in consoling the character Boethius must be assumed to be complete. The apparent changes of direction noted in Section [3] will be taken either as stages in Boethius's re-education or as unintended effects of the author's wish to make this work into a compendium of a syncretistic philosophical system, and Philosophy's own view that she has resolved the problem of prescience will be accepted as that of Boethius the author.

Yet there are a number of reasons which suggest that Boethius's intention as an author was more complex. First, it would have been hard for his intended audience of educated Christians to ignore the fact that in this dialogue a Christian, Boethius, is being instructed by a figure who clearly represents the tradition of pagan Philosophy, and who proposes some positions (on the World Soul in III m.9, and on the sempiternity of the world in V.6) which most Christians would have found dubious. Boethius the character says nothing which is explicitly Christian, but when in III.12 Philosophy says, echoing the words of Wisdom viii, 1 that 'it is the highest good that rules all things strongly and disposes them sweetly', he expresses his delight not just in what she has said but much more 'in those very words' that she uses—a broad hint to the reader that he remembers his Christian identity even in the midst of his philosophical instruction.

Second, the genre Boethius chose for the *Consolation*, that of the prosimetrum or Menippean satire, was associated with works which ridicule the pretensions of authoritative claims to wisdom. Elements of satire on the claims of learning are present even in the vast, encyclopaedic *Marriage of Mercury and Philology* by the fifth-century author Martianus Capella, which Boethius clearly knew. Ancient authors thought carefully about genres, and it is hard to think that Boethius's choice was not a hint that Philosophy's authority is not to be taken as complete. And, third, in the light of these two considerations, the changes of direction, incoherencies and ultimate failure of the long argument about prescience, when the question is suddenly recast as one about predestination, all suggest themselves as intentional features, for which the interpreter must account.

Some recent interpreters, such as Joel Relihan (1993, 187–194), have gone so far as to suggest that the *Consolation* should be understood ironically as an account of the insufficiency of Philosophy (and philosophy) to provide consolation, by contrast with Christian faith. Such a view seems too extreme, because Boethius the author has clearly taken great pains with the philosophical arguments proposed in the text, and the main lines of Philosophy's thinking fit well with the metaphysics glimpsed in the theological tractates and even, at moments, in the logical commentaries. It is plausible, however, to hold that Boethius wished, whilst acknowledging the value of philosophy—to which he had devoted his life, and for which he presented himself as being about to die—to point its limitations: limitations which Philosophy herself, who is keen to emphasize that she is not divine, accepts. Philosophy, he might be suggesting, provides arguments and solutions to problems which should be accepted and it teaches a way of living that should be followed, but it falls short of providing a coherent and comprehensive understanding of God and his relation to creatures. Boethius the character should be satisfied, but not completely satisfied, by Philosophy's argument. And if this is Boethius the author's position in the *Consolation*, then it fits closely with the theological method he pioneered in the *opuscula sacra*.

* * *

Boethius: A Chronology

395	Establishment of the two Roman Emperors governing the Eastern and Western Empires.
476	Romulus Augustulus overthrown by the barbarian general Odoacer. Odoacer becomes Western Emperor.
476	Approximate date of Boethius's birth.
485	Symmachus (Boethius's adoptive father) becomes a Roman Consul.
487	Boethius's natural father becomes a Roman Consul and soon dies.
493	Murder of Odoacer by Theoderic, who becomes Western Emperor.
495	Boethius marries Rusticiana.
503	Boethius writes *Principles of Arithmetic* and *Principles of Music*.
504–505	He writes *First Commentary on Porphyry's* Isagoge.
505–506	He writes *Introduction to the Categorical Syllogisms* and *On the Categorical Syllogism*.
505–509	He writes *On Division*.
507–509	He writes *Second Commentary on Porphyry's* Isagogue.
509–511	He writes *Commentary on Aristotle's* Categories.
510	He becomes a Roman Consul.
512	He starts *Theological Treatises*.
513	He writes *First Commentary on Aristotle's* On Interpretation (Peri Hermeneias).
515–516	He writes *Second Commentary on Aristotle's* On Interpetation (Peri Hermeneias).
516–522	He writes *On the Hypothetical Syllogism*.
520	He writes translations of Aristotle's *Prior Analytics*, *Posterior Analytics*, *Topics*, and *Sophistical Refutations*.
521	He completes *Theological Treatises*.
522	He completes *Commentary on Cicero's* Topics.
522	He becomes Master of Offices under Theoderic.

Selected Bibliography

• Indicates items included or excerpted in this Norton Critical Edition.

Amory, P. *People and Identity in Ostrogothic Italy, 489–554*. Cambridge, UK: Cambridge UP, 1997.

Bark, William. "*The Legend of Boethius' Martyrdom*." *Speculum* XXI (1946): 312–17.

• ———"Theodoric vs. Boethius: Vindication and Apology." *American Historical Review* 49. 3 (April 1944): 410–26.

Basik, Nathan. "The Guilt of Boethius" <http://pvspade.com/Logic/docs/GuiltOf-Boethius.pdf>.

• Chadwick, Henry. "Introduction." In Gibson, ed., *Boethius: His Life, Thought, and Influence*.

Courcelle, P. *Late Latin Writers and Their Greek Sources*. Cambridge, MA: Harvard UP, 1969.

De Rijk, L. M. "On the Chronology of Boethius's Works on Logic." *Vivarium* 2 (1964): 1–49; 122–62.

Gibson, Margaret, ed. *Boethius: His Life, Thought, and Influence*. Oxford: Blackwell, 1981.

Jefferson, B. L. *Chaucer and the 'Consolation of Philosophy.'* Princeton: Princeton UP, 1917.

Lewis, C. S. *The Discarded Image: An Introduction to Medieval and Renaissance Literature*. Cambridge: Cambridge UP, 1964.

• Marenbon, John. *Anicius Manlius Severinus Boethius*. The Stanford Encyclopedia of Philosophy: <http://plato.stanford.edu>.

———. *Boethius*. New York: Oxford UP, 2002.

Matthews, John. "Anicius Manlius Severinus Boethius." In Gibson, ed., *Boethius: His Life, Thought, and Influence*.

Minnis, A. J., ed. *The Medieval Boethius. Studies in the Vernacular Translations of 'De Consolatione Philosophiae.'* Cambridge: Brewer, 1987.

Patch, H. R. *The Tradition of Boethius: A Study of His Importance in Mediaeval Culture*. New York: Oxford UP, 1935.

• Pike, Nelson. *God and Timelessness*. Eugene, OR: Wipf and Stock, 2002.

Relihan, Joel. *Ancient Menippean Satire*. London and Baltimore: Johns Hopkins University Press, 1993.

Stewart, H. F., E. K. Rand, and S. J. Tester. *Boethius: The Theological Tractates; The Consolation of Philosophy*. Cambridge, MA: Harvard UP, 1973.

Index

202